D1289990

FIRE UNDER THE ASHES

FIRE

UNDER THE

ASHES

❀ ❀ ❀ ❀

THE LIFE OF

DANILO DOLCI

❀ ❀ ❀ ❀

By James McNeish

BEACON PRESS   BOSTON

Etna, an isolated active volcano . . . Its
form is a domed cone . . . The cone is
not perfect . . . The height and form
of the crater constantly change . . .
According to age and composition,
some lavas and most ashes have disinte-
grated into fertile soil . . .

—*Chambers Encyclopædia*

Published in 1965 in Great Britain by Hodder and Stoughton, Ltd.

Library of Congress catalog card number: 66-14489

Beacon Press books are published under the auspices of the Unitarian
Universalist Association

Printed in the United States of America

FOR FLICKA
WHO HELPED
MORE THAN SHE KNEW

It is true that in other countries great men have also occasionally been persecuted and put to death. Nowhere else, however, has this happened with the same discrimination, regularity, and determination. . . . Italy instinctively neutralized all the men who tried to foist moral greatness on their countrymen.

—Luigi Barzini (*The Italians*)

ACKNOWLEDGMENTS

I AM INDEBTED to the following for permission to quote copyright material:

Danilo Dolci, for the poems, letters, speeches and other private documents.

Ilys Booker and Professor Ross Waller, for their private letters.

Laterza & Figli, Bari, for *Banditi a Partinico*.

Giulio Einaudi, Turin, for *Processo all'articolo* 4.

La Nuova Italia Editrice, Florence, for *Fare presto (e bene) perché si muore*.

MacGibbon & Kee, for *Inchiesta a Palermo* and *Spreco*.

The line-drawing prefacing the three sections is from Borgo di Dio, drawn by one of the children of the men killed by bandits.

Grateful acknowledgment is made to the Danilo Dolci Trust, 29 Gt. James St., London W.C.1, for its constant help.

Scores have helped with this biographical excursion. My especial thanks are due to: Annie Kalldal, of Kallrör, Sweden; Robin Dixon, Oxford; Don Zeno Saltini, Nomadelphia; Giorgio Pecorini, Milan; Norma Slevison and Bill Pepper, Rome; Marcello Cimino and Gino Orlando, Palermo; Franco Alasia and Vittorio Geraci, Partinico. Also to Diana Fussell, of Wellington, New Zealand, who took the picture of Dolci playing the accordion, translated the poems, and transcribed many tapes; and Elizabeth Morton, of Auckland, who typed the MS in record time. Lastly, my deepest gratitude—to Pasqualino, whose mill, wine cellar, and genius at unscrambling the Sicilian dialect were always forthcoming; to Kerstin and Eyvind Hytten, who bravely entrusted me with Borgo di Dio—and even Amedeo—when the furies were at their height; and to Totò, of Cammarata, who finally managed to convince the district police officer I was not a Communist spy.

CONTENTS

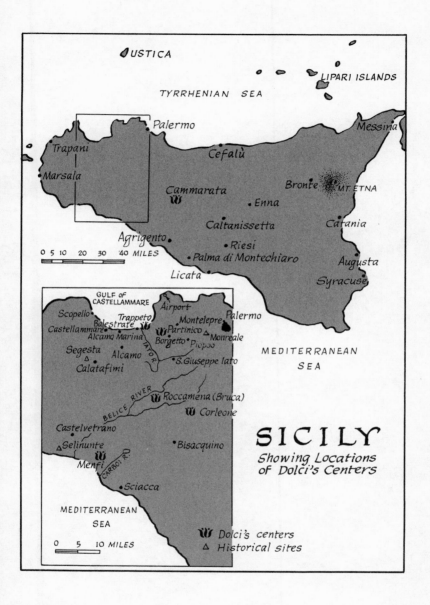

USTICA

LIPARI ISLANDS

TYRRHENIAN SEA

Palermo

Trapani

Messina

Cefalù

Marsala

Cammarata

Bronte

MT. ETNA

Enna

Caltanissetta

Catania

Agrigento

0 5 10 20 30 40 MILES

Riesi

Palma di Montechiaro

Augusta

Licata

Syracuse

GULF of CASTELLAMMARE

Airport

Palermo

Scopello

Trappeto

Montelepre

Balestrate

Castellammare

Partinico

Monreale

Alcamo Marina

Borgetto

Piopso

Segesta

Alcamo

S.Giuseppe Iato

MEDITERRANEAN SEA

Calatafimi

BELICE RIVER

Roccamena (Bruca)

Corleone

Castelvetrano

Selinunte

Bisacquino

Menfi

CARBOI R.

JATO R.

SICILY

Showing Locations
of Dolci's Centers

Sciacca

MEDITERRANEAN
SEA

0 5 10 MILES

Dolci's centers
△ Historical sites

INTRODUCTION

DANILO DOLCI is that rare person, the intellectual who does things.

At the age of twenty he was unknown. At thirty-one he was a world figure. Now in his forties, he is as controversial in Europe as Martin Luther King is in the United States.

Sicilians sometimes call him "the professional misery man." He is still attacked for having revealed Sicily's tragic underside to the civilized world; indeed, he is still attacked for almost everything he does. It is partly the lot of the pacifist reformer. It is particularly the lot of the reformer who is brave enough, or stupid enough, to choose this unresponsive soil as his seeding ground. Sicilians seldom forgive, and, as the prince in *The Leopard* points out, "The sin which we Sicilians never forgive is simply that of *doing* at all." "Doing" is probably the simplest way of describing Dolci's philosophy of life.

Ever since 1956, when he led a group of unemployed peasants out to repair a broken-down Government road, gratis, and was put in prison for it, Dolci's prestige outside Italy has soared, in inverse proportion to that within it. Nowadays, the official Italian press hardly mentions him, except occasionally to applaud when there appears a likelihood of his going to prison again, being put on the Index or, as in his 1962 fast, going into a coma. It is generally the way with saints and revolutionaries. We love them all, from a distance. Close to home they are embarrassing.

Many observers consider that the *Eminence Grise* be-

hind much official hostility to Dolci is not the Mafia but the leading ecclesiastical authority on the island, Cardinal Ernesto Ruffini, Archbishop of Palermo and Primate of Sicily. When I called
at the archbishopric on 7 September 1963 His Eminence declined to receive me. He said he did not consider it opportune
and authorized his secretary, Monsignor Longhi, to speak on his
behalf. Monsignor Longhi described Dolci as an upstart, a dis-
graced Christian, an imposter, a dishonest and ambitious man
whose aims were evil, grasping, and immoral. To put these re-
marks in perspective it should be remembered that the broad
Church criticism of Dolci is that he is "a defamer of his country
and his people." "It is a Christian duty not to speak badly of
your neighbor," priests have told me.

Monsignor Longhi gave me a confidential report on Dolci,
completed in 1962 by the Palermo police. It is eight and a quarter-
er foolscap pages closely typed. Part of it seems based on a newspaper article by a former senator from Partinico, Savarino,
which the police attempted to use as evidence against Dolci during his trial in 1956. Monsignor Longhi said I was to treat the
police report as His Eminence's "personal opinion." It is not
actually libellous. I shall quote from it, from time to time.

Aldous Huxley has called Dolci "the ideal twentieth-century saint."

It is one of Dolci's misfortunes that he does not look the re-
forming type. He is a towering man who always seems on the
point of bursting out of his clothes which are too small for him,
and indeed is fated to split his trousers at the most awkward
moments. He reminds me of an unorthodox provincial business-
man, in the act of clearing his desk before flinging a shoelace
round his neck in mistake for a tie and departing at a hand gallop for a well-earned holiday. Dolci is a conventional reformer
only insofar as he never takes a holiday. Only the strong hazel
eyes, limpid and penetrating behind the cut spectacles, and the
uncanny moral armory limning the quiet reassuring voice, betray the poet and mystic and the man of conscientious action.

One of the paradoxical things about Dolci is that he is criticized most by those farthest from him—those who understand him least, or do not want to understand him at all—like Cardinal Ruffini; and by some of those who have been closest to him —those who, one would think, understand him best—like Giovanni and Gerrit and Bianca and Pasqualino, all former colleagues and once staunch advocates. This is part of the riddle of Dolci, the man. For these latter people the close-focus of the man himself, his shortcomings, especially his failure as an administrator, are paramount. Each of them could write a separate, perhaps equally valid book on Dolci. But they would be writing about a different Dolci. For me it matters less that his private figure often falls short of his public figure. For me his limitations are secondary. I am concerned primarily with the man and the gesture; with Dolci in a world context, with the man of ideas and the influence of these ideas. I see him as a symbol, as a positive living force.

To write about Dolci it is also necessary to write about the Center. This is the curious organization he founded in 1958 which, from a renegade warehouse visited officially only by policemen, has become a sort of moral launching-pad visited today by world authorities in the social sciences and by Italian ministers of state. But this is not a history of the Dolci movement. Many names are omitted; and for this reason the stories of Goffredo and Ilys should not be taken as isolated epics. Others (Raffaele Maiello, Riborg van der Felz, Mariapia Pieri, Fiorella Viola, Marco Marchioni . . . the list is a long one) have achieved as much, and suffered more. I would like to have written more about these people, for they, too, are symbolic—of young men and women everywhere who fire themselves for an ideal, only to find that the more sacrifices they make the more it blinds and exhausts them. It has exhausted Eyvind. It killed Teresio Bonini, the young statistician who was found dead in his room, the gas-heater still burning, a letter he had been writing to Professor Waller, half-finished, in his typewriter.

My own connection with the Center is oblique—I am of it but not in it. The connection has grown from a casual meeting

with Dolci four years ago to a present attachment in the mountains, a field study blessed jointly by the Center and Stockholm
University. I should also explain that I am not a sociologist or
an economist and have not attempted a close appraisal of Dolci's
technical studies or the scores of monographs his specialists have
prepared. They belong to a different kind of book. I have also
omitted Dolci's more theoretical writings on what he calls the
technology of nonviolence, for the same reason.

This is principally the account of a man's life. It is not ex-
haustive. I regard it as an extended portrait rather than a full-
scale biography. It is official in that I have had Dolci's willing co-
operation, though this is almost a euphemism. Lately he has
been travelling so much that the only occasions when we have
been able to get together for more than a day at a time have
been, significantly, when he has been flat on his back, starving.
I still have a guilty feeling that I had him at a disadvantage.

To delve into a man who has already changed course three
times in his life and is still maturing may seem impertinent. But
when I remember how Gandhi and Kennedy died, when I pick
up a Sicilian newspaper and see almost every day how casually,
and sometimes carefully, lives are shattered here virtually by
force of habit; when I drive across the island to the Partinico
plain, near Palermo, where Dolci lives—that is, the long valley
road which begins in the hills behind Santo Stefano and passes
through Corleone and San Giuseppe Iato, skirting graveyards
where lie the remnants of over two hundred Mafia murders, all
recent and almost all unsolved—then I am not convinced that
this book is premature. It is one of Dolci's achievements that he
is alive at all.

Perhaps nowhere do the social revolutionary and truth
have such short lives as on this melancholy island. Sicilians say
that the truth does not exist. Their torn and beautiful land is
littered with the tombstones of rebels who have sought truth
and tried to build on it to bring about justice and change. I can
think of only one other would-be reformer who provoked the
Mafia and lived. He is a priest and the Mafia doesn't usually kill

priests, and in any case this young man was made to sign a confession, under duress, retracting everything he had said. Nobody is sure why Dolci has been allowed to live. "I don't know," he says. "I really don't know."

Eduard would say that this is overplaying the Mafia's role, and he may be right. But Eduard, who is Dolci's liaison officer with the German-speaking world and the extension work in Africa, is himself something of a vagabond from death. He is one of the few surviving organizers of the *putsch* against Hitler and he should know how slender is the hair-line between luck and oblivion.

Some of Dolci's life is already studded with myth. It is not too soon to get at the facts. I can think of no better reason for making them known than Dolci's own reason for publicizing the facts about Sicily—"For when they are deeply known, other people may then work."

J. McN.
Cammarata, West Sicily, 1964

PART ONE

There will always be the sound of thunder, and chaos and ruin and death, in the affairs of men and nations until they achieve God and enter into his tranquillity

—LAO-TSE

BEGINNINGS

HE had always been a maker of dreams. They were the sort of dreams that had to do with a reality that was just round the corner, that had to do with people, always people, and with faith in people. Faith-dreams, you might call them. He didn't look like a dreamer. He had that pathetic formal seriousness of the small boy who listens gravely to the parental word of command, and then strides off to carry it out as if the Papal dignity were at stake. "Oh, he is such a *good* boy," an elder aunt used to say. When he was four he was standing on a balcony wearing his sailor's cloth cap when he noticed an even smaller boy standing on the pavement below, gazing wistfully up at him. He took off the cap and gave it to his threadbare admirer. He never understood why his father spanked him so hard afterwards, because his parents had always told him it was right to help the poor. Once his father sent him round to the tobacconist with a letter and the money to buy the stamp. The tobacconist who sold the stamps was closed, but he posted the letter in the pillar-box just the same, and then he posted the money for the stamp. He got a spanking for that too. He was always dreaming: about seamen and spacemen and starmen, about his paternal grandfather, Pietro, who had travelled even to America (and that was *something*, in those days)—dreams about poets and painters and great musicians. When he was fifteen and studying at technical school his dreams took the form of fantasies, lie-fantasies; sometimes he told lies from fear to avoid another beating, but the dream ones, he always said afterwards,

Danilo Dolci and Franco Alasia

were a part of his own private world of evasion and he had a need
to kiss fantasy. The worst dream of all began after he was twenty-
five and had left the university and the family home in North Italy
and gone away to live in a paupers' community run by a thickset
dumpy man whom people called "the mad priest of Nomadelphia." This dream was to outlast even the revelations of Nomadelphia and to follow him down to Sicily. "For several years
I went on having this dream, until I was about thirty. I dreamed
with anguish that I hadn't taken my architectural degree, a sort
of guilt dream, afraid of not being strong, of not building these

things." The dream was true; in fact, he hadn't taken the degree. Some ten years later, during a hunger strike, he had a different type of dream. It was short and, apparently, vivid. It was 14 September 1962. He was almost at the end of a nine-day fast in a poor part of the Sicilian town of Partinico. I was sleeping between his bed and the door, which was shut, and Franco his secretary was sleeping on the other side of the room. He'd put the light out about ten o'clock, and we lay back talking. He was worried and weak from lack of sugar. We all dropped off. It must have been about two in the morning when he woke suddenly and shouted to Franco, "Quick! There's a police car out there." I'd heard nothing, nor had Franco. Franco bolted outside in bare feet, holding his pajama pants up with one hand and rubbing his eyes with the other. After a few minutes Franco was back. Yes, it was a police car, he said. The carabinieri had called at a house sixty yards down the street and taken a man away.

I am not sure if these dreams, if you can call them dreams, have any great significance. If they have, though, they belong more to the Pirandellian world of reality intertwined with illusion than to any Kafkaesque world of nightmarish hallucination. Perhaps this is just to say that they belong very much to the private world of Danilo Dolci.

He was born on 28 June 1924, at Sesana, a village near Trieste, which is today in Yugoslavia. He grew up in a typical middle-class Italian environment, or rather a series of environments, in which there was great affection, without real intimacy, and rather too much religion. The religion came from his mother, who was Slav: Meli Kontely. His mother first spoke to him in Slovenian, and the prayers that were said every morning and evening were in that language. She gave him a Slav name, Danilo. As a boy he spoke Slovenian, the only foreign language he has mastered. From his mother he inherited a gift for music and a balanced artistic temperament. His father, Enrico Dolci, was a railway employee, of Italian and German blood, and, by reaction

against Signora Dolci, a religious abstainer. The veil of astrin-
gent Catholicism, formal and uncritical, which tinged the family atmosphere had no influence at all over Signor Dolci's heavy
hand which always seemed on the point of rising or falling,
usually in the direction of Danilo. Yet Danilo was closer to his
father, and from him gained a love of the country and of walking. Signor Dolci was a wiry, handsome man. Being attached
to that vast machine, the Italian State Railways—which, like the
state police, was in the habit of suddenly transferring its em-
ployees from one end of the republic to the other—he kept his
family in a sort of perpetual motion, steering them on his modest
railwayman's salary through a succession of self-contained four-
roomed bungalows, with and without flower gardens, from Trieste to Lake Maggiore, to a town near Alessandria, and to points
south. Otherwise, apart from the weekly rows that civil servants
the world over have with their wives over matters of upbringing,
life held no major problems for Enrico Dolci. He was not an
ambitious man. There was no aspidistra in the Dolci bungalow.
The only status symbols were the upright piano in the living
room and a battered leather suitcase which had belonged to
Grandfather Pietro, the traveling salesman. Danilo recalls the
musical evenings as "nice moments." Signora Dolci sang and
played, Danilo played and sang, and two or three uncles were
usually on hand to ballast the choruses. When Danilo was eight
a sister appeared, Miriam, who thereafter seems to have become becalmed in the Italian middle-class existences of doing
exactly what was expected of you, which was what everyone else
did. Life was quiet, modest, and "traditional." The Dolci household appears as an oasis of conventionality rising out of the unorthodox past of their fathers and leading into the outrageous
future of their only son. Both Danilo's grandfathers were rug-
ged men, with the spice of originality. Both travelled. Josef
Kontely, his maternal grandfather, was a law clerk. He was a
linguist, a 'cellist, and a man of fiery honor. In 1928, when Danilo was four, Josef refused to doff his hat before a fascist banner
at Brescia, and for that was beaten and made to drink castor oil,

the stock fascist purgative. Josef returned to Yugoslavia and never
set foot in Italy again. Danilo never knew his paternal grandfather, Pietro. He only knew there was a famous leather article
in the house known as "Grandfather's bag" and from time to
time messages would arrive from the most improbable places,
saying "Send the bag—I'm off to America." Grandfather Pietro
was a cheese salesman. He came from Rovato, near Brescia, married a German woman from Nuremberg, and travelled half the
world in the cause of *gorgonzola*. He was in partnership with a
man called Arrigoni. Pietro died young and left a modest sum
to be divided among ten children. Enrico, who had wanted to
study, started work at seventeen and became a railwayman by
mistake. He determined that his son would study and get an
important post.

Danilo was more interested in music. At six he began with
Marusi, the organist at Milan Cathedral, and fell in love with
Bach. By his midteens he was accomplished on three instruments. If he didn't play well Marusi used to rap him over the
knuckles. An unstated hatred of violence was instilled early.
His education was formal and undistinguished, though occasionally his essays were read aloud to the class. But he was not
an outstanding pupil. He was not always present. If he didn't
like the teacher he used to wander off into the fields and sit,
through the long enigmatic afternoons, staring at the pebbles
of a favorite stream-bed. He would take a book and read, or he'd
just sit, staring. His father reacted typically when he found out,
but the beatings Danilo received only drove him farther into his
books. He read old library books, his father's books, anything he
could lay hands on; all his savings went into books or music. He
had his first calf-love affair (with a teacher) at nine, went through
technical school in three different towns, played basketball,
clambered up mountains, and became an excellent swimmer.
It was all "very normal," he says. Above all through his adoles-
cence, he read.

Born into the cynical twenties, he was growing up in a world
slowly emptying itself of spiritual values, against a background

of mounting violence and empty slogans. Education glorified male supremacy, fighting terms, and the state. Along with millions of other Italian children he learned by rote the slogans, "Mussolini is always right," "With book and gun, true fascist son," and "Better to live one day as a lion than a hundred years as a sheep." At six he put on the black shirt, black belt, black fez, and gray-green socks of the *balilla* and at fourteen became a *marinaretto*, the sea-scout version of the *avanguardisti*, by means of which Mussolini was spinning a paper web of efficiency for the first time in the history of a united Italy. His father was an early conformer to the facile acceptance of a dictatorship few believed in or even understood, and as the mood of life subtly altered through the thirties, and youth took sides, Danilo acquiesced, without criticizing. But he remained uncommitted. In 1939 when Hitler marched into Czechoslovakia, and Mussolini, not to be outdone, invaded Albania, Danilo was flirting with the heroes of Jules Verne. He experienced his first instinctive revulsion for the régime at sixteen, shortly after Italy entered the war. His father refused to let him listen to the BBC from London. They argued bitterly. Then there occurred a small, almost routine event which was later to reshape his life. His father was sent from Tortona near Alessandria, where they were living, to become stationmaster in a remote village at the other end of Italy, the village of Trappeto in Sicily. None of the family had ever heard of Trappeto before.

Signora Dolci and the children remained in the north. Danilo studied mathematics and drawing at school and at home plunged deeper into his reading. It had become a ritual. He would rise at four, slip an overcoat over his pajamas and read for two hours; after a break for a hot drink he would go on reading until it was time for school. In three, three and half hours, he would devour a major work. In his sixteenth year he read close to three hundred titles—all the Italian classics, Goethe, Schiller, Tolstoy, Ibsen, Shaekspeare. Simultaneously he studied the history of art and crossed into fresh religious worlds, wanting to understand how so many other millions outside Italy might live according to vastly different, yet firmly established patterns of conduct. He read the Bible and the Koran, turned to Tao, Confucius, and the teachings of Buddha. He read all seven hundred stanzas of the *Bhagavad Gita,* the work which half a century before had become Gandhi's spiritual reference book. He soaked up knowledge drunkenly. But there was no correlation between theory and the practice; the growing intellectual had no platform.

In the summer of 1941, when he was seventeen, he took a sketchpad and went south with his mother and sister for a holiday. After two nights and a day on the train they came to the fishing village of Trappeto, in western Sicily, where his father was stationmaster, and rented a house by the sea.

Trappeto, like most southern villages, was half-starved. People were living on locust and carob beans and whatever herbs they could scratch from the countryside. There was no grain for bread—it had either been requisitioned by the military or hoarded by the rich. But as the war had so far not ruffled Danilo's conscience, so the poverty of Trappeto failed to touch him. He read and sketched the painted boats, made friends with the black-garbed fishermen, with Paolino and Toni and Peppino and Leonardo, "son of the blind one." They spoke a loud gravelly dialect he couldn't understand, took him fishing at night, and Toni "the philosopher" talked of Alaska, showed him the stars, and introduced him to the magical world of the Biblical night fisherman. It was the world they lived in and the world of *Moby Dick,* and it excited him. "They translated what I'd read into reality, gave me a new dimension of the world." But it was an artistic dimension. The primitive boats, the crusts of bread, the tumbledown dwellings—he saw it all pictorially.

His father was something of a hero, he discovered. Fishing was officially prohibited in wartime right round the coast. "We told your dad, Signor Dolci, we couldn't take the boats out when he came," Paolino said. "And off he goes and speaks with the carabinieri [the state police]. The carabinieri sent him to the

military and the military sent him to the mayor and the mayor
sent him back to the carabinieri ... what a business. But he
sorted it out, your dad. He came down one night and he says,
'It's all right, boys, you can take your boats out.' He fixed it."

Danilo felt no longing to emulate his father. He knew him
to be a *good* man. It was enough. His father wanted him to get
on quickly, pass his surveyor's exams and take a job with a big
construction firm, perhaps in Africa. Danilo read *The History
of Italian Art* and went on a pilgrimage to the southwestern
corner of the island, to Selinunte and Segesta, to study the Greek
glories of the past. He saw the temple of Segesta alone on a summer's morning. The massive frontal columns, set starkly on a
hill above the cavernous goat country which fell away behind,
seemed far more important to him than Trappeto. He saw the
temple, above the blue thistle and the somber green esparto
grass, with a kind of greedy curiosity, made several sketches, and
went away. He was in love with the idea of becoming an architect.

He returned north with his mother, jumped a year to take
his surveyor's diploma, and gained a cultural diploma as well at
the Brera Academy, Milan.

By autumn 1942 the tide of war was turning. German troops
were taking over the north, antifascism was spreading, and Mussolini was losing control: his mistress' relatives were rumored to
be sidling into the country's affairs, from posts in the diplomatic
service to professorships at Milan University and the Polytechnic,
where Danilo was now a first-year architectural student. Fascist
leaders began listening to the BBC in London to find out what
was happening, and Danilo began his first serious love affair.
But study remained his real passion. Against a background of
mounting chaos he continued the early morning ritual, rising at
four, reading the Greek dramatists and the Utopians. He earned
his first money, teaching in the evenings. By the late spring of
1943 half Mussolini's armies in Russia were lost, his forces had
surrendered in North Africa, and, with the allies about to in-
vade Sicily, Signor Dolci had left the Sicilian railways to their

fate and returned north. Before he did so, however, he cemented
the Dolci prestige in Trappeto by persuading the carabinieri to
break into the warehouses of the landowners and distribute the
hoarded grain among the fisherfolk.

Danilo, studying fifteen hours a day, collapsed from over-
work. His parents found him in a faint on the sofa. It was the
first of a series of frights he gave them. The Allies landed in the
south, the Nazis occupied Rome, and Mussolini set up his pup-
pet state in the north centered on Salò. It was late 1943. Rebellion was in the air. Danilo, until now exempt from service because he was a student, was picked as officer material and knew
he would soon be called up. He was nineteen, and already sym-
pathetically involved in the growing resistance. Emerging from
the idealism of Plato's *Republic* he realized he wanted nothing
to do with Mussolini's so-called Republic of Salò. He saw himself as a combatant in a hypocritical school of murder. He went
round ripping down Nazi posters—"those horrible Nazi posters"
—wherever he saw them. His parents were terrified. Danilo went
on ripping down the posters. Then he decided to reach Rome.
He left a note for his father, and with the money he had earned
from teaching, took a train south. He had two books with him,
Mazzini's *The Rights and Duties of Men* and Thomas à Kempis'
The Imitation of Christ. Before Genoa there was a train check
by the Nazis. He was arrested, handcuffed, and taken to Sturla
jail where he spent the next ten days in a cell, 18 ft. by 9 feet,
sleeping under straw and blankets with twelve others and a small
army of lice. His companions were port thieves and partisans,
and included a Jewish factory owner who had tried to escape by
jumping out of the window when the Germans arrived. The
Jew was taken away from the cell and not seen again. Danilo
used his brains. At the prison hearing, he mentioned casually to
the officer-interpreter the name of an obscure German sculptor
he'd read about in a doctor's waiting room. The interpreter was
impressed: he knew the sculptor. Danilo played his advantage
and appears to have convinced the interpreter that he himself
was an architectural genius, for the latter spoke to a superior,

handed Danilo a *laissez-passer* note, and Danilo walked out of the gate.

He walked up into the Ligurian mountains, went south by truck and foot, came to the Abruzzi, and again took to the mountains. He passed Gran Sasso, the highest peak in the Italian Apennines, and above L'Aquila was chased by a German patrol. He hid in the snow. He had a close shave with a fascist patrol and then in the woods found a loaded pistol. It came in handy, scavenging for food. Then he thought about it and threw the pistol away. For a week he lived on diseased and dying hens which the peasants had thrown out. "I skinned them and boiled them. I had fowl for breakfast, fowl for dinner, and fowl for supper. I never had so much poultry in all my life." He was sheltered by a shepherd family in the village of Poggio Canelli, where escaped British prisoners were also hiding, and learned his first words of English from a New Zealand infantryman who'd just captured a runaway pig. "Such is life," the Kiwi said with a grin, and proceeded to slaughter the pig. The Germans were now retreating north from Naples, but were still in charge of Rome, as Danilo discovered when he drew near. He returned to Poggio Canelli and stayed with the same shepherd family, teaching their son to read in return for food. Early in 1944 he crossed over the lines, hidden in the back of a truck carrying merchandise, and reached Rome. The war for Italy was virtually over.

THE FIRST FEVER

A PHOTOGRAPH taken about 1947 when Danilo was twenty-three
and in his fourth year of architecture in Milan shows a shock of
wavy brown hair, a lean dedicated face, impeccable collar and
tie, and expensive rimless spectacles. There is an air of groomed,
assured professionalism. There is no hint of an internal struggle
which had begun a year or so before, a poet's rebellion against
the sophisticated society in which he was living. He'd given up
reading altogether and begun writing poetry, seeking in the battle for the control of words themselves a way out of rhetoric and
into reality. And then, one October, he went out into the country. Years later he told me of the experience:

"I went out from one October to the next, because I wanted
to verify directly the things I'd been reading. I saw all things
born and I saw all things die. And I realized that everything became, could become, a parable. I saw that when the leaves fell
from the trees you could see farther. I saw that you could see the
sun only when it was hidden by mists. I saw, as we all do, that
from afar the grass seems luxuriant and it's only when you're
close that you see the patches of dry earth. I saw that when the
leaves fall only the seeds remain, that the seeds then return to the
earth. I saw that in the act of wasting away they become reborn.
And continuously the seeds fell and became fruit, ready for eating. And I saw all the seasons like this, from *inside*, as it were. I
forgot everything else. I wanted to live them, just once; and I
did. I saw the whole cycle of life. I *felt*, I didn't reason it, that

nature, that everything, was a tragedy where the living devoured
the dead. I didn't know why, I only knew it was so. And then
slowly, very slowly, I felt the need to be consumed, like the seeds,
to become manure myself.

"And then I understood the value of communion, that everybody must be together. I understood God's purpose in creation."

Out of a synthesis of bookish culture and mystical experience
he had discovered a meaning in life. But he was not yet to collaborate with it. His head continued to go one way, his body another.
As he wrote in a poem, there were

> *demons of the flesh*
> *placed in positions of command.*

Yet the Hyde of his dual personality wasn't a very ribald fellow.
At parties he was often to be found at the piano, playing Bach.
He had the body of an athlete and warm friendly eyes which
his girl friends found endearing, but he had a disconcerting
mode of expressing his feelings. According to a contemporary account, one affair ended rather abruptly when he turned
up at a rendezvous on a crowded Milan thoroughfare at promenade time, pulled a piece of paper from his pocket, saying,
"Just a minute, let's look at this poem," and with that sat down
on the pavement and began to read it aloud. He became engaged
to an attractive arts graduate, Alicia, and they courted formally—
every Sunday, mostly by reading poetry together—talked increasingly of marriage, of property and children, and of entering the
società illuminata of Milan when he had qualified and set up in
practice. Alicia was the daughter of a well-to-do provincial building contractor. Danilo was well-endowed artistically and press-
ing to the front of the new generation of resourceful and
energetic designers. They were both good Catholics and went
regularly to church with their respective parents, Danilo going
home to Tortona and visiting his fiancée in a nearby town every
weekend. It seemed an ideal match. His parents in particular were
delighted.

He had rented a room in Milan, filled it with a rented piano and books and music, and was paying his way by teaching at the Milan Polytechnic at night and by giving lessons on the theory of construction to his architectural colleagues. He is "ashamed to admit" nowadays that he took money from fellow students. It was at the Polytechnic that his rebellion against the shallows of intellectualism took hold. He began to admire qualities, such as the capacity for sweat and work, in ordinary people about him. He was teaching literature to lads of seventeen and men of thirty, all bunched together, mostly laborers and factory hands. Among them was a young mechanic, Franco Alasia. Franco was three years younger than Danilo, and working ten hours a day in a motor-assembly plant. He was a raw young man, handsome in a finely chiselled way, and gawkily enthusiastic for knowledge. He had come through the fascist education-mill of being taught not to think, and was trying to make up the gap at night school and also to overcome a deep-seated inferiority complex about girls who wouldn't dance with him because, he told Danilo, "I'm not cultured." Somewhere between the mechanic's striving to get up and the intellectual's yearning to climb down, the two found a relaxed meeting point. Danilo was the first intellectual in Franco's life. "I felt this respect on his part, this equality between teacher and pupils," Franco relates. "He had a humility before each person, irrespective of their amount of culture, just because they were people. All I waited for were his lessons. Often he'd go well beyond the subject and we'd continue the discussion walking home." A deep bond sprang up between them.

Danilo, meantime, was coming more and more to despise intellectualism for its own sake. He was restless. Ideas, he felt intuitively, should be made a function of life itself, not merely a means of analyzing it. In the summer of 1948, not long after he met Franco, he heard of a Catholic community run by a man called Don Zeno—"the mad priest of Nomadelphia." Nomadelphia was a self-supporting charity for destitute orphans in Emilia. Perhaps in community life he might find the transition he was seeking from theory to application. He decided to go and see.

In fact, he wasn't much impressed. Scattered over a few flat acres at Fossoli, near Modena, on the site of an old concentration camp, Nomadelphia had an air of desolation. Pictorially, it was a mess. It was far from being the perfect society he had imagined. He spent a day there and went back to Milan to prepare for his finals.

He had already published two architectural monographs, *The Science of Construction* and *The Theory of Reinforced Concrete*, had designed a church, been offered further commissions, and was delving into research on tensile strengths and beam structures with a young engineer with whom he planned to go into practice. He was regarded as "more than promising." Friends predicted a bold career and his fiancée was enthusiastic. They made plans, began building a house of their own, and he rented a studio in Corso Sempione, the Champs Elysées of Milan. But as the time for taking his finals approached fresh doubt arose. At lectures his mind wandered to Utopian visions, beam structures were blurred, and behind them he saw the faces of the orphans of Nomadelphia and the crinkled leonine face of the priest who'd given them the first real home they'd ever known. He went about in a sort of coma. For two days, in fever, Nomadelphia tormented him. Did he really want to become an architect? To build houses for the rich, creating more privileges for those who were privileged enough already, while all around him...? "The mad priest of Nomadelphia," people said. Was it so? Was the priest mad?

Almost on the point of taking his final exams, Danilo said, No.

"I suddenly realized that I was about to become fossilized," he says. "I was about to bury myself in a materialist society which glorified intellect to the point where it killed feelings, those very feelings which could become actions. And I felt the *need* of action. I suddenly realized that reinforced concrete and drawing boards weren't enough. A home, a car, and all the rest—they weren't enough. Better to be penniless and in shirt-sleeves and a nobody, merely alive in the midst of life, alive in the midst of the perfect community which was still maturing within me"

Alicia broke down when he told her of his decision. He asked her to come to Nomadelphia with him. She returned the engagement ring. Only Franco, the young mechanic, was sympathetic to the idea.

Signor and Signora Dolci had always listened to their son's theories, his talk of a better world, with nods of approval, even with admiration. After all, the ideas had come from them in the first place. "The true Christian, Danilo, is the one who lives for the next man," his mother had always said. But now, at home in Tortona, faced with a 25-year-old son about to act on these ideals, they rebelled. It was late one autumn morning in 1949 when Danilo took out his grandfather's bag and put it on the spotless drawing-room table where the vase of flowers normally stood, and began to pack his belongings. Most of the town's prosperous farming community was in the fields, getting in the wine harvest, a few wives were nodding away the sultry morning in the market square, and Signor Dolci was home from the railway station. He was standing by the sideboard mirror watching his son pack, shaking with rage and weeping. Danilo had never seen his father cry before; he went "quite green." Signora Dolci was in the kitchen, weeping and cutting up bread and salami so that her son might want for nothing on the journey. Signor Dolci gripped his big-boned son by the shoulders and began shaking and abusing him. When Signora Dolci came in from the kitchen bearing a handful of salami and cheese her husband was swearing and pummelling the table so that the suitcase jumped. He grabbed the salami and stuffed it in with the underclothes and sweaters, and then the bread and the cheese, and all the time he went on swearing at his son and throwing things into the bag and shouting that the world was what it was, and there was no sense in trying to change it. Danilo—tense, yet almost detached—spoke of renunciation and said you had to start somewhere. He kissed his mother goodbye.

His father went with him to the station. He bought a single

ticket for Modena and waved to his father out of the third-class carriage window. It was a tearing away of the flesh on both sides. The older man remained standing on the platform. He felt emptied out, betrayed.

One of the last things Danilo did before he went home to pack was to go through all his books and music, and the hundreds of poems he'd written in Milan. He kept the books and the music. When the next tenant moved in he found what was left of the poems in various corners of the room—so many pieces of paper, torn to shreds.

❦

❦ III ❦

❦

THE PERFECT WORLD
OF DON ZENO

DON ZENO, the founder of Nomadelphia and, after thirty-three years, still its guiding light, is not a Gandhi. In moments of priestly anger he has been known to break chairs and lesser pieces of furniture across his knee and, in matters of community administration, to deliver judgment with a kind of brute spiritual violence verging on moral totalitarianism. Once he confronted a newly arrived young woman with twenty children, saying "This is your family," announcing in a few seconds the sentence which was to seal the rest of her life. When Danilo arrived, wearing an old sweater and carrying his grandfather's bag, both traits—the moral and the physical force—were in full evidence and Don Zeno was, like his thriving community, in the prime of life.

Don Zeno Saltini was born in Emilia in 1900, one of ten children in a rich peasant family. He spent his youth skipping school and hobnobbing with delinquents, and almost became a criminal lawyer; but he changed his mind and became a parish priest, deciding that instead of defending delinquents it was more sensible to try to prevent the delinquency. On the day he said his first mass in 1931 he adopted a nineteen-year-old orphan, just released from prison, who was in the congregation, and spent his entire inheritance on an orphans' home in his parish of Mirandola, near Carpi. He waited almost ten years before his first "mother," an eighteen-year-old girl called Irene, turned up—she was given 46 children as her first family. When Italy entered the war, the "little apostles," as they were then known, became fly-

Don Zeno Saltini

ing angels. Don Zeno was arrested for his antifascist outbursts,
and jailed, and the children became scattered. Then the people
of Mirandola rose up and threatened to sack the village, and Don
Zeno was released. He went on campaigning against the régime.
Six of his followers, aged sixteen and seventeen, were caught in
possession of his propaganda leaflets, and either shot or hanged,
and Don Zeno had to flee with a price on his head. At the same
time as Danilo was hiding with British infantrymen among shep-
herds in the central Apennines, Don Zeno was hiding somewhere
in the Maremma, living rough with two escaped prisoners-of-
war, one of them an Englishman. In 1946 he turned up in his
home country again with a crowd of orphans and a kettle-and-
washboard band, piled on top of a truck full of bedding and old

furniture. He took them across the fields and marshes of the Modena countryside to Fossoli, to an abandoned concentration camp where five hundred Jews and many British soldiers had lost their lives. Without waiting for permission he led them on to the site and occupied the camp. They breached the walls, ripped up the barbed-wire enclosures, and put dovecots on the four watchtowers, in place of the machine-gun posts, as a symbol of faith in their new world. Nomadelphia proper had begun. Nomadelphia was, by its name, the place "where fraternity is law."

From that day on children flocked out of the war-torn Emilian landscape into the ready arms of Don Zeno. Institutes made over their "impossibles" to him and he combed the streets, bringing in colored children, scavengers, thieves, the children of prostitutes. He rescued one child as the mother was about to throw it off the Fossoli bridge into the canal. When Danilo came back in 1949 he found fourteen hundred children in the care of sixty mothers and three thousand more abandoned children waiting to be admitted. "This isn't a Boys' Town," Don Zeno told him, "but a reconstruction of ordinary family life." Nomadelphia had its own pilot cooperative farm, church, school, store, and recreation room. It was a creative society, a primitive work-and-prayer colony where everybody worked and money was never used, and there was one fixed point—great love.

For the first year Danilo was "drunk" with the place. He worked as Don Zeno's secretary, borrowed his accordion and began a small orchestra, emptied rubbish, joined a woodcutters' party in the scrub, and then was put in charge of seventy of the rougher youngsters. He took his group on fortnightly camps to the woods above Grosseto and there he won their trust quickly. Occasionally he would read to them from the Gospels—some of them later complained he wore them out with religion.

"Sometimes I came to feel as if I had God in my hands," he says, and this is evident in almost all the poems he wrote at Nomadelphia. They were published in 1951 as *Voices in the City of God*. Not masterly poems, but they show clearly the mystical intimacy of his thought:

In order to live I must be brother to You
And father
And wipe Your dripping nose
Support Your faltering steps
Build You a strong house of stone
Solid and upright, and revive You
When Your helpless forehead
Burns on my knees
And get bread for You, soup,
And the honey and fruit You like:
This is my worship

Danilo regretted nothing. He went about in black—patched and torn pants, black jersey, black beret; until they got to know him the mothers took him for "one of them newfangled American priests." Priests who did come to Nomadelphia for the experience were put to work emptying septic tanks or scrubbing out latrines. A Professor of Holy Writ from Milan was given the job of overseeing the pig pen. Don Zeno was a great believer in Christian communism. Franco visited Danilo three times. Signor Dolci came to see him. They were building a road at the time. "If I'd known you were going to take to this sort of thing, Danilo," he grumbled, "I'd have brought you up to be a railroad-crossing guard."

Most nights he flopped into bed exhausted, almost too tired to eat. They were short-staffed, burdened with debts, and the kids were far from angels. Some of them hid in a watchtower, electrified the doors, and roasted and ate every dove they could lay hands on. But he saw that nothing was hopeless. "I discovered that even the dumbest, the most monstrous child, if I really loved him, became more beautiful, more intelligent. He became transformed." After a time even the most dissolute youngster responded. "I remember one essay, by a boy of about eleven. He wrote, 'Our parents are the trunks and the roots and the branches. We are the leaves and the flowers. Without us they can't live.' Usually we think that a child can't live without *us*, but this lad had understood perfectly the reciprocity of life. *Incredible* intuition."

The whole environment created by Don Zeno nurtured intuition. Don Zeno became Danilo's *guru*. The two were almost always together. Don Zeno at fifty was a formidable figure, pouchy, squat, with a gnarled terrifying stance and the energy, in full cassock, to chase and catch a recalcitrant youngster less than half his years. He wore a thick black sweater, which emphasized his bulk, a beret pulled aggressively down over his thick brows, and when he was angry retired to his room, tipped his beret slantwise over one ear and played the accordion. The kids loved him, and claimed that the moral impetus he radiated penetrated even the stoutest partition. Many a troubled youngster, about to knock on his door with a problem, would suddenly stop, and then turn confidently away without entering, the solution having already "arrived" across the threshold. Danilo loved him because of his rustic simplicity: when Don Zeno built his church, for example, he put the altar at one end and a cinema screen at the other, and on film nights had the smaller children sit on top of the altar to watch. The pair of them went for long walks, often out all night, railing under the stars, and Danilo tested the widening horizon of his ideas against the leathery sounding board of the older man's profounder Catholicism. Once he rebuked Don Zeno for not admitting more children. "Here we have order," the priest rumbled. "Open the doors out of blind love and we'll have chaos." Danilo says, "I made such acts of faith in him I lost the capacity to criticize, I began to think as he did. He was nearly always right." Don Zeno talked of his vision, to construct *the* Christian Society, based on his three imperatives—love, brotherhood, and justice—as an example to the world; and Danilo gave the vision substance, translating it into a kind of radial city on paper. As a first step he took forty of the older youngsters down to the hilly scrubland overlooking Grosseto, where Don Zeno had bought two hundred acres of wild pig country, and they began building a nucleus village.

The site was known as Ceffarello. It was a high wilderness, stony and rooted in tussock and heavy scrub, looking out over the olives and tidy vineyards of Grosseto plain to Elba and the north

tip of Corsica. They tented down and worked by hand, quarry-
ing their own stone, cutting a road up through the scrub, laying
down foundations for eleven houses, a school, and a church,
working like madmen, eighteen hours out of twenty-four. Don
Zeno visited them, well pleased. He was beginning to feel he had
found in Danilo someone who might eventually succeed him.
Danilo said that some unemployed workmen from the village of
Battignano had called, asking for jobs. "We're not an employment agency," the priest said, emphatically. A young laborer
turned up and pleaded to be taken on. "Either you take me, or
I shoot myself," he said. "We can't take you," Don Zeno said.
Danilo argued with him. It was their duty to help *all* the poor,
he said. "That's your idea, Danilo. I don't even accept this principle; we're not an employment agency." Danilo persisted, stubbornly. The older man relented, almost huffily. "All right then,
give it a try—but that's not my line." It was the first serious difference between them.

Danilo went ahead and engaged a dozen laborers, on contract. He was in his element, designing, supervising, surveying
fresh sites, holding group discussions in the big recreation tent
when it was too wet to work. Eleven buildings were rising and
the electric-light tower was completed. The hillside swam with
the hot sweat of fraternity in action. "Men, not merely stones,"
he ruminated, looking out across the valley. Before him rose a
vision of the city of the future.

> *High up, by the groves of marine olives*
> *In the scent from the vine-flowers*
> *We will build the city of God*

he wrote.

But Danilo was not, as it turned out, to be its architect. One
of the reasons was that the world outside, the one he'd left behind, sent him a reminder notice, and he was called up to do his
military service with the postponed 1924 class. When he reported to the barracks at Siena and was handed the regulation ques-
tionnaire, he filled it in:

PATERNITY: God
NUMBER OF BROTHERS: About a billion
NUMBER OF SISTERS: Ditto
PROFESSION: I'm learning to be consumed.

He was the strangest recruit they'd known. He told his superiors he considered military service a polite expression for organized murder, refused to do "anything soldierly" and said, point blank, "No shooting, no bayonet practice." He stuck to his point, and won. He consented to do fire drill and gymnastics. After Don Zeno came to plead Nomadelphia's case Danilo was given liberal weekend leave. Once he came back a week late. He was called before the commanding officer, Colonel Sebastiano Camboso. He explained the needs of Nomadelphia and pointed out that Don Zeno was in trouble. Colonel Camboso was a cultured man and, by chance, had read some of the recruit's poems published in a national anthology. "Never let it be said," he remarked, "that here brute force is a mightier weapon than the spirit." He shook Danilo by the hand. What with Don Zeno's continued efforts, the help of friends at Siena University, the influence of the poems, and Danilo's stubbornness, he did very little service of any kind. In desperation they put him to work as a designer and offered him a commission. Danilo refused the officers' course and stayed with the ranks. During the whole of the token three-months' course his single achievement appears to be an assignment carried out in Rome, abetted by friends from Siena, when he was ordered to design a new regimental standard. It was to show all the battalion emblems, mostly eagles' heads. He was given a car and a driver to go out and buy materials and paints. He finally produced a monstrous caricature—the eagles' heads were enormous, the talons fiercely predatory. Nobody noticed. It was hung proudly in the regimental officers' mess in Rome and, presumably, is still there.

Don Zeno was worried. In 1951, when Danilo was in camp, Don Zeno had many enemies. He was not an anarchist, nor, as some cardinals in the Vatican and leading members of the new

Christian Democrat Government considered, was he mad. He was a Catholic firebrand and a proud descendant of the unorthodox holy tradition of the Piedmontese Don Bosco and the Veronese Don Calabria and the most that could be said of him, in the political field, was that he was bizarre. He despised cant and clericalism, thought all the political parties were tarred with the same bourgeois brush—and ever since 1946 had said so, publicly. It did not endear him to the Vatican, especially after 1948 when the Christian Democrats, the official party of the Church, became all-powerful. Don Zeno, with seventeen Emilian priests, led a minor political revolt, on Nomadelphian principles. It failed. Emilia was militantly Communist. Mario Scelba, the equivocal Home Secretary and Minister of Police (1947–55), and the members of the Rome Curia were hysterically anti-Communist: it was the era when parish priests were encouraged to tell their congregations how the Reds would cut off boys' heads and gobble up little girls with the *hors d'oeuvers*. Don Zeno's revolutionary Christianity—revolutionary, because actually put into practice— was too much of a bad thing. Inevitably he was suspected of being a Kremlin spy. In 1951, up to his eyebrows in debt, he asked the Government to help him settle his creditors, adding that he had rescued hundreds of children from crime and starvation whom no state institute had wanted or even known about. He had an ally in the Countess Maria Albertoni Pirelli, daughter of the tire magnate, and to her Scelba made the enlightened statement that he did not approve of Nomadelphia "from the moral, the social or the political point of view." He tried to buy the priest out, offering to fix his debts if Don Zeno gave up Nomadelphia. Otherwise . . . the Minister made a firm threat. Don Zeno refused to be blackmailed or neutered, called the Christian Democrats "heels" and "anti-Christian" and quietly began ferrying some of the children from Fossoli down to Rosellana, a desolate woodland valley belonging to the Countess and directly underlying the hill of Ceffarello where Danilo was building. But he wasn't quick enough. The cold war with the Government became a hot one. Scelba sent a massive police force to Fossoli, blockaded the camp and, on a pretext of red tape, loaded the children on to trucks, and took them to official religious colleges. Don Zeno lost a thousand children in a morning. His creditors took their cue and closed in; his assistant-priests, one by one, were recalled by their bishops. But Don Zeno had not trained as a lawyer for nothing. He spiked both Scelba's and the Vatican's guns by invoking the Italian decree which says it is against the law for a priest to go bankrupt—and promptly went into voluntary liquidation. "Creditors can wait," he thundered— "children can't!" He went to court, shouting, "It's not Nomadelphia that failed, but the State!"—won the case, then threw off his cassock, and became a layman. He dispersed the remaining children all over the north of Italy and then mustered them again at Rosellana where the Countess made him a gift of 2,000 acres. Nomadelphia is there today, a thriving creative colony, more than self-sufficient, and the nearest thing to nonmarxist communism outside the *kibbutz* system in Israel. Don Zeno is once more a practicing priest—he said his second "first mass" in 1962—and Scelba is no longer in a post of importance.

Above the new Nomadelphia, near Grosseto, today can be seen the scored hill of Ceffarello, and on the skyline the ruins of Danilo's "city"—the walls of eleven buildings, including the church, which he had intended to call Agape, and the completed light tower, on which someone has chiselled with a pick the motto of the Portuguese Catholic colonizers in South America, *Pasamos por aquí*—"We were here." From time to time, whenever Danilo's name crops up, a shadow crosses Don Zeon's animated leonine face, and he says as though muttering to himself, "If he'd stayed with us, he would have been precious."

Danilo came out of camp in the summer of 1951 when the cold war between Don Zeno and the Government was at its height. A first colony of mothers and children from Fossoli was already tenting in the valley of Rosellana. They didn't use the dwellings at Ceffarello—Don Zeno had bought this land but never got around to paying for it, and when the credit squeeze took hold building stopped abruptly. Reluctantly Danilo dismissed the workmen and abandoned the site.

He took his building force on to the valley floor below, joined up with the others, and they all began hacking a third Nomadelphia out of the wilderness. There were half a dozen mothers and a communal force of about a hundred and fifty, nearly all youngsters. The majority lived in tents. There was a farmhouse and one or two outbuildings. The rest was bush and stone, hill scrub and fenland. The scrub ran for kilometres. "We must have order!" Don Zeno pronounced. Boys of fourteen drove catepillars, loaded stone on to trucks and assembled prefabs. ("Who knows?" Don Zeno told Danilo. "We may have to move again.") Danilo's group grew to sixty and was the new agricultural arm. That autumn there were freak rains and throughout the district peasants walked off their land and declared the sowing of wheat and barley impossible. At Rosellana a tractor was bogged down and lost from sight. Danilo's group went on to the hillsides and sowed the entire crop by hand.

Gradually out of the wilderness came the breath of life: the children were repatterned into families, the stones became foundations of new houses, the scrubland became grainfields.

Don Zeno was then confident he could evacuate Fossoli completely in time to avert the coming storm. Danilo missed that battle. He was locked in a private war of his own. For the second time fever gripped him. "Every day," he reasoned, "there are men from the villages with destitute families coming here and asking to be taken on. We have two courses—to accept or to refuse. We refuse them. Why? Because their moral convictions are different. We don't even *try* to solve their problem." Finally, he went to Don Zeno and said, "I'm thinking of leaving," Don Zeno was sitting in his tent, writing. There was a brief exchange, pungent, not bitter. Danilo said he wasn't responding any more, that Nomadelphia was committed to a limited Catholic morality which argued only to the converted and which took no account of social problems outside. He felt he had to get out and help

All that is left of Dolci's "city"
at Ceffarello above Nomadelphia

all classes of men. The older man snorted and advised him not
to put the cart before the horse. "You want social change—that's
not a religious problem at all, Danilo. Everywhere you find social improvements and bad societies. We say—first, fraternity; then
social change. In that order. Don't mix them up. To build a social
revolution *and* a new people there's only one way—and that's *here*."

They were two obstinate men. Don Zeno took the young
plant and nurtured it; Danilo wanted to straighten out the jun-
gle. Their paths were quite different. It was painful for both of
them.

Danilo said later: "It wasn't so much that Nomadelphia excluded non-Catholics. Sometimes it seemed so good, so perfect, that

bit by bit the children and adults formed the opinion they'd *achieved perfection*; and this perfection became enclosed, and a kind of pride—not in him, but in the others. It was mistaken, it was lost—and I felt empty."

Don Zeno said later: "We're not a closed shop—we're closed only to non-Catholics. With Danilo his idea was you could form a community even with different religions. It was a case of seeing and not seeing. But he had this driving force inside him, this force to be useful to humanity. And he *had* to go because of this—this in him."

Danilo left Nomadelphia at the beginning of 1952. He gave all his books and music, several hundredweight of them, to Don Zeno for the library and caught a train, third-class, to Tortona. He went home, had a fresh row with his parents, and then north to look at the area around Ancona. But the villages he saw "weren't poor enough." He remembered Trappeto, in Sicily. He wrote to some of the fishermen to say he was coming.

He left Nomadelphia as he had come, quietly. The youngsters, who'd come to look on him as a kind of father, heard that he was not returning from Virgilio, one of the Ceffarello builders. They took Virgilio's news gloomily. "He told me to tell Don Zeno not to worry. 'Not to worry,' he said, those were his words —'Tell him I'm going to become a priest.' The group listened. Virgilio went on: "All he had with him was a woman's basket, a skiddly *woman's* basket, and some olives and dried figs. And he got into third. I felt somehow ashamed, seeing him go off like that, like a—"

"Like a what?" someone said.

Virgilio hunched his shoulders and thought about it. "Like a Gandhi," he said at length.

PART TWO

Who shouts loudest, is right
—SICILIAN PROVERB

AMONG
THE UNTOUCHABLES

DOLCI stepped off the one o'clock train at Trappeto in February 1952. He was wearing an old jersey and a pair of baggy pants and carried a few old clothes in Grandad's case. He had thirty lire in his pocket—five cents. Some of the fishermen were there to meet him—young Paolino, Toni "the philosopher," Leonardo, "son of the blind one," Peppino Russo, Giuseppe Scardino, and one or two others. They were all related. They embraced him warmly and he told them he'd come to stay. The fishermen scratched their ears. "I've come to live among you, as a brother," Dolci said.

They took him off round the village. He agreed, after persuasion, to spend the first few nights with the Scardino family. They squeezed him into a back alcove and he shared their single-room dwelling with the hens and three other sons. For the first two days he did nothing but walk round, talking to people. The knot of fishermen clung to him.

Trappeto, facing Castellammare Bay, thirty miles from Palermo, had some 2,800 inhabitants. People were living in conditions which no qualified veterinary would recommend for animals. He saw cubist patterns on sheets hanging over the alleys, looked closer and saw they were patches of patches of patches over patches. Rooms four yards square had beaten earth floors, ark-like sticks of furniture, and no water. The word "lavatory" was practically unknown. Antediluvian dressers leaned up behind pale fly-screens, laden with the monstrous bric-a-brac of the poor:old tools, outdated calendars, empty cans, combs as big as rakes, clocks which had stopped when the Americans landed. Women who had never learned to sew sat mending on the step, using stitches half an inch long. Chairs which nobody used sat funereally round the walls. The rooms were dark and smelled. Most were partitioned for the mule or the pig; hens skittered under tables and larger animals emerged from the shadows. From behind the fly-screens the children and the elders watched. Everywhere blank faces, watching.

There was something else, something beyond the mere smell of poverty. Dolci couldn't put his finger on it.

A woman with five children said—Paolino was translating the dialect into Italian: "We eat twice usually—bread, straight, in the morning; at night a plate of spaghetti, sometimes colored with sauce or beans. Today we haven't eaten yet." It was a quarter to six in the evening. "Do you ever have meat?" Dolci asked. The woman snorted. "At Christmas." She went on, "At night we stand outside to get away from the smell. The kids play outside in all kinds of weather—over there, in the Vallone. It stinks there too, but it's a better stink than the one inside."

The Vallone was an open canal, almost wide enough for a small boat, which ran through the middle of the village. It was drain, sewer, dump, and children's playground. The kids played among hens and pigs at the bottom of the filth, often naked. "Down there," Paolino said, "where Giustina's standing, the stuff often comes into the houses." Giustina's husband was in prison, Paolino said. Dolci looked at her, nodded, and went on walking round.

"If we hadn't been baptized we'd be no better than animals that talk," someone said.

"Why are so many men in prison?" he asked. "When the young ones cry we steal for them," he was told.

A woman whose husband and four sons had earned a total of eighteen dollars in the previous four months said they had been waiting to be put on poor relief for twenty-nine years.

In one family of seven nobody had had as much as a day's schooling. "I was barefooted, so the teacher used to send me home," a girl of fifteen said.

"What do you do when you're not working?" Dolci asked everywhere. "I go to bed," one said, suspecting a trap; "I'm not the sort of man who goes out to steal wood." But the invariable reply was "Nothing."

"Do you have a bit of land?" he asked one man. "Yes—in the cemetery, when I'm dead."

Everywhere despair, a deep brooding on injustice, the feeling—real and imagined—of being forgotten, left out, of being put upon by the *signori*—the proprietors, the local authorities, the Government. By *them*. The feeling of being an untouchable.

Did they want anything then? he wondered. And if so, what? He asked, "What do you want most?" A young girl smiled, without replying. A man of sixty seemed at first not to understand; then he decided: "I'd like a pair of shoes, size nine." A woman said: "I want a new bed, complete with bedding." A neighbor explained: "Her husband died in it, you see, and they burned the bed and everything on it."

Don Zeno had said: "If you go south, Danilo, I think these are places you have to live in for a long, long time before you begin to understand them . . ."

Not everybody was poor. This too he noted, moving round.

He learned to talk with his mouth almost shut. "When you walked along," he says, "the flies rose up and settled again after you'd gone. All the streets were streets and drains at the same time. People didn't know what a sewer was. And always a halo of flies. Black stains on the ground where the mules had passed. They rose and settled, rose and settled. You had to be careful how you opened your mouth . . ."

There was no druggist and no telephone, no library, no nursery school, no newsagent; and when he went into the only café it was unable to muster a cup of coffee. Children of seven regarded him curiously when he said "Hullo," and he saw in their tired eyes the expressions of adults of forty. Others, the spindly results of malnutrition, looked only half their years. He suspected that child mortality was high.

The fishermen took him down to the tiny rock beach. He remembered it well—the gawdy colored boats, drawn on to the beach, painted and chipped with religious legends, the big kerosene lamps, the black nets. On the parapet above, fifty or sixty men gathered round him; there were warm words of recognition, handshakes, smiles—and general incomprehension when Paolino said he'd "come to stay."

They offered him tobacco. Dolci said he didn't smoke. "Once I saw my father get in a rage because he'd run out of cigarettes, and I decided then I'd never take it up, for this reason." They thought he was a bit odd.

They fished at night, they said, and sold their catch on the beach at dawn to the Palermo buyers. Most of the village took its livelihood from the sea. In winter they doubled as peasants. There were only the two jobs. Everyone did a bit of both.

Dolci explained his idea of opening a house where the needy would be fed and clothed and live together in brotherly love, which was the basis of true religion. A kind of community. There was silence. A community? What was that?

"You won't get far if you try to change things in this place," someone said.

"Well, it sounds very fine to me, whatever it is," Toni observed.

They began talking, all at once.

"If we're lucky we get fish on a hundred days of the year."

"You see, Danilo," Leonardo began, "the Sicilian is born with this system, he—"

"A hundred and fifty at the most."

"The fishing's being ruined by the trawlers."

"He's born with this system, he grows up with this system, and—"

"They come within the limit, against the law."

"Nobody cares."

"We ask God for good health and providence, but nothing's ever done."

"They come right inshore. Farther out they use bombs."

"Bombs?" Dolci asked. "How long's this been going on?"

"Ever since the war, since Signor Dolci left."

Leonardo said again: "We're born with this sytem, we grow up with this system, and the responsibility for every darn thing falls on the man."

For the hundredth time Dolci asked: "What do you want most?"

"Work," the fishermen said.

When Gandhi arrived back in India from South Africa in 1915 he spent his first year there with "his ears open but his mouth shut." It was the wisest thing he could have done.

Circumstances in Trappeto did not allow Dolci to follow Gandhi's example. He had little time to stop and consider his motives. Though he sensed, beneath the resignation, a kind of stoicism, his first reaction was that the situation was critical. He had to act, and act quickly.

When the confusing grains of evidence whirring in his brain had subsided, he picked out the two biggest bits. One was the desire for work. Of this he was convinced, in spite of a basic northerner's prejudice that southerners, especially Sicilian southerners, were "idle." The other problem was malnutrition. Children were wasting away in the alleys, were slowly starving. There was no money to buy medicines. Many were orphans. Food was needed, clothes, shoes, bedding, shelter. Quickly.

"We need a house to take in the needy," he told the fishermen.

"Yes, yes, that's right," they said.

"But there isn't one," Paolino added, with Sicilian logic.

"We'll build one."

"But you haven't got any money, Danilo."

"I'll get some," Dolci said.

They found him a site just outside the village. It was a wide shelf on top of a hill, harbored by olives and facing the sea. The

owner wanted $588 for the land. Dolci borrowed enough money
for his train fare and went north. He went home, and then to
Milan where his former professor of architecture gave him one
hundred and sixty-eight dollars. With this he returned to Trappeto, put it down as deposit, signed promissory notes for the
rest, and took possession of the land. He put up a tent and became a Sicilian "resident." From that day, in the spring of 1952,
his troubles began.

The following Sunday many villagers came up to see the
stranger in his tent. Even the mayor, and the archpriest of the
next village, Balestrate, came. Describing this later, in *The Story
of Borgo di Dio,* Paolino and Toni say: "Everyone was pleased
and they asked him what he planned to do. He told them everything and the mayor said he, for one, would do all he could to
help.

"The next day Danilo fixed it with a mason to start on the
house and the mason said he would work even if there were no
wages—he was willing to wait on Providence, he said ('Until it
rains,' as we say round here). A man in Alcamo and another in
Balestrate gave Danilo the lime for the mortar on credit . . . Two
days later he went to Mazzara del Vallo for two wagonloads of
tufo building stone, asking them to send it COD, trusting that
the money to pay for it would arrive about the same time as the
stone did—otherwise he would have had to pay for the stuff to
sit in the wagons at $6.50 a day. But when the time came some
friends lent him the money. And that's how it was with everything.

"When the stone was unloaded he was the first to grab a
pick and start working, him and two others. There was a bit of a
mule track up to the site, but when the horses were laden with
stone they couldn't manage the last bit where the track petered
out so Danilo and the others carried the stuff the rest of the way
on their backs."

Giovanni Piergallini, a wiry, drifting orphan from Lom-
bardy, arrived out of the blue, and fresh from prison. This pal-
lid footloose youth, an atheist, had had several stopovers in jail,

for want of means and a fixed abode. He found his first spiritual
home in Dolci's tent, and for more than three years gave himself
to the work as no other volunteer did. Giovanni was the first veteran helper. He was followed almost immediately by Franco,
the young Turin mechanic. Franco had written down, saying he
was married and had a child, but little money. Dolci replied,
saying, "Come and look round." Franco came for a month and
stayed until his money ran out six months later. In 1956 he came
back again, for good.

They worked on the house for a month and a half. As soon
as the roof was on Dolci and Co. moved in.

He was in and out of the village every day, often sleeping
there. He saw terrible quarrels. People fought each other in the
ditches. A woman of 47 whose first daughter died of an abscess
at eighteen months said: "A year and a half later I lost a little
boy of six. His throat was hurting and the doctor said it was
meningitis, but at Palermo they said it was tetanus. When this
one died I was pregnant and the shock took hold of the heart of
the one unborn. Eight days after birth its feet were all swollen.
The doctor said that it had a sick heart: 'He'll die sooner or
later,' the doctor said. When the doctor came back he did die.
Two years later I had another baby and as it was wartime, what
hope was there of finding a doctor? At four months he got dysentery and sores all round the mouth. His sucking infected my
breasts and the milk gave out altogether. At the children's hospital in Palermo they told me to leave him there, but I didn't
want to leave him alone and brought him home again. I took
him round the neighborhood to be fed and after four days he
was dead."

Dolci began to believe it was possible for despair and hunger and blind animal ignorance to drive people to anything.

He began fetching medicines from the drugstore at Balestrate, five miles away. He told the druggist what he told everyone else—that he'd pay when God was willing. If the druggist
refused him he'd bang on doors and badger people until he got
what he wanted. Children now recognized his beret from a dis-

tance and would run after him, shouting "Hullo, Danilo!" With the youngest he'd bend down and wipe their noses, as Don Zeno had done at Nomadelphia, and then he'd kiss them. The village watched and wondered.

He and Franco were sent for one day and brought to a basement at the bottom of the Vallone. The sewage water sludged past and seeped over the doorstep into the room. The room was dark. He made out humid stained walls and, in a corner, a slender young woman holding a baby a few weeks old. Her name was Giustina Barretta. She was 22. It was her first child. Since the baby was born she had eaten only a bit of bread and pasta the neighbors had given her. Her milk had dried up and the baby no longer had the strength to suck. Dolci ran to get powdered milk. They tried to give the milk to the baby, but at every attempt it vomited. They put the child on the bed, a palliasse laid on planks, and Franco went for the doctor. Dolci sat with Giustina.

While they were waiting for the doctor the child died.

The incident haunts Dolci still. "I would never have believed if I hadn't seen it that a child might actually die of starvation," he says. "I can still see that woman—her hair, wild, her features, quite yellow; she no longer had the strength to shout or scream. She'd lost even the capacity to react. And this was the terrible thing—I didn't realize it till later, of course—that underneath ordinary misery was this hidden layer, a deeper stratum; and this was a mass thing, it had to do with the very *structure* of poverty."

Although the incident, only one of a series of shocks, was not traumatically decisive for him—as is usually written—it was to affect his attitude to the whole Sicilian situation.

In the village people said Giustina's child had died of "the black sickness." It was "just tiny," they said, as though there were some natural law by which tiny babies had to die.

BORGO DI DIO

OFTEN when Dolci went to Palermo for materials for the house he had to borrow his train fare from one of the fishermen. His father kept sending down money and toilet gifts, but just as he found it impossible to accept food from fisherfolk if it meant their going without, so he would not accept gifts. He gave them away.

As the house grew so did his enthusiasm, and poetic fancy. Giovanni says: "He'd told me there was already a cooperative of fishermen, a school, a house ready—everything. But when I got there in May there was a tent and two pieces of wall just off the ground, and nothing else. I didn't worry. I realized that the things he'd planned were still only in his mind."

Dolci laid in beds, furniture, bathroom fittings, all on installment. Initially, the local assistance board helped.

He was down in the village one day when he heard screams. A woman was holding a child with one hand and tearing at her hair with the other, shrieking in the street as her husband was being taken off to prison. He had stolen a bunch of grapes. Dolci persuaded the police to release the man and gave him a job.

They began work on a road up to the house. "At first about twenty men came along," Paolino and Toni relate, "and he said to them: 'I haven't a bean to pay you with, but if you want a job I'll give you wages just as soon as Providence sends me the money.' The storekeepers staked the men in food, trusting that Danilo would eventually make good his promise ... A few days went by and there were no longer twenty laborers but forty. In the end eighty men a day came to work there, until there was hardly enough room between them to swing a pick. There was no other work available . . ."

The house was low and L-shaped. It rose 150 feet above Castellammare Bay on a secluded shelf of carob and olive trees. It was simple and unostentatious.

He called it *Borgo di Dio*—Hamlet of God. It was constituted as an official organization, with three aims: to house the needy, to find work for the unemployed, and spread the Christian doctrine.

Even before Borgo was finished the first occupants moved in Giustina and her husband Mimi. The following day Vincenzina arrived with five children. Vincenzina Mangano was in heavy mourning. She was a peasant widow in her late twenties, handsome, with sturdy features and a resilient pose. Her tiny legs made her seem stockier than she actually was. Her husband, Luciano, had died at 34 following an attack by masked bandits. He was surprised in the fields while ploughing, made to lie down and heavily beaten when he refused to blackmail his employer. The shock, with recurrent fever, brought a slow and painful death four months later.

Vincenzina's five children were the first to be taken in. Within a week there were fifteen children at Borgo. They came from Trappeto and Partinico and Borgetto, the children of bandits and the children of the men the bandits had killed. When they saw whole loaves of bread on the table they took half a loaf and put it under their pillows to keep for the morning, because they couldn't imagine waking up and having still more bread the next day. "These children," Dolci says, "you had to teach them to wipe their bottoms. When they were taken to the lavatory they screamed. To wipe their bottoms they used their fingers and then they cleaned their fingers on the wall. So we had to start their education from there."

Giustina and Vincenzina kept house and looked after the children. The news of Borgo spread. So many women with husbands

Once the land was rich in timber, citrus, and grain. All too often only stones and eroded hills remain. The people live high up in crowded hilltop towns. In places the Government is building better houses.

in prison brought their children that Dolci had to put them off until he had enough workers to start day sessions. Visitors from the north came and went, a little mystified by what Don Zeno's young revolutionary was hoping to achieve. Dolci yet had no clear idea himself. He was like a giant harbor of love, with the entrance lights constantly flashing, praying to God to send him cargo and no more freight charges. There were prayers daily, family visits to mass on Sundays, and the Gospel of brotherly

love. "If we try to think and live as God wishes," he told everyone, "sharing everything alike, then we *shall* live together."

The lesson didn't always go home. Giustina's parents came
to Borgo, leaving their house in Trappeto empty. Dolci suggested they give it to another family whose house was falling
down. The parents objected; the other family was "dirty," they
said. Giustina's parents went back to live in Trappeto.

Borgo was the first building in Trappeto to have a bath.
When the furniture and fittings were finished half the village
trooped up again to see.

Dolci asked the priest, Father Angelo Donato, if he might
try the small organ in the church. The priest agreed. Dolci became the official organist for mass. On other occasions he would
slip down to the church in the daytime, a score under his arm,
and bestir the wheezy cottage organ. The locals passing by would
stop and listen, marvelling at the sound coming from within.
They had never heard Bach before.

A nucleus of fishermen, however, was coming to regard
Dolci as a deeply religious man with high moral principles; a
man of continence, who never smoked or drank and, most remarkable, in an environment where everybody shouted or
screamed, never raised his voice. He was always going somewhere, doing something, thinking something; yet his unlined
Nordic face was almost always in repose. He never seemed in a
hurry. The fishermen saw him as someone who could overcome
any obstacle and his pensive voice gave them a feeling of security. It had a saintly quality.

The children at Borgo found they were not neglected or
beaten, but were treated as individuals. Matteo, Vincenzina's
second son, was then about eleven. He had been in a religious
college run by nuns. He says: "If we didn't say our rosaries right
we were put to bed without supper. One mealtime I was caught
talking—or I didn't like the food, I don't remember—and they
made me come out, me and another boy, and kneel down on
the refectory floor in front of everyone, with our hands cupped

under our knees—like this. Under our hands they put the shells of broken almonds. Then one day my mother fetched me and brought me up to Borgo. I didn't know how to take Danilo at first, but then suddenly I felt happy there, lifted up—free."

Dolci bought a secondhand accordion, on credit, and gave the children music; he began to stock a library for the villagers in Borgo's big room, 20 feet by 18 feet, and to plan another building to house the volunteer helpers.

He acquired a blue motor scooter, on which he and Franco, sometimes both, swathed in old overcoats, berets, and scarves, would career over the low hills to Partinico and elsewhere on errands of mercy. "Once," Franco says, "we had to go to Palermo and there was no money for gasoline. I borrowed a litre here and a litre there and put in a bit of olive oil, and in Palermo a friend lent us twenty cents for a meal. Then we hadn't enough gas to get back. So I found three stamps in my briefcase—three five-cent stamps, right?—and we sold them back to the tobacco shop and got fifteen cents' worth of gas. But it wasn't enough and we pushed the scooter the last few miles."

Often they were days on end without money; bread was short at mealtimes, the children without shoes. Once their plight was so bad that when one baker refused credit Dolci wept at the counter, it is said, until he was given bread. His debts grew. Two men arrived from Palermo and demanded the furniture back unless he paid up on the spot. They grabbed him by the shoulders and tried to bang his head up against the library wall. Dolci, strong enough to hurl both men through the window, shook them off and told them they could have the motor scooter as part payment. The men took the scooter and went off cursing. Later, when he was able to pay for the furniture, they gave him back the scooter, and he bought more fittings from the same shop.

The children were taken into the country, shown the flowers, the stars, were taught to design. The etchings young Matteo did then, today symbolize the Dolci organization on post-

cards which are sent all over the world. Matteo, the son of an
illiterate peasant killed by bandits, is now a professional designer in Milan.

There was a danger in all this. Dolci had begun to create a
kind of oasis, removed from the reality he was hoping to change.
The revolution of Borgo, with its individual hand-to-mouth
charity, its mixed bag of helpers, all untrained, all plunged urgently to work before they had time to understand the complex
morality of the place, was to cost him dearly.

Giovanni and others had begun an inquiry in Trappeto
and were bringing back incredible reports. People were living
on as little as seven and a half cents a day. Children at ten or
over didn't know how to write their own names or make the
sign of the cross. Schoolteachers arrived halfway through the
morning and some did not bother to come at all. Gaspare, a peasant, who had developed fluid on the lung, told them he had
been given a cursory examination at Balestrate and sent back to
Trappeto, where a local doctor came to draw off the fluid. "He
came along with his instruments, not a kitful, just a syringe and
an old needle, and he began to poke into me. The first jab got
me in the ribs. The second one was all right, but didn't manage
to find the fluid immediately and he began to waggle the thing
up and down until the needle broke off inside. Then he panicked
so much he didn't even think to make a small cut to remove the
other piece—you could see the broken bit. But he was terrified
and had me sent off to the first-aid post in Palermo. There they
X-rayed me for over two hours, twisting and turning me about
until they located the needle. They said it meant an operation
—they said they'd operate before midnight. Midnight came and
they didn't operate. Nothing happened. The needle stayed put
and I've had it inside me for more than five years ..." In the
hospital, Gaspare said, he was treated for pleurisy. After twenty
days he went home to help his wife through childbirth (the
baby subsequently died of leukaemia) and took up cobbling.
After a few months he had chronic tuberculosis. He went back
to the hospital and an operation was proposed, "but neither the

family nor any of my relatives would hear of it." When Giovanni found him in Trappeto he was propped in bed in a narrow alcove, spitting up blood. The roof was falling in, and when it rained the water fell directly on to the bed. His wife was also ill. The family had no regular assistance and didn't know how to set about getting a pension.

Reports like these roused Dolci anew. "Must we wait," he wrote in his diary, "until they rise up in revolt, maddened by hunger and misery, before we turn to and help them find work so they can save their families? Must we wait until they end up in the sanatoriums and the prisons?"

Autumn came, then late autumn, and the brief harvest of strong white wine led into the dead season on the land. "The worst season of the year is still ahead; there are many unemployed; and what hope have they of finding work?" Unemployment rose. Sporadic crime increased. A middle-aged farmer, when he refused to pay two million lire ($3,360) extortion money, had his mule killed and a little later his vines cut down; above the limp vines was left a bamboo cross warning him not to go back to his land or he, too, would be killed.

And at Borgo: "Oil, tomatoes, pasta, must be bought. Who cares? There aren't enough bunks; there aren't enough mattresses; there aren't enough sheets. Who cares?

"The tiny ones, who still mess in their pants, need several changes if they're to be kept clean. Who's going to buy the stuff? And the spoons and forks, if they're not to eat with their fingers? And the pens and pencils and the writing-paper, if they're not to grow into suspicious half-savages? Who *cares?*"

He saw that there was a solution to one of these problems, perhaps both. The people had only to use the waters of a stream, the River Iato, which ran to waste in the sea, and there would be work for everybody. He drew up plans for an irrigation scheme. In summer, he reckoned, a forty-horsepower pump could raise the level of the water 180 feet in 150 seconds, irrigating 750 acres of dry land. Year after year the priest had been holding a special service, *"ad petendam pluviam"* (to pray for rain) and all the people knelt to pray *"ad petendam pluviam,"* murmuring Latin words they did not understand, to solve a problem which a forty-horsepower pump could have solved in two and a half minutes.

Men *could* intervene to change things, he told the peasants.

For centuries they had been growing grain and beans on arid plainland in unvarying rotation. "Look," he said, "an acre of land growing grain needs only twelve working days a year. But if it's irrigated and produces vegetables it can stand perhaps as many as two hundred and fifty days a year. Don't you see?"

The peasants did not see. Irrigation and "things like that" belonged to the *signori*. Water belonged among the saints. "Water is another God," they said.

The priest did not see either. Dolci made application for the right to use the water. The local authorities were not interested.

Men came to Dolci asking for work, and kept on coming. He had none to give them. He called a meeting at Borgo and told the men there was no work and no possibility of any. In that case, they said, other children would die of hunger.

Dolci prayed.

Finally, he knew what he had to do. He sat down and wrote a letter. In it he asked for enough money to provide immediate work and relief for the village. Then he walked down to the village and into the basement that had been Giustina's house at the bottom of the Vallone. He lay down on the palliasse where the child had died and refused to eat until help, or death, came.

VI

FIRST FAST

Trappeto, 14 October 1952

Dearest friends,

I am a sinner but God will bear me out when I say I want nothing more than that I may die in order that you may all live . . .

We can stop these children being forced to leave school at seven or eight to become assistant-breadwinners.

We can very largely stop the prisons from filling up.

We can stop the ravages of death.

Would you pummel a person to cure him of pneumonia?

We must redeem and repent for this sin of omission towards our own brothers. We must save them and save ourselves by learning to love.

We must act at once. Urgent cases mean urgent treatment. I want to do penance in order that everyone may become more perfect. In the meantime rather than see another child die of hunger I would rather die myself. As from today I will not eat another mouthful until the $50,400 required to employ the neediest and help the most urgent cases has arrived.

When someone is about to shoot down a child, and there's no other way, shouldn't you throw yourself in front to save it? . . .

Then, at once! It is too late to go on waiting. Waiting only means more corpses.

If I, by living, cannot awaken people's love, then by dying
I will arouse their remorse.

Yours in God

DANILO

The letter was printed on a small handpress in Palermo and
sent off to a few friends.

Giustina's room was eight feet below ground level. In the
upper part someone had made a kind of window, an escape
hatch in case the sewage discharge should flood the place suddenly. The floor was earth. Dolci, clad in trousers and a sweater,
spent most of the time lying under a blanket, meditating and
talking to Franco. Franco had borrowed a bed and was sleeping
in the same room.

"Danilo, you must get up and eat," a woman said. "You'll
never get well lying down like that."

Women came, with babies in their arms; some brought him
food and when they saw he had no intention of eating they broke
down and wept. He told them: "If my own mother came I
wouldn't want her in here crying. When you sow grain and the
seed is scattered, and you know that the seed will waste away in
order to bring forth fruit, aren't you cheerful then?" The women
nodded. "Well, then—a fast is the same. It's a strong thing, a
joy." He forbade them to come in weeping and told Franco to
bring down the accordion from Borgo. Thereafter he played
the accordion—dance tunes, mazurkas, and waltzes—daily. He
told everybody he felt calm and happy.

The village women never quite understood. They never got
past the idea that he was doing penitence for the Madonna.

The news did not travel quickly or well. This was not surprising. Under fascism northerners seldom heard of the poverty
of southern Italy and in 1952 they were scarcely better informed.
Italian sociology and culture seldom probed beyond Naples.
Sicily was that pernicious appendage at the bottom, land of rob-
bers and policemen. Who in 1952 was likely to get worked up by
skimpy reports about an accordion-playing crank, starving to

save a tin-pot village alongside Africa? The answer was, almost nobody.

On the third day Franco and others went to Palermo to try to raise the money. They came back downcast. "There are other ways of setting about things than fasting," officials told them. The Trappeto authorities were no help. They were not all there. The priest and the police sergeant had vanished, and were not seen in the village again until the fast was over.

Dolci was outwardly cheerful. He wrote, talked, got up, walked about, played the accordion, and thought about everything except conserving his strength. As the days passed the villagers noticed that the tunes were becoming sadder and sadder. Women began to pray in the houses for him. "He's too young to die," they said. Vincenzina, the young widow, and Giustina took turns to visit him. Some of the fishermen proposed a public demonstration in the capital. "Where is your faith?" Dolci said. They then pledged that should he die one of them would carry on fasting in his place. First Paolino, then Leonardo. "Him first, and then us," they said.

The mail brought little hope. Hardly any of those to whom the letter was sent bothered to reply. This upset him more than the indifference of the authorities. "It shows you, Franco," he said, "that we must put our trust in God, not in men."

The only significant reply was from the pacifist, Aldo Capitini. Capitini had already founded at Perugia a movement for peace. He advised Dolci to stop fasting immediately. "You've no right to throw your life away like this without first informing the public properly of the facts," Capitini wrote, beginning a correspondence which was to have a big effect on Dolci's development.

Franco went to see Cardinal Ruffini, one of the most powerful men on the island. Not long before this, Ruffini had denounced the squalid conditions of many Sicilian families, granting land and money for rehousing in Palermo and calling for "Christian action ... to wipe a horrible reality *immediately* off the face of the earth."

When he called at the archbishop's palace, Franco says, the Cardinal refused to see him because he was "improperly dressed."

After five days Dolci was visited by a young man called Mignosi, secretary to Alessi, an eminent Right-wing politician and a former Sicilian Prime Minister. Alessi (the present Senator) had a key post in the Christian Democrat party. Mignosi had read some of Dolci's poetry and, convinced he was not a crank, was moved to act. The case recalls that of Oscar Wilde whose *Salome* was produced in Paris while Wilde was in Reading Jail. On release Wilde said: "In prison it had been entirely forgotten that I was a literary person; but when they saw that my play was a success in Paris they said to one another 'Well, but this is strange—he has talent, then.' "

Mignosi told Dolci he had taken on too much and that nothing could be done unless he stopped fasting.

"Less than an hour's drive from here, where you've just come from," Dolci said, "there are bright lights, motorcars, and luxury by the windowful. Go for a walk round Trappeto and see the difference." He added: "These people are all sons of God, like you and me, and children are dying here. Whoever knows this—and now the authorities *know*—and leaves them be, is an assassin."

Mignosi said he would do all he could. "But you must stop fasting."

"Before anything will be done, someone's got to die," Dolci said.

Dolci became weaker, and the accordion tunes petered out altogether. He continued to tell Franco that he was well.

Normally, given a relaxed body and adequate mental preparation, a fit person can starve for up to ten days without danger. Dolci had read *about* fasting. That was all. His preparation had been wholly religious. His technique was nil. This was a hunger

Much of a woman's life is spent in church or in processio
praying for better conditions—or simply for ra

strike in the raw and it frightened the wits out of young Franco. The Turin mechanic ministered to Dolci like a mother and grew pale with worry. Villagers hung about outside in small whispering groups. Many were now afraid to enter the room. Police constables watched the house day and night.

Towards evening on the seventh day Dolci became light-headed. It amazed him that he could still think lucidly—he said so to Franco. They put the light out at ten and dropped off to sleep with the noise of the sewage waters, rushing over the door-step, in their ears. Dolci slept soundly. About half past two in the morning he woke suddenly and called out hoarsely to Franco.

"I turned on the light and went to his side," Franco says. "His hands were cold, his feet were cold, he was shaking all over. His breath came in gasps and his right arm and part of the right leg were paralyzed." Franco ran out in his pajamas for the doctor. When the doctor arrived Dolci was unconscious. The doctor took the pulse and the heartbeats, declaring the one "hanging by a thread" and the other "imperceptible," administered some drops and a camphor injection, and, when Dolci came round, harangued him at length about the need to begin eating. Dolci closed his eyes, opened them, and said, No. The doctor sat down and wrote out a memorandum stating that the patient was dying and the fast had to be stopped immediately.

"How long . . .?" Franco started to say.

The doctor squeezed his upper body and jaw into one of those Sicilian gestures which disclaim responsibility, say nothing and everything at the same time, and went back to his bed.

Franco took the memorandum straight to Alessi. Late that afternoon, the eighth day, Dolci, resting fitfully, was roused by the arrival of Mignosi. With him was a welfare priest, Monsignor Arena, who said he was acting for the Prime Minister, Restivo.

"The Hon. Restivo wishes me to assure you of his full co-operation to relieve the desperate plight of this zone," Arena said.

"Thank you," Dolci said softly.

Arena said the Prime Minister guaranteed to grant $2,800 immediately, to care for the extreme needy whom Borgo could not accommodate, to open a work depot for 67 men, and to subsidize a project to harness the waters of the Iato for irrigation.

The last was the vital point. Above Trappeto the irrigation of a stony plain could transform 1,200 acres of sterile land into market gardens and orchards, providing work for over a thousand men and ending the unemployment.

Dolci thanked his visitors and asked them to wait outside while he talked it over with the others. A small group of fishermen came in. They had to strain to catch the words. "Now don't accept this offer just on my account," he told them. "But if you're satisfied, I'm satisfied, and I'll get up and start eating."

"What does it all mean?" Paolino asked.

Franco had scribbled down some figures. "If these men are sincere," Dolci said, "the Government will meet nearly all the expenses of the works: Franco's worked it out—about $50,400, which is what we asked for. This is what they have promised."

"We think it's fair," Paolino said.

Dolci did too. He called the visitors back, accepted their pledge, and said he would break the fast the following day.

"You're a brave man, Signor Dolci," Monsignor Arena said. "The Prime Minister asked me to say also that when you are well he would like to meet you in Palermo."

Dolci had not fasted merely to save Trappeto. He fasted for a creative principle—to redeem those who were blind to, or ignorant of, the sin of their own omission. There is a similarity to Gandhi's first fast in a public cause, in the foothills of the Himalayas in 1917. Gandhi fasted—his biographer, Fischer, writes —not so much to improve conditions for the textile workers as to cure the employers of their unwarranted objection to an arbitration system which would promote peace in the textile industry. "I fasted to reform those who loved me," Gandhi said.

More than anything Dolci's first fast was an act of love.

Villagers reported afterwards that when the two intermediaries, Arena the priest and Mignosi the state official, came out of the room, before walking up to their car they stood for a few moments looking across the mire of the Vallone where the children were playing; and that one of them made the sign of the cross. But whether in a spirit of blessing, or exorcism, the villagers said, it was too dark to tell.

VII

THE TWO DOLCIS

Dolci returned to Borgo. After a few days he went to see Restivo and Alessi, both Christian Democrats. The Prime Minister said he would never have dreamed that a river might run to waste in the sea while, alongside, people starved. He praised Dolci's "statesmanship" and said he had chosen a tragic area. Alas, he said, all of Sicily was poor.

It was to be more than six years before a Roman doctor, Silvio Pampiglione, revealed to both of them that, compared to the *miseria* of a town like Palma di Montechiaro, Trappeto was just a fleabite.

Works officials came to Trappeto and made preliminary surveys to pump the water from the Iato. Dolci drew up the deeds for a development syndicate among the farmers whose land would be irrigated. The promised twenty-eight hundred dollars arrived and in 1953 Trappeto got its first streets, its first drains, its first telephone, and a drugstore.

At Borgo, they dispensed clothes, medicines, and powdered milk which dribbled down from friends in the north. "Simple charity," someone said. A wagonload of old clothes sent by Quakers arrived at the station one night. When they had sorted it the stuff filled the big room at Borgo, over forty feet long. Next morning at six the villagers came up the hill at a gallop for their quota. Paolino attempted to distribute the parcels fairly, through a window, but got jammed and was nearly lynched.

Already there were two Dolcis in action, more or less irrecon-
cilable. There was Dolci the apostle, community-builder, organist, and good Catholic. There was Dolci the technician, irrigation-
planner, sociologist, and freelance trade union unto himself. In
practical terms the only common meeting-point was his creed,
"*Participate,* in order to understand." It wasn't enough. A year
after coming south he was still beside the same crossroads he had
found on entering—one signpost said immediate Christian need;
the other, long-distance social planning. Dolci, no longer directed
by a Don Zeno, veered off on to a lone, if inspired, path of his
own somewhere down the middle. Unwittingly, he compromised.

With anyone less single-minded it would have been fatal. As
it was there were rifts. The do-gooders—in Dolci's words "those
who came to share but not to change"—were always at odds with
him. They saw the contradiction in him and criticized his insistence on technological change *as well as* Christian charity. One
or the other, they said, echoing Don Zeno. Carlo, a Roman helper, wanted to build a vast chicken hatchery; he thought you could
combine meditation with making a living. Dolci pursued his
own path. The critics invariably left. They said they did not understand him.

Reflecting now, he says: "Nomadelphia—the fraternity ideal
—matured inside me like a raging fire; and I imagined that at
thirty I'd be dead. Then at Trappeto—I was already nearly thirty, and I realized that I was still very much alive, that what I had
to do was long-term, that I had to reconsider a lot of things. This
much is certain—I chose a path between that of giving myself to
the people and putting my feet flat on the ground."

In 1953 Dolci did not even realize there was a hard choice
to be made. This ambivalence was to be his private bogey for years
to come.

Even without this confusion of motives there were obstacles
enough. Dolci's visitors, including the women, went swimming.
Before 1952 Trappeto had never seen a modern female bathing

suit. The people were scandalized. After the visit of Lamberto Borghi, Professor of Education in Florence and one of the leading pedagogists in Italy, Dolci was ridiculed. "You told us he was a professor," the Sicilians said, "but he can't be. No professor would go walking on a beach in *bare feet*." Dolci's own team contributed to the view that it was all a kind of vaudeville act. Simply because he hadn't learned that it was sometimes important to refuse the needy stray (and many early volunteers were as much in need of help, one way and another as the Sicilians themselves), hadn't learned tact, and selection—because of this Dolci found himself within a year surrounded by a collection of "types" whose record cast impressive doubts on the sincerity of his aims. One, ironically enough from Nomadelphia, robbed Paolino of most of his money, then vanished. The first Sicilan helper was straight from prison. There was Carlo, a Roman orphan. A dedicated fascist at fifteen, Carlo had ploughed into trouble since, ending up at Borgo a thin, anarchical youth, out on his feet, and spurred by a guilt complex and an indefinable blend of mysticism. "There's good in everybody," Dolci said. He was right, of course —in theory. As a working principle in Sicily it was calamitous. "You, Signor Dolci, I've no complaint about you personally," the police sergeant said to him. "But the company you keep... it doesn't, you might say, appear to heighten your own *honor-r-a-b-i-lll-i-t-y*."

Thus whenever Dolci's helpers went to the priest to inquire about local customs or to the carabinieri to discuss the crime rate, they got nowhere. The priest replied that Signor Dolci had no authority to take such a deep interest in the situation. The sergeant replied that he was not authorized to give a reply.

Sicilian officials have long been trained in the art of gentle rebuff. Additionally, Dolci came from "the Continent"—that is, the mainland. He was a foreigner. And thus, automatically, an "exploiter." He found himself in a little Ireland. Much as the Irish used to resent prying English officials, so the encrusted layers of local bodydom resented Dolci. "If you go to the town council," he wrote, "you find that member X is still on holiday, that his private secretary Y is nowhere to be found. Day after day. Is nobody deputizing for them? The doormen as a rule behave like dumb beasts set to protect the tranquillity of their masters."

Yet this was nothing to the barrier the villagers sent up when Dolci married the widow, Vincenzina, and adopted her five children. In any northern community the act would have been cheered, as indeed it was later overseas. In Trappeto it was resented. It is not easy for an outsider, and no more for an Italian, to grasp the stiff taboos of the Sicilian moral code, ingrained as they are with pagan and Moslem superstition. Normally, if it is known that a woman has been alone with a man for half an hour her reputation is ruined. If marriage follows at once, it is saved. "To elope does not bring shame," the proverb says, "but preservation of life." Vincenzina's first marriage was typical of many. She was a child bride at fourteen: a brief flight with her peasant-fiancé, Luciano, to relatives; enraged parents; return home, reconciliation, and a speedy marriage—and all was well. Luciano died in 1949.

When Dolci arrived in 1952 Vincenzina and the eldest boy, Turi, then eleven, were working in a sardine factory to keep the family. Between them they were earning less than $1.10 for a fourteen- or fifteen-hour day. Vincenzina was desperate. Borgo was her salvation. She went there as housekeeper. Technically, she had once again "eloped"; but the role was eventually accepted. Now, more than a year later, there had been a delayed marriage. The villagers felt that their moral applecart had been upset twice over. Others had imagined Dolci to be the complete ascetic: "We felt this way," Leonardo says. "He'd never said to us that he wouldn't get married, but he'd never led us to believe that he *would*, either. And somehow, by intuition we felt that he wouldn't. So when he did, it seemed wrong. I'd been away. I found him up at Borgo, planting tomatoes—and when he told me he'd married Vincenzina I got furious. 'You'll have the whole village against you now!' I said. Then he got furious. We almost hit each other. After that I didn't speak to him for months.

"But now—that was years ago—now I see that I was wrong. He did well to marry Vincenzina. Now she's got a vocation, whereas before she was lost."

Half-truths have recently appeared in Italian newspapers about the marriage. Many in Trappeto were against it at the time, especially the respective parents. On Dolci's part it was a sacrifice, even a necessary sacrifice, an earnest of his pledge to live among these people in brotherly love and share their conditions—and, in particular, to suffer with someone who spelled out in stark human terms his mission. That mission was Sicily, and Vincenzina, the uncomplaining yet volatile young widow, was every fibre *of* Sicily. Dolci told me: "As a girl she'd saved up, lira by lira, for a small chest of drawers, and when she came to Borgo she wanted to have it up there too. It was everything to her. But her people objected. There was a scene. She didn't say anything, but I knew she was terribly upset. That dinner-time I didn't eat, again saying nothing. I couldn't, out of respect for her. When I saw her next she had two black eyes—the face of a pirate! She'd done it to herself, with her own fists. Why? Because she'd upset *me*. And that was what stunned me. This, I suddenly realized, was also Sicily, and I knew that if I was ever going to really understand this place I had to identify myself with it *thoroughly*."

Dolci does not believe, with what he calls "the big things," in doing by half-measures. "Not in quality, not in love, nor in commitment," he says. "These three things with me are crucial. Quality—to give it you must make sacrifices, even sexual sacrifices. Love—you make love seriously, it's not a second-hand operation. Commitment—whatever your pledge, you carry it through."

In Vincenzina there was a fusion of all three elements. Certainly Dolci did not marry for love in the conventional sense. He was poet, intellectual, and mystic; she was a peasant woman, a year his senior, and barely literate. At the same time there is a very deep and special bond with this heroic woman of alien culture. Vincenzina was two months pregnant when they married. The marriage would have taken place a lot sooner if family pressure on the priest had not caused him to "lose" the papers. Father

Donato succeeded in "losing" them for some months and might never have found them again had Dolci not confronted him in the sacristy with an ultimatum. "Are you going to marry us or not?" Dolci demanded. The priest managed to find the papers.

Dolci and Vincenzina were married by Father Donato in Trappeto church in August 1953, and returned to Borgo to make of it a home and a creative community which would, they hoped, command the respect of the village. But the affair had driven a wedge between Borgo and a section of the people, and a few splinters would always remain.

They went on with the house-to-house inquiry, often under fire. "We have even been spat on," Dolci wrote. "Real spit, saliva —not merely insults." More than ten people worked on the inquiry, including Vincenzina and Giustina; with not more than seven years' schooling between them, the pair became valuable helpers. The team memorized questionnaires which, with variation, were to become the blueprint for hundreds of Dolci workers: "Do you usually read newspapers or books? Are you interested in the social conditions of the area, of the nation, of the world? Why? When is your day off?" And so on. They discovered that nobody bought books or newspapers; that people were often resigned to things because they were told it was the will of God; that social and religious questions were not understood. One woman, asked how she tried to live religiously, answered abruptly: "We're honest people. In all these years I've only been with my husband." Only ten houses had running water. Infant mortality was nine times higher than in the north.

The facts alone were bad enough. They were underlined by a wide belief in the *maaríe*, the spirits, who the people said always functioned; and wide disbelief in the *professori*, the state schoolteachers, who Dolci discovered almost never did.

Belief in the *maaríe*, for example, led people to consult Ninuzzo rather than the doctor. Ninuzzo was of indeterminate sex and "spoke" with the spirits. She, or he, had remedies for everything—especially love aches. On Ninuzzo's advice girls without suitors often mixed a little of their menstrual blood in some pasta or wine or in a cigarette, and gave or sent it to the man they wanted to marry. The alchemy is said to produce devastating results.

On the *professori*, Dolci noted: "Not one of the ten teachers lives in the village . . . Today is 6 November. The schools began almost a month ago. This morning, out of ten teachers, two arrived. Yesterday, the same, and there are two hundred pupils. The children roam the muddy streets. It's been like this for weeks: out of ten masters two or three have turned up—exceptionally, four." On 1 December he wrote: "Soon it will be Christmas, and the schools have not yet begun properly."

He sent an open letter to Alessi in Palermo, and another to the Italian Prime Minister, the Home Secretary, and the national secretary of the Christian Democrat party in Rome. He told them it was the law itself which stood between an honest man and his right to eat. He said: "In the Montelepre zone as far as Balestrate the fifty-five or sixty cents a man earns for twelve hours' labor— since he can find work only for six months of the year—come down to thirty-five cents a day, which has to keep an average of five or six people; and this, as you well know, comes down to six cents each; six cents a day is not enough to keep one person." He pointed out that banditry was increasing, and that carabinieri were risking their lives daily for starvation wages. "Do you think you can resolve this problem by increasing the number of carabineri? Do you think you can resolve it by increasing the wages of the carabinieri?"

He called for one, just one, agricultural expert to be placed at the disposal of the peasants in each of the thirty-seven Sicilian communes; "In a few years the agricultural face of the island would be transformed."

Dolci told Alessi: "A public administration which shirks dire needs is preparing tombs."

The Trappeto inquiry was finished by Christmas and published in January 1954, as *Act Quickly (and Well) for People Are Dying* [*Fare Presto (e Bene) perchè si Muore*]. It is the most spontaneous of Dolci's books and embodies the core of his religious thought. Small and tightly packed, it contains the open letters and a series of case histories, presented as running shorthand-autobiographies, and is remarkable for its head-on poetic accusation and a complete absence of rancor.

An Italian, looking at a forgotten part of the south, had dared to produce a document of shame and accusation. It was difficult for Italians to believe they were reading about their own republic:

> Yesterday and today a woman told us that her husband got well by drinking a glass of urine; neighbors have praised this . . . therapeutic aid.
> Meantime in a citrus orchard a couple of miles from here another man has been found shot dead.
> And this is another day like all the rest.
> Giovannino, aged five, left alone to shepherd a flock, when he got really thirsty used to drink his own urine.
> We have taken in two more children: one of three, one of five. They were living in a pigsty less than three yards square with two young sisters (another child about to be born), their father and mother, and the pig, titleholder of the establishment. As well as several hens. The tiniest child was wearing a piece of canvas so tight that to get it off we had to tear it: she had been wearing it for a long time.

The authorities were worried. There were signs that this man had big ideas. His fast had confined itself to 2,800 souls. Now he was talking about a whole *zone*; worse, he mentioned "the Sicilian situation." Had the Government not recently conducted its own parliamentary inquiry into southern destitution? It was embarrassing to have this very inquiry thrown in its face by a religious upstart who quoted, to his own advantage, the Government statistic that "in these provinces about nine of every hundred children die among the poor, compared to one of every hundred among the rich." The moral was clear: social insecurity killed eight children out of one hundred every year.

Here was a self-appointed missionary who had suddenly

Much of a peasant's day is spent riding to and from his plot, which is seldom near his village.

turned social detective; who spoke mystically of God as though
they were fellow masons, and in the same breath called for agrarian *technicians*. What was he?

An agitator? Yes. But what *kind* of agitator? The authorities
were not certain.

The fact that Dolci was not sure either did not console them.
The missile was "dangerous." Intangibly, and quite suddenly, an
official barrier of hindrances began to go up.

Dolci appealed for workers, in Churchillian tones: "And
whoever feels it in his bones to be consumed in order that these
people might live, let him be prepared to find himself, almost
isolated, dragged under water by those he is trying to save."

At the end of 1953 he was desperately worried. He told a
Florentine friend that though the promised money had arrived
—every penny—the work depot had not been opened, the sixteen children in need of immediate care had not been provided
for, the irrigation syndicate was still in bureaucratic limbo, and
every day there arrived at Borgo more orphans, more widows,
more unemployed, asking for help. "We're building a kindergarten," he said, "but we need timber, we need whitewash, we
need ... everything. We need more helpers, men of courage.
The furniture isn't paid for. We spend over fifteen cents a day for
every child. The shopkeepers are too poor to give much credit.
The baker says he can give credit only to the end of the week. . ."

Missionary or sociologist? The dilemma was clear. He was
in a blind alley, caught between the fires of his own creation. He
marched along it, confident of his path—and certain of his faith
in the Sicilians. "There is God in these people," he wrote, "like
the fire that smolders under the ashes."

VIII

SENT
TO COVENTRY

TODAY at Borgo di Dio there is no community. There are some outbuildings, including an enormous hall inhabited by rats and old mattresses; there is squint-eyed, lovable Domenico, the peasant who patrols the grounds in the summer with a rusty shotgun, and who, every time I stay there, promises to take me rabbit-shooting but never does—for, he says, "the rabbits are more cunning than delinquents," and he hasn't got one himself yet; and alongside the kindergarten, in Borgo itself, there is Eyvind, the Norwegian philosopher who is Dolci's valued colleague, his wife Kerstin, their three children, a tame dog called Amedeo who understands Swedish, and a zebra-like donkey on whose back Eyvind may sometimes be seen, thinking, and moseying about the olives.

But for roughly eighteen months, between 1952 and 1954, there were sixty children and adults here and Dolci's dogged faith in the miracle of multireligious brotherhood was not misplaced. When the kindergarten was finished, Paolino and Toni relate, "All of us from Borgo went out and grabbed the poorest and the dirtiest and the hungriest from among the hundred kids of kindergarten age. We could only bring back thirty because there wasn't room for any more." More than a thousand villagers came to some of the concerts in the great hall, called the People's University; repeat performances were called for; Chekov's *The Bear* was a big success. Vincenzina called Borgo "my garden." From the prolific garden she had an uninterrupted

view of the whole gulf. The children had health education on a
Greek pattern under the olives. Volunteer helpers donated books
and teaching aids, chairs, tables, and rubber aprons, records, and
a hand-cranked German phonograph. Doctors and musicians
came regularly from Palermo. An upright piano was freighted
from Rome; legend says the instrument reached Borgo still upright, but that the three-wheeled Vespa which lugged it up the
Borgo switchback was never the same again. All this reached a
peak in 1953 when there was a flood of private generosity from
the north. Giorgio La Pira, Mayor of Florence, cajoled friends
and journalists to visit the stone hamlet; Ignazio Silone, the novelist, sent over twenty-five hundred dollars for the library and
nursery school; and Elio Vittorini, author of *Conversation in
Sicily*, donated the royalties of a fresh edition (they paid for the
roof of Borgo). Maria Sacchetti-Fermi, sister of the Nobel sci-
entist, sent her teenage daughter Ida to give a hand. Later, Maria
Fermi came herself. She washed dishes. "Whenever I feel depressed," she told a friend in 1957, "I simply take a trip down to
Sicily and visit Dolci, and that always restores my sense of values."
A Swiss 'cellist, Claudio, arrived and went out with the fishermen
every day for six months. He was the first foreign helper. Tullio
Vinay sent a young Protestant couple from his alpine community
in the north to staff the nursery. Vinay is Waldensian, the original
Italian Protestant order. He is Florentine. In the last war he
saved the lives of scores of Jews and earned the nickname "the
Rabbi of Florence." In 1953 Dolci was already turning to Vinay
for spiritual help and then, Vinay says, "was praying every night
near his bed."

Dolci's helpers were of both sexes and of every political and
religious creed. When a dapper Palermo medical student, Vincenzo Borruso, turned up he found that segregation was strict
and that when women stayed in Borgo, the men moved out and
bunked in the People's University. Dolci went too.

The community had adopted fifty children, seventeen of
whom lived at Borgo. It fed them, clothed them, and doctors came
fortnightly to examine them. The children, who lived by the

sea, had been told that sun and salt air were "harming." When a party of them was taken to the beach the sun healed their running sores in a few days. Their designs and linocuts were collected and published to raise funds. And they were learning, slowly, when they quarrelled, not to reach for the nearest blunt object. Fraternity was sinking in.

Paolino explained it this way: "When the sardine lamps for the boats came from the factory I read the instructions and couldn't get the hang of anything. But when someone showed me how to light them it was easy. It's the same with the Gospel—it was only when I saw them actually *living* it that Danilo's talk about brotherly love sank in."

Dolci believed that all official attempts to repress banditry concentrated on attacking the symptom rather than the disease itself. The creative work at Borgo, among the children of the bandits, supported his theory that you had to begin underneath, with the disease itself. It was token proof, but it was a practical living expression for those who wanted to see.

When, in *Act Quickly (and Well)*, he invited the reader to eavesdrop on the confidences of these children—the "tremendous vendettas" some were brooding—he was speaking for the growing generation of a whole zone: four villages and a town, fifty thousand inhabitants. The Establishment remained puzzled by his intentions.

Democratic authority when puzzled is often deaf, and sometimes blind as well. Thus it was that it decided to close down Borgo di Dio.

There was no warning. They came at dawn in a small truck, between 30 and 35 carabinieri from Palermo, commanded by a staff officer. They carried rifles and submachine guns.

On 22 January 1954, Matteo was up early. He says, "I went into the garden and looked down the hill. It was cold. There was white on the trees. I saw one of the bushes move, and another, and then I saw the uniforms coming up the hill. I ran in and told Danilo. He was writing. He put down his pen and came out. He talked with the officer and then the officer and some of the men came in." The children were roused and as the carabinieri entered they ran screaming down the corridor. They knew what "police" meant. Some jumped out of the windows, but Borgo had been surrounded and they were brought back. The officer was the second Government representative to visit Borgo in an official capacity The first was also a police officer; he had interviewed Dolci in the library with his pistol placed between them. The present visitor came straight to the point. He told Dolci that as there was no guarantee of financial security the premises were to be closed. Dolci replied: "I've no intention of obeying any orders of the police or the prefect which contradict God's law."

"We'll see," the officer said.

He turned to the volunteers. He examined their papers, taking pains over Ida Sacchetti-Fermi and a young Tuscan teacher. The latter was bearded and had a bandage on one foot. "What's wrong with your foot?" the officer said. The teacher replied, "I cut it." There had been an armed robbery on the Alcamo road and the culprits were at large. The teacher was told to remove the bandage. The officer peered closely at the cut and then tugged at the teacher's beard. He was disappointed to find both genuine.

When the police left they took away those children whose fathers were in prison. Aged from seven to twelve, the children cried, screamed, and fought all the way to the trucks. They were outnumbered, four to one. They were taken to Palermo and put into religious colleges. The parents were not consulted. Dolci learned later that at least two children were kept in a cell in a reform college where iron chains were set into the walls.

It is possible that had Dolci confined himself to schooling and medical aid he might have been left alone. But having finished the first inquiry, he had begun paddling in dangerous waters. He had begun campaigning against the pirate trawlers whose crews were destroying the livelihood of the local fishermen, from Trappeto to Castellammare del Golfo. Behind the trawlers there was a big business syndicate, and behind the syndicate was a branch of the Mafia.

The Mafia is the most single-minded organization in the whole of Italy. It is also the most efficient. Concentrated in the west of the island, it has a cloak of mystique, fear, and pseudo-legality, and a heritage of thousands of murders. Two-thirds of an officially estimated five thousand Mafia trials in history have come to nothing, for lack of proof.

Dolci had no idea the Mafia was a refined organization of family cells, protected by Right-wing political forces. "I'd heard of Mafia, of course, and I knew I was in a Mafia area," he says, "but like most northern Italians I thought of it as robber bands and delinquency, nothing more."

At the time of the police raid on 22 January piracy of the inshore fishing grounds had been going on for eleven years undisturbed, under the nose of Customs and Excise police. The law laid down a three-mile limit. Outside this, motorized boats from Palermo and Terrasini used bombs. Inside it, they used fine linen netting to cream off thousands of pounds of sardine fry in a night. "And all the fry of the sardine mature," Dolci noted. The fry were sold openly on the Palermo market. Dolci calculated that over forty days the earnings for the sixteen shareholders of one Trappeto boat amounted to 272 lire, a total of forty-five cents among sixteen families.

Many fishermen were too discouraged to take their boats out at all. Some were in an ugly mood.

Dolci went north to seek advice. In Perugia he met that cheery pacifist, Capitini, who, with Tullio Vinay, gave him great courage. "It's a popular pastime to decry efforts towards spiritual regeneration," the tubby professor of nonviolence told him. Capitini's paternal interest in Dolci remains. In 1954 he did two things for him. He put Dolci in touch with a wide circle of distinguished lay friends—among them Einaudi the publisher, Calamandrei the lawyer, Calogero, the grand old man of Italian philosophy, and Levi the writer—so that Dolci was helped immediately by powerful intellectual forces. And he widened Dolci's intuitive Gandhism, planting the seeds of a more integrated Christianity. Writing to me, Capitini says, "I think that these two elements, plus the backwardness of the Sicilian clergy, helped to enlarge Danilo's whole moral and religious horizon."

On his trip Dolci kept a diary. In Turin he records: "What a relief not to see carabinieri spying on you at every turning."

In a series of public discussions he posed the problems, and said: "Back there in two small towns of less than eight thousand people there are some fifty police, including ten Customs and Excise men, and a naval petty officer—although I get on very well with him I can't quite see what use he is. This means that every month $2,800 goes in police salaries alone. The local assistance board spends only $33.60 a month for the whole of Trappeto."

His facts were disputed. "I don't wonder," he records. "Even in Trappeto people who live only a few yards from the grimmest poverty say: 'It's because the brutes are too lazy to work.' It's a question of getting your perspective right. . . . Revolution then? All right . . . But it's the form of revolution that counts. If we sow peas we don't reap fish. If we sow death and untruth we don't reap life."

On 11 February at Vicenza he learned that the police had again visited Borgo, sending home the thirty nursery-school children and closing down the kindergarten. "Why?" he asked. "Ever since I was so high I never understood why Jesus was persecuted and murdered. Now I'm beginning to understand."

The kindergarten was closed following the visit of a health inspector. He noted a mildewed stain on one wall and declared the place "insanitary."

Friends formed groups to send more funds. Everywhere he asked them, "What do you advise me?" They answered, "Go on."

He returned to Sicily. Arriving at Borgo he found that the police had threatened to banish his helpers if they persisted in their inquiries among the fishermen. One had already been sent away—Ida Sacchetti-Fermi.

He wrote to the press. He called for speedy action on the

Iato River project, publicized the fishing abuses and republicized the crucial facts, enclosing a petition covered with signatures stating that the situation described was "the actual state of affairs." To his surprise people began collecting signatures on their own initiative. "It's perhaps the first spontaneous action of the kind here."

In *Notes for Friends* he records: "While I'm writing to you, fishermen and peasants are in the library listening to Bach's *Second St. Matthew Passion...*"

The 1954 raid on Borgo was a replica, in miniature, of the Scelbian police operation against Nomadelphia at Fossoli in 1952. Once again the Government only partly succeeded. Borgo was registered as a charitable institution and could not be wiped off the map. Dolci's marriage to Vincenzina gave him resident-status and he could not be served a *foglia di via*, the old fascist method of exiling "prostitutes and other undesirables." The kindergarten was soon reopened. Dolci handed control to an official welfare organization (who have it today), run by a friend, Senator Zanotti-Bianco.

Then he calmly resumed his attack on the fishing abuses. By March the local fishermen were so desperate they were breaking the law themselves, driven by hunger to use fine netting which all but scraped the sardine eggs off the sea bed. Dolci despaired. "Why is it that certain people, instead of meeting our arguments with facts and figures, instead of treating us as colleagues, want us thrust aside and slandered? Why do they waste their time on flowery words when so much is crying out to be done?"

The answer was, in a word, Mafia.

Throughout this period his diary reads like a piece of Zola. But it was not fiction.

> Sunday 21 March
>
> The fishermen are walking the streets, their eyes lidded with sleep
>
> The night before last they were fishing until three-thirty in the morning. Some until four. Then they dried and repair-

ed their nets: that took until eleven: the share-out was $1.20
per man.

They ate some bread and a few sardines and went to bed
at noon. Two hours later they were up again making ready
the nets. At four o'clock they had some bread and pasta and
at five they were at sea. They stayed out until three this morning. An hour later they began repairing the nets and they
are still at it; it's now eleven o'clock. And so it goes on, day
after day. Today's earnings were eighty cents per man.

11-13 April

Two trawlers are fishing illegally. Last night a boat from
Terrasini landed 100 cases of fry—1,400 pounds of fish destroyed like this in a single night. Four other boats were fishing too...

10 May

A Customs launch appeared—at last—towards eleven
o'clock and caught a trawler within the limit. Let's hope
something happens. The locals are sceptical. "They'll bribe
their way out with a case of fish," they say.

14 May

A trawler has been fishing illegally all day, only 300 yards
out. We rang the Port Captain at Palermo: he promised
to send a launch tomorrow morning.

15 May

A trawler fishing illegally all day long, undisturbed, a
few hundred yards offshore. No sign of the Customs launch.

On 17 May Dolci wrote to the Port Captain: "My dear Captain... After receiving ample evidence of the continued flagrant
abuse of the fishing laws in Castellammare Bay; after being warned
of the risk that the fishermen, losing patience, might start firing
on their aggressors; after being advised that, thanks to you, Italy
loses over a quarter of a million dollars a year in the Gulf of Castellammare alone—after all this, you continue to side with the
culprits...

"This letter of ours is not meant as an insult: it is simply a

recommendation that you should not allow things to get any
worse." The letter was signed by hundreds and, with documentary evidence, was sent to twenty-two of the authorities concerned in Italy.

18 May

A trawler is fishing a stone's throw from Trappeto beach.
At Balestrate knots of fishermen are planning to board a
trawler, beat the crew up, and throw them over the side.
Some want to tie the crew up and sink the vessel, others just
want to cut the nets loose . . .

They're expecting a lawyer to talk the whole matter over
with them at nine in the morning.

19 May

The lawyer did not turn up.

The lawyer came the following day. Three days later a Customs cutter arrived. But the trawler had been warned and was
outside the limit. The captain of the cutter pointed out that the
penalties, when applied, were inadequate anyway. He promised
to return that night.

24 May

The cutter did not come back: but the trawler reappeared,
it came almost on to the beach. First with lights doused and
then, about ten o'clock, with all lights blazing.

The local fishermen, armed with knives, began circling
round the trawler and prepared to board it. Dolci went out in
a motorboat and advised the trawlermen to clear off before
blood was shed. They hauled in and went.

A month later the trawler was back. "A few days ago," Dolci
wrote, "the Head of the State was awarded the Order of Christ:
'as a defender of Christian civilization.'"

In mid-August the Fisheries Board finally alerted all port
captains in Sicily and called for "decisive action" against the
raiders. On 7 September Dolci records, laconically:

Three trawlers continue to fish illegally.

8:30 A.M.   Telephone the Fisheries Board. A girl's voice
                replies that the chairman is abroad and that,
                at this hour, nobody is able to speak for him.

8:40   Telephone the naval officer in charge at Bale-
                strate.

9:00   Attempt to telephone the Port Captain; the
                book gives the wrong number. Various
                attempts over the next 70 minutes. We get the
                Deaf and Dumb Institute, a doctor, and other
                private numbers. Finally (at 10:15) the Bale-
                strate naval man calls back: he'll go out to-
                morrow after the trawlers; today he's not feel-
                ing well.

10:30   The Port Captain's office, his deputy on the
                line: the captain isn't there.
                A sailor goes off to look for him. We hang on
                for five minutes. He can't be found but another
                person speaks to us who, on hearing what it's
                about, says he'll pass it on to Customs and Ex-
                cise, as the Navy hasn't any vessels available.

Three days later Dolci was at the seafront at dawn to see
four trawlers fishing close in, undisturbed. When a fifth arrived
he went straight to the head of police in Partinico. The inspector
told him to submit a complaint in writing. The complaint, with
61 signatures attached, was submitted to the main police and port
authorities of the province. "We disown violence and bloodshed,"
it ended, "but we will not leave our families undefended. We beg
you therefore to come to our aid *quickly and well*."

That spring there were five murders in the area, several kid-
nappings, two armed robberies, and an outbreak of petty thiev-
ing. By the end of the year trawlers had fished illegally for 350
out of 365 days without interference. Dolci had achieved nothing.

The complaint was archived.

(As I write these lines in 1964, ten years later, at Alcamo
Marina, just round the coast from Trappeto, I am looking out

on Castellammare Bay. It is late at night. The bay is lined with the kerosene lamps of pirate fishermen, working 250 yards from shore. I can count thirteen boats. None of the crews is local. The local fishermen are not be found in the villages. They have gone away, northward, in search of work—untrained, unhappy, resentful. The population of Trappeto has fallen from 2,800 to barely 1,400. Almost all the able-bodied men have gone. The fishermen began leaving in the spring of 1954, after their collective complaint to the police went the way of all the rest.)

Such was, and is still, the power of a minor branch of the Mafia.

It was the first and last time that Dolci was to limit himself to a protest that expressed itself entirely on paper. He had been rendered almost as impotent as the law itself. He was down, but not out. He would make more mistakes, but not again would he be so ingenuous as to tackle the Mafia single-handed without ascertaining first what Mafia actually was.

❧

❧ IX ❧

❧

THE EMBATTLED TOWN

IN 1955 Dolci moved from Trappeto to Partinico.

There were many contributing factors. Vincenzina says they were under constant attack for living "in a villa." Many villagers continued to regard Borgo as a cross between a vaudeville act and comic opera. The kindergarten was flourishing again, but the fishermen had begun to drift away and the People's University had fallen silent.

There was the priest. Not to be outdone by Dolci's kindergarten Father Donato opened one himself, in opposition. Dolci sent 10,000 lire, more than he could afford, wishing the venture well. The money was returned. Dolci tried again. "Please accept it," he said. "This is a good thing you're doing." The money was refused a second time. "We do not need your help," he was told. Little by little, he was edged aside. Father Donato, bred in an antique reactionary mold, is a typical Sicilian figure. "There's no poverty in Trappeto," he told Dolci. "It's only a few fishermen who aren't well off." He came from another village where, he said, the poverty was far worse. That was hardly the point, Dolci said, suggesting, in vain, that the priest accept barefoot children in church. The priest suggested that Dolci ban non-Catholics from his community—also in vain. As Dolci's religious horizon widened, through Capitini, Vinay and others, he found no meeting point with the other's limited Catholic

Dolci, near Partini

view. It wasn't long before the latter was preaching openly
against the "godless foreigners." Such is the distortion of gossip
which follows village sermons in Sicily that locals came to believe not only that Dolci was in the pay of the Communists
(Giovanni Piergallini was an atheist), but also that he was hand-
in-glove with the bandits whose children he was attempting to
succor. After Dolci's first child, Maria-Libera, was born in April
1954, and the baby was not baptized, the priest called him a heretic.

Of the Sicilian clergy Vinay has said: "They are souls of
their traditions and of their past. They are unable to understand that the task of the Church is to incarnate the words of
God in the life of the people—are *unable* to understand. They
are keeping, saving, preserving—and personally I think that the
greatest sin of the Church is the sense of preservation; where
there is preservation there is not faith.

"Danilo always considered himself a Catholic. But the
Church denied it. How often it pushes out of the door the best
men it has. And Danilo—little by little, he was out."

By the end of 1954 Dolci had left the Catholic Church. But
at Christmas he was given the *Premio della Bontà* (the Prize of
Goodness), an award made annually by a group of Milan industrialists for Catholic social work.

The main reason for the move to Partinico, however, was
practical. The Iato irrigation scheme, magnified now into a dam
to serve the whole area, was based on Partinico, where lived the
majority of farmers whose land would be flooded. Also, more
and more bandits were coming from Partinico to blackmail the
Trappeto folk. Partinico was the administrative and geographic
center of the whole homogeneous area, the headquarters of the
police and the law courts as well as the bandits. Dolci wanted to
get to grips with peasant suffering on a wide scale. If he was going
to start with *gli ultimi*, the lowest, he had to live with them.

Partinico first shocked him, then drew him, irresistibly.
Working, as usual, one step ahead of himself, he had already be-
gun an inquiry here, with Giovanni and some graduates from
Siena, travelling daily from Borgo by the seven A.M. train, on a

spartan diet of breadcrusts, hot powdered milk, and rock sugar.

The winter of 1954 brought more unemployment. Banditry flared. Behind the Partinican hills the crackle of machine-gun fire from police maneuvers grew. On 13 December a man of 24 was shot dead ten yards from the square. A fortnight later Dolci and Giovanni were in Partinico, returning from discussing the dam in Palermo, and heard shots fired just in front of them. "They sounded like squibs. Instead, they were three pistol shots, fired at a young notary. We saw him lurching about, his hands clasped to his abdomen. The evening promenade on the Corso —it was a Sunday—was momentarily interrupted, then, as soon as people saw he was 'only shot,' not dead, they went on promenading as if nothing had happened."

By the time Christmas, and the Prize of Goodness, came along, Dolci knew he must break with the little oasis of goodness that was Borgo. It was the end of the Nomadelphian vision. It was inevitable. Slowly he was coming to feel the weight of Don Zeno's words: "Fraternity and social change, they're two different things. Don't mix them up."

There has always been something special about Partinico. The place has a martyred look. In 1955 the only standard things about it were an abiding preoccupation with death and a passionate mistrust of the outsider. The town is spread flat white in a broad basin. The basin is checkered in vines and olives and joins forces with the grizzled surrounds of Borgetto and Montelepre near by, and, farther out, with the fields of Trappeto, San Giuseppe Iato, and Alcamo. From afar the houses appear herded together, in the shape of a tuatara lizard, uneasily united under the shadow of nude ocher mountains. They are of white and stippled blue wash. Above the houses tower the harsh reds and dun browns of King's Mountain, its shaggy pinnacle looming directly over the church and the town square. The Corso, the main street, is a mile long and dead straight. Every second shop seems to be a barber's, and every third a bar. The rest are mostly butchers. In summer when the flies appear and alight on the blood-red meat hanging outside, the flies are sometimes sprayed with DDT. Paunchy, white-jacketed policemen stand about chatting in pairs, unbothered by the traffic jams of the mules, which outnumber the motor vehicles. Even today it is difficult to find a man about town who cannot produce a knife or a gun on demand. But for the absence of hitching rails, it is a classic Wild West setting.

For seven centuries Partinico has been a nerve center of revolt. It is distinctly non-Christian, which may derive from Greek times, when its thick forests were sacred to Diana. The name itself comes either from the Greek *Partenos* (Diana) or the Roman *Par Iniquia*—under the Romans it was a penal colony. Only the Arabs, who planted sugarcane and quilted the basin in market gardens, gave the Partinicans a sense of civic pride. None of the other invaders, spilling overland from Castellammare Bay or wreaking havoc on the plain-dwellers from the hills, except the Spaniards, stayed long enough to give the people anything but a rigid sense of social insecurity. For six centuries Partinico was an enormous church fief, a status-less ragamuffin outpost, and as late as the beginning of last century, when the Bourbon King, Ferdinand II, built his summer castle on King's Mountain, the only municipal authority was the archpriest's. The archpriest was everything from sheriff to undertaker. Ferdinand found the Partinicans scornful of church rule and pandered to them. He created the Great Royal Wine Cellars, planted a park with 3,600 rare trees and shrubs, and put a cross on top of King's Mountain which he visited, on a horse, whenever the heat of the plain grew oppressive. He made the town a commune, planted more dependents than he did trees, and founded *The Academy*, where the local poets foregathered and fought out marathon battles of extempore verse.

Unfortunately, Ferdinand's dizzy patronage didn't last. The castle, and the Great Royal Wine Cellars, fell into decay; and so, once more, did Partinico's civic pride. A rigid Bourbon régime settled. There was bitterness and unrest. Partinicans spat at the sight of a Bourbon tunic. By the time the century was out they

had risen seven times against unjust land dues and each time
had been savagely put down. Typically, in 1860, they did not
wait for the invasion of Garibaldi and his Thousand, but rose
spontaneously against the Bourbons almost a month before.
When Garibaldi marched through Partinico and on to Palermo,
to liberate the island and unite it to Italy, Partinicans had already
baptized their new citizenship in blood. Cesare Abba, one of the
Thousand, gives this description of Partinico:

> 18 May 1860, between Partinico and Burgeto
> It would have been better to break our backs and cross
> the mountain rather than glimpse Partinico ... The col-
> umn we had routed at Calatafimi had run into the rebels of
> Partinico, heroic folk indeed. Having razed the village the
> Bourbons massacred the women and helpless of all ages.
> Corpses of soldiers and peasants, of horses and dogs, some
> with their guts torn out. As we rode up the bells were ring-
> ing, but whether in ecstasy or in rage I do not know; the
> houses were still smoking; the people in tumult among the
> ruins, priests and monks screaming frenzied "Evviva!" The
> women were flailing their arms and around a funeral pyre
> of seven or eight singed and festering bodies large numbers
> of young girls were dancing in a crazed round, holding
> hands and singing. Those corpses were soldiers. The Gen-
> eral spurred on through, wrenching his hat down over his
> eyes. We followed, all of us, deafened and miserable. Now
> we are far off, but the bells are sounding still. It is four-
> thirty. I would like to lie tonight among these olive groves
> and not lose from sight Castellammare Bay which sunset
> will shortly transform into who knows what heavenly radi-
> ance of colors.

From that day Partinico has been known as "bandit town."
The *Giornale di Sicilia,* the Bourbon mouthpiece, called Garibaldi a bandit too, but changed its verdict to "blond hero" when
a few days later he slipped in by the back door and took the city
by surprise.
Partinicans pinned their faith on the blond general and

made him an honorary citizen. Garibaldi accepted "with pride."
But his arrival, the end of one era of repression, only ushered in
another, that of the Mafia.

Mafia had been conditioned by a gradual impoverishment
of the island under successive invaders, growing up as a peasant
self-protection movement long before Garibaldi. Altruism soon
vanished. The *mafiosi*, the bailiffs on the feudal estates, were
happily placed—they blackmailed the absentee landlords on
one hand, and terrorized with armed bands the peasants under
them on the other. Garibaldi promised the peasants ownership
of the land, and they followed him. So did the Mafia. It put its
auxiliary police force at his disposal and then, having seen him
safely off the premises, availed itself of his lieutenant, Nino
Bixio, to shoot down the peasants. Under the soft new Kingdom
of Italy it joined up with the reactionary landowners (both of
them now had a vested interest in anesthetizing social revolt)
and eased itself into power.

The so-called Liberation was the deathblow to peasant faith
in the justice of the outsider.

"Change everything in order to change nothing," says the
prince in Lampedusa's Garibaldian novel, *The Leopard*. Garibaldi was not the peasant's savior, but the Mafia's. It is from
1860 that organized Mafia as we know it today really took hold.

Sicilian peasants continued to revolt, without ever achiev-
ing a revolution. In the bloody nineties Partinicans were among
the first to demonstrate, parading the streets with placards saying, "BREAD, WORK, REFORM." A Partinican woman of 35 led an invasion on the town hall, ejecting the mayor bodily into the arms of
counterattacking cavalrymen, and Crispi, the Prime Minister, was
moved to confer on the zone the title, "Crown of Thorns."

A section in the *British Encyclopaedia* about 1900 notes
that "in organized form the Mafia survives only in isolated dis-
tricts." At the time the Mafia was entrenched throughout the
four provinces of the west, its "friends" resided in town councils,
in police barracks, in law courts; and collusion flourished behind a mutually protective smokescreen. In 1911 the economist

Lorenzoni, wrote: "The scent of the orange groves in flower badly conceals the stench of gunshot smoke . . ." Political rivals were simply eliminated by hired Mafia assassins.

In 1918 a Partinican, Vittorio Emanuele Orlando, was Prime Minister of Italy. He became famous by uniting the people to drive out the Austrians and Hungarians and win the tail of the war; and in 1919 was one of the Big Four at Versailles with Lloyd George, Woodrow Wilson, and Clemenceau. Orlando also granted favors to many Partinicans. Later, asked why he'd done nothing to improve his town's social conditions, he explained: "You only asked me for jail passes and warrants to carry firearms—you didn't say anything about streets."

As manifestoes in his electorate proclaimed in 1946, Vittorio Emanuele Orlando was "*l'amico degli amici*," or "the friend of friends." Everyone knew who the friends were.

On an island of the forgotten, Partinico stood out as a scabland of the iniquitous. Mafia fingered its wine, olive, citrus, and market garden produce. Its death roll was second to none. In 1924–5 there were some two hundred murders in Partinico. Emigration was restricted. Honesty meant starvation. Faced with the age-old dilemma, "serf or bandit?", Partinicans chose banditry. This fringe activity naturally disturbed the Mafia. The Mafia declared war on the bandits. The state police were rendered almost superfluous.

During fascism, Mafia went underground. Mussolini's prefect, Mori, exiled or jailed many *mafiosi*, and tortured hundreds of innocents. In Partinico there were so many arrests the churches had to be used as tribunals. After the war the Mafia rose again, stronger than ever. As it had used Garibaldi, it used the American Seventh Army, paving the way for a smooth advance in 1943 and then, with the eager aid of the Americans, hoisting itself into key administrative posts. It entered the drug and contraband rackets, and politics. Mafia thugs came home from exile to become mayors, and the Church did not publicly lament their appointment. An American officer nominated Don Calò Vizzini Mayor of Villalba. Don Calò was undisputed Head

of the Mafia, a picturesque illiterate and a notorious criminal.
On the day he became mayor priests and dignitaries, among
them a representative of the Bishop of Caltanissetta and Dr.
Calogero Volpe, the present CD deputy in Rome, greeted him
with acclaim; and a select chorus of friends, lined up outside the
police barracks, shouted tumultuously: "Long live the Mafia!
Long live delinquency! Long live Don Calò!" Don Calò opened
his term of office by arranging for the extinction of the district
police officer.

One of Don Calò's close associates was the head of the Partinico Mafia, Cavalier Santo Fleres. Fleres began life as a cowherd. His five-year reign, 1943-8, coincided with the rise of the
famous Giuliano and an era of social banditry which gave the
Trappeto–Partinico–Montelepre zone yet another title, "Triangle of Hunger." Fleres ran the town, and paraded the Corso
in company with the local draper, the spaghetti merchant, and
others who are today prominent citizens. Giuliano worked from
the Montelepre–Partinico hills. And whenever these two were
resting there was always the Lombardo gang to keep up the
terror of daily Partinico living. The Minister of Police, Scelba,
tried hard to catch Giuliano—or said he did. Giuliano's men,
under Mafia protection, walked the streets openly in their
hooded cloaks, and Giuliano occasionally lodged with Signor
Giordano, the present draper, jeweller, and church benefactor,
who gave the outlaw-king the gold belt buckle which appears
in so many photographs.

Fleres died, assassinated by Lombardo behind the municipal bandstand in 1948. Giuliano died, betrayed by the Mafia, in
1950. "When Giuliano died part of Sicily died with him," Her-
bert Kubly wrote. Partinicans agreed. His band was recruited
from Partinico. Hunger drove the cowherds of the Via della
Madonna to join him; they followed his banner as a beacon in
the long deluded search for social justice.

Once again the peasants gained nothing, save a bad reputation and long prison sentences.

The Mafia stayed in business. Having adopted Giuliano,

"Even if we make a just remark it's always wrong because we haven't any money."

then cast him off, it returned to its old love, the forces of reaction, and when Sicily was granted a form of home rule in 1948 backed the Christian Democrats. The CD party adopted as its emblem the cross. Half a superstitious peasantry was won over automatically—"We always vote for the cross," Dolci was told, "because God told us to carry the cross." Others took the slogan "Vote CD—or Starve" at face value. Those who didn't see the cross as a political symbol of divine justice had the theory explained from the pulpit. The Mafia displayed "friendship" in several ways. The elections coincided with the peasants' symbolic occupation of the estates, under the new reform laws; and with the rise of a primitive Left-wing, largely in support of peasant rights. Trade unionists had become popular heroes, threatening to undermine the Mafia's rural dominion and a CD majority. The Mafia began systematically to assassinate them. In Partinico peasants were forbidden to enter the Left union, the Camera del Lavoro, on pain of death; and on the Sunday preceding the 1948 national elections, having murdered eleven key unionists and socialists in three months, the Mafia conducted a punitive expedition which, beginning outside Palermo, took in Monreale, Pioppo, Borgetto, and San Giuseppe Iato, and ended in the center of Partinico with a hand bomb and bottles of benzine tossed into the Communist headquarters. The death roll rose to thirteen. The Mafia clinched its liaison with the Church party by rigging candidates and, in cases—where illiterate peasants needed a "guide" to mark the voting slips—also the polls.

In Sicily, in both regional and national elections, the Christian Democrat party was overwhelmingly victorious. In Partinico in 1947 the combined Left-wing parties polled a total of 27 votes.

By 1955 when Dolci moved to Partinico the whole mutually protective network between Palermo and Rome, the foundation of Mafia inviolability, had been secured. Mafia was urbanized. Mafia was in building and banking, television, Government contracts, food distribution, and water control. The only business it left alone was prostitution. In these few years social and economic progress on the west of the island was sterilized —indeed, if anything, it went backwards, for northern industrialists, to avoid graft and sabotage, were forced to move to the east. The *capo-mafiosi* wore business suits, frequented the Massimo Opera House and had "friends" in the highest places—in the professions, in the Church, in the Regional Government, and in ministerial office in Rome. Political murders by hired assassins could still be arranged for a mere hundred and fifty bucks. Palermo by now was a second Chicago of the Al Capone days. The murder rate was climbing to eight times that of any city in the north.

Around Palermo, outlying cliques were partly assimilated to the new urban pattern. Elements of these, the Water Mafia, the Mafia of the Gardens, and so on, were to affect Dolci's later work.

There was a separate Mafia branch for every activity. Partinico boasted six, of a possible fifteen. The business end of these activities, the *lupara* shotgun, the traditional killing weapon, was presented by a series of middlemen—armed "tax collectors" and reprisal merchants, able to turn their hand to an anonymous letter, a bomb, or some other such ritual warning. The real *mafiosi* were few. They were the rustic heritage, the former rivals or bodyguards of Santo Fleres, and when not protecting their monopolies or leading religious processions were usually engaged in a tin-pot vendetta among themselves. They were second-rate. The only figure was the absentee Frank Coppola. Francesco Paolo Coppola, after Orlando, is Partinico's most famous citizen. He was born there in 1899. As a youngster he went to America, became a gangster, and was mentioned in the Kefauver congressional report on the American underworld. It is said he lost part of one hand while burgling a bank. The hand was jammed under a safe door just as the police sirens sounded, and in order to escape he cut off the trapped fingers. He was charged with drug-trafficking and extradited as undesirable, returning to Partinico in 1950 a conquering hero. On the welcoming committee were clergymen, among them the parish priest of the Church of the Holy Sufferers. Coppola then moved to Anzio, near Rome, spent nearly $95,000 acquiring and improving a

125-acre property and, as a gentleman farmer, was occasionally
seen driving about in the company of a high-ranking Customs
officer. His intimacy with Liberal and Christian Democrat politicians was not concealed; Palazzola and Savarino, successive Liberal and Christian Democrat members for Partinico (1953–58),
addressed him by letter as "My dearest Don Ciccio." In 1951
Coppola was sought by Interpol as a growing rival (some say a
partner) to Lucky Luciano, his Sicilian contemporary, who was
the mastermind of the intricate drug-trade routes operating between the Middle East and the United States, via French and
Italian pharmaceutical suppliers who refined the raw opium and
morphine base into heroin. Luciano, jailed in America in 1936
on 62 charges of compulsory prostitution, was released and sent
home in 1946 for his "contribution to the war effort" (he arranged the bloodless American advance across Western Sicily in
1943 and the Americans in return arranged [unwittingly] the
Mafia's return to power)—and resided in style at Naples where
he rejoiced in the title of Ex-Whoremaster General of the United
States. Luciano was suave and versatile. Coppola, operating from
Anzio, was leathery and brash but equally adept. In February
1952 one of his men was arrested at Alcamo carrying thirteen
pounds of heroin for shipment to the United States in crates of
salted fish; records found in the possession of his gang incrimi-
nated 23 prominent underworld figures, and a respected pharmaceutical dealer in Milan. Coppola was prosecuted, but evaded
imprisonment. An official Italian Custom report of 15 May
1952 describes him, somewhat flatteringly, as "supreme organizer" of the illicit narcotics traffic emanating from Italy. There
is a photograph of Coppola taken about this time at an intimate
gathering in Partinico where he was invited by the Partinico
branch of FUCI, the Italian Federation of Catholic University
Students. After that body had bestowed its honorary member-
ship on him, he distributed spiced cakes to the gathering. In the
photograph Coppola appears short and dumpy and somewhat
tasselled, for he wears the white medieval tricorn of the Faculty
of Philosophy. He lives nowadays at Pomezia near Rome, still

farming. Since Orlando bequeathed Partinico to the nation as a
safe Mafia seat Coppola has allegedly continued the tradition.*
Italian newspapers denounce him repeatedly as the "grand electoral patron" of the district; and an impressive number of affi-
davits before the present Parliamentary Commission of Inquiry
into the Mafia link his fortunes more or less exclusively with the
promotion of Right-wing senators. He is usually seen in Partinico only at election times.

In 1955 when Dolci arrived, Partinico may have had only a
second-rate Mafia, but it boasted first-class connections.

A CD administration ruled 25,000 inhabitants. Day laborers,
small landholders, cowherds, outlaws, dawn-scavengers. There
was a small shopkeeping class, a smaller professional class, and
a parasitical élite known as "armchair Mafia." The mayor was
Mario Mancuso, a robust lawyer, friend of the police and also of
Coppola. Senator Santi Savarino, also head of the powerful Government organ, the *Giornale d' Italia*, was in office.

Three years in the area had taught Dolci that the Honored
Society, as it is known, had a vested interest in social decay, and
that, as a social *reformer*, his mere arrival in a town like this was
tantamount to an open declaration of war. Trappeto fishermen
tried to stop him going. Some called him a traitor. Most, like
Leonardo, reminded him that there was such a branch as the
Mafia of the Coffins. "They pop men off like flies in that place,"
Leonardo said. Dolci expostulated in his earnest way. "Ah well,
perhaps—but I'm going." He had studied the island's history.
He had studied the peasants and would study them further. He
would understand them. He would continue to renounce violence. And he would work in only one direction, the way he believed to be right.

* Mafia leaders have openly bragged about their support for CD and Liberal (extreme Right-wing) candidates. In *Vita di Capomafia*, Nick Gentile,
former gangster of the Luciano–Anastasia–Capone school and today a gentleman farmer in Agrigento province, discusses his electoral campaigns for the
former Sicilian President, La Loggia, and the Liberal senator, Battaglia. There
are many more examples.

His belief was strong and profoundly Christian. This was the foundation of his own private inviolability.

On 16 May 1955 the last and greatest of the peasant leaders, Salvatore Carnevale, was murdered in the village of Sciara, not far from Palermo. Carnevale was thirty-two. He was the thirty-eighth trade union victim of the Mafia in less than ten years.

Dolci the outsider was slightly younger when he moved to Partinico in 1955. He arrived in June.

AN INSTRUMENT
FOR ACTION

HE found a house in Spine Sante, in the poor part. At first he lived alone, one of the workers cooking for him; he didn't believe in wasting time preparing meals. Spine Sante (Holy Thorns) was one of three emaciated quarters. On the north side was the Mulini area, where prostitution flourished. In the southwest, running off the Via della Madonna, were the outlaws and cowherds, the men who'd followed Giuliano, living in uneasy juxtaposition with the *mafiosi*. And just behind the church and square was the tight little bunch of smelly alleys known as Spine Sante. Even in Partinico Spine Sante was looked down on. Of a total of twelve quarters in all, it was the saddest, the retreat of the underdog, the half-bandit, the snail-picker, the mentally deficient. Half its numbers got by on expedients—one of Dolci's neighbors, for instance, kept his family by unbolting the brakes from the trains in the station yard and selling them for scrap iron.

His rooms, at Number Ten, Via Iannello, were empty. The occupants had declared them haunted and cleared out. The "ghosts" were a hen and her chicks who used to peck at their feet as they lay in bed. The rent was $1.15 a week. There were three rooms, two up and one halfway down the stairs. When Dolci's family arrived later in the year they all squeezed in—he, Vincenzina, Maria-Libera, and their second child Cielo (born in June), Vincenzina's first five children, and six orphans: thirteen children in all. "It could be worse, Sariddu," Dolci told the

Sicilian who lived opposite. "There are fifteen people sleeping in the room just below us."

The house was furnished with hard chairs, five-buck wire beds bought on instalment in Palermo, Vincenzina's girlhood dresser from Trappeto, giveaway oddments, and one or two of Matteo's paintings. Dolci's office was the room off the first landing. It was divided by a curtain behind which he and Vincenzina and the two youngest slept. He rose every morning at four, when the peasants were beginning to clatter their mule carts out for the two-hour ride to their plots. Upstairs, where the other children and occasional helpers slept in bunks round the walls, the rooms were divided by a toilet the size of a telephone booth. This was a luxury. Sariddu's toilet, typical of the quarter, was a hole in the floor normally covered by the kitchen burner. The lavatories in Spine Sante, those that existed, went straight down into the "drains" underneath. Dolci had left a Swiss and a young Italian graduate to carry on at Borgo; Giustina and her husband had found fresh quarters; the other volunteers, plus the seasonal Siena students, slept in another house in Via Iannello. But they ate at Number Ten. Vincenzina fetched water from the fountain, cared for the thirteen children, and cooked on a three-ring gas burner for the entire team. Pasta at noon, minestrone at night, wine on Sundays and when there were guests. At mealtimes half a dozen usually had to sit on the floor. For the next four years Vincenzina served a minimum of twenty people twice daily, kept house, did a good deal of the washing, parcelled out charity gifts, and bore Dolci three more children. She never asked him for as much as a new dress.

From this base at the bottom of society they launched their new nonviolent attack.

Dolci moved easily among the poor, a big man in a Basque beret and an old woolly sweater. He looked rather like a Quaker farmer. His clothes were too small for him, his trousers shabby, his gait ambling and a bit lopsided. Partinico was a noisy place, even for Sicily. The people expelled their dialect in ringing

Spine Sante: The area where Dolci lived from 1955 to 1960. He was accused of "living in luxury." The fountain serves one hundred and fifty families.

shouts. Beneath their gravelly poetic speech and extrovert manners he detected an individualism and an abrasive cynicism. Everywhere their history showed—anarchical pockets, religious action groups, street-corner informers, mental enfeeblement, insensitivity to violence, a wayward caste system. An Evangelist movement was almost tolerated. The men dressed up on Sundays, let their women go to church for them, and rotated between the cinema, the card halls, and the brothels as their main sources of escape. One brothel charged as little as six cents a time. Knots of unemployed men were forever glued to the stony Corso. A few yards off it, wherever he wandered, he was in a perpetual farm-yard, where hens and goats wandered in and out over beaten earth floors. Mounds of dung and rubbish lay about like booby traps. The town seemed poised uncertainly between dumb nar-cotic stupor and revolutionary flashpoint. It was, as somebody said, a sociologist's dream.

His first foothold was with the chronically unemployed, the obdurate half-workers, who scrabbled a few lire from the wild life and herbs of the hills. Sariddu lived by gutting and spitting frogs and selling them in the square at three cents each. "It takes an awful lot of frogs to keep a wife and three children, Danilo," he said. Sariddu was a lithe young man with a vicious toothbrush moustache; he had been waiting nine years for a regular job. Dolci next concentrated on the outlaws. They were not the west-ern kind. They were men who'd rubbed the police the wrong way or got into trouble over a petty theft or a vendetta and had joined the bandits in order to stay alive, while their families were left to starve, or were jailed. In many cases they were those who'd been questioned, beaten, and tortured for no crime at all. "Society bans them," he told a friend. To him an outlaw was anyone who'd been banned from the possibility of living with others. They had earthy backwoods nicknames—Corn-eater, Three-day-Peppino, Shit-his-pants, Fifteen-lire (his mother sold him at three for fifteen lire), Donkey-dropper. But the lone-liness of the great empty piazza by the town hall, leading to the Via della Madonna, was more intense than in the mountains of West Virginia. This was an introverted *town* misery.

It would be too much to say that the peasants trusted the Mafia. But it conditioned their behavior pattern and commanded a sneaking respect. For if the state couldn't find their stolen ani-mals (which it couldn't) the Mafia always could, provided it was paid well enough. He did not worry particularly about Mafia.

When a trade unionist from Alia, Salvatore Comparetto, came
to see him and said he was afraid to return to his village for fear
of being murdered, Dolci hid him in a hayloft, below his house,
for a month. Comparetto was a close friend of Carnevale, the
latest Mafia victim. Dolci was concerned with Mafia only as a
state of mind contributing to the culture of the people and the
repressive attitude of the police. The police sent for Dolci and
invited him to clear out. "You've come to the wrong place at the
wrong time," he was told. Dolci took no notice.

A Right-wing journalist of the day describes "a lively charm-
ing town with white celestial houses . . . a modern rejuvenated
little city." The authorities had done "their utmost" to relieve
the sufferings of the poor, he says. The article appeared in *Voce
Cattolica*, the voice of the Palermo archbishopric. The correspondent remarked on the "calm, intelligent character" of the people,
spoke with the mayor, and, after a glance down the side streets
for "the terror of Partinico"—which, he said, he couldn't see—
returned to the capital.

At the time two-thirds of the male population were unemployed, and the mayor was running a cosy gambling den among
whose patrons were leading police officers of the district, Inspector La Corte and Lieutenant Petralito. The mayor's CD administration was spending over $84,000 a year on rural guards to watch
over the acting mayor's private herd of cattle; and municipal funds
were augmented by a novel tax involving the creation of a ten-lire
stamp bearing the image of the local Madonna. There was also a
municipal tax on the brothels to help with the expenses of the
annual religious *festa*.

Dolci bored into the facts. He noted that madmen, cripples,
and delinquents numbered more than a hundred, that illiteracy
and absenteeism from school bordered on fifty per cent, and that
public amenities—baths, lavatories, an efficient health service, a
library—were nil. Infant mortality was nine per hundred—as
against six for Italy as a whole and three for Britain. Residents
of Spine Sante said they hadn't seen a street sweeper for years,
which was not surprising considering that two-thirds of the town

rubbish collectors had been diverted to wait privately on the mayor, his friends, and the friends-of-friends.

Dolci's most startling discovery was that 350 outlaws had received from the state only 650 years of schooling as against a total of 3,000 years in prison. This simple juxtaposition of facts—documented, case by case—was to make the Government pink with rage.

"Moral pressure must be brought on the politicians from below," he ruminated.

Some visitors did not want to believe what Dolci told them. He showed them just the same. "Come and see for yourself," he would say jauntily, propelling them to the handiest quarter. It saved hours of explanation. A British correspondent, hearing that there was a madman living in Spine Sante in the same room as his parents, asked the mayor if this were so. "Oh yes," Signor Mancuso said, "but this situation's much improved now. We've put a partition down the room." The partition was a row of iron bars. Inside his cage Pasqualino, aged 32, paced up and down like a wild animal, roaring at intruders, black eyes flaming.

Volunteers came and went. Those who stayed were given questionnaires, rudimentary guidance, few questions asked, and were sent out as itinerant cullers-of-fact. Some complained of woolly instructions, others of autocracy—if they didn't come back with the right kind of information they were substituted. "Danilo took almost anyone on," one says. "He wasn't fussy. He tried to direct the good in everybody. Sometimes he changed his mind ten times in a week, but as a team we got along."

In his poky office Dolci began a kind of school where the men came assiduously in the evenings. He taught several of them to write, fathers of big families, and encouraged them to talk about their own lives. Some came begging. He gave his coat to a man who sold it and drank the proceeds. Vincenzina and the team continued to give out dried milk, medicines, and old clothing. Half-samaritan, half-documenter, he was unable to say No, unable to break the vicious circle with which they were now utterly enclosed. Files grew, autobiographical accounts multiplied, and the police sent a couple of spies, got up as bums, to discover exactly what the foreigners were up to. It should have been obvious. Dolci was diagnosing the disease points of the town. But even such a harmless task as mapping the municipal drains turned them into "subversives"—the Siena students went out with an enormous sheet of blank card, to mark up all the sewers, fountains, and amenities they could find: a few hours had elapsed, and then it was all round that Dolci was planning a "foreign invasion."

"Memories of Garibaldi and the Thousand," Dolci chuckled.

"Or the Allied landings," Giovanni grunted.

"Cretins," one of the students said.

Finally, it was obvious what Dolci was up to. He was finding out too much and he was doing too much. Like the new recruit to union rules he was working far too hard and making the foreman feel uncomfortable. Dolci was called one day to an appointment at a warehouse. He went alone. He knew the men. Five of them were waiting for him, smoking, their berets pulled down hard at the corners. Two or three were relatives of a lad who was working for him, a local medical student; the others were their friends. One family had been instrumental in obtaining Coppola's safe passage home from America. Dolci had already been under pressure to release the lad. The men ushered Dolci to an inner room. One of them locked the door and pocketed the key. Dolci sat down on a crate and the men sat on crates facing him. They said the boy was degrading himself working amid poverty. They worked on Dolci for almost an hour, cajoling, threatening, raging purple. "He's losing his *honor!*" they said. Dolci used simple moral arguments and repeated, "The lad's free to do as he likes." Both sides ran out of breath. They sat facing each other in sticky silence. Uncertain what to do next, Dolci reached down and took an orange from the crate he was sitting on. He began to peel it and when he had finished broke it into pieces and offered them round. The men took the segments and sat holding them. Dolci ate his and, after a bit, so did his captors. Not long after, mumbling something he didn't catch, they opened the door and went out. Dolci did, too.

He took the advice of a Palermo lawyer and for some time was careful not to go about alone at night.

It was a stock situation, the sort of warning appointment many had gone to, and then later disappeared. Dolci recounts the incident with an air of childish puzzlement. The student stayed with him, then gave up medicine. He is now a trade unionist in Palermo.

Mafia usually strikes when the atmosphere is still. Dolci was then working in comparative silence. It was a good moment to neutralize him. Yet the local Mafia hierarchy—whose opportunities for exerting friendly pressure on Rome were excellent—waited, well used to swatting inquisitive gadflies when the time came. They made a mistake. Soon Dolci would be more than a mere gadfly.

"When Danilo arrived," Sariddu says, "he and Vincenzina and all those children, they didn't have a lira. A few days after they moved in a woman brought along her baby, something like a year old. Imagine! A skeleton on legs. A ske-le-ton. You could pick up the skin in handfuls. When Danilo came downstairs and saw it he threw up his hands, and shouted to Carlo: 'Carlo, how much've we got in the kitty?' 'About three dollars.' Carlo yelled. 'Bring it here,' Danilo said. He gave the money to the woman and sent Carlo with her to see she got the right medicines. And that child, that piece of ragwort—it got better and better, it got so fat in the face it was like a *bull*!

"That night, after the woman came, I took Danilo and his family over some bread and cheese. They needed it. Because I saw that this was a charitable man."

"Some families go for days on end without ever tasting bread," Dolci told Carlo Levi. Levi, who was making his island trip that resulted in the book, *Words are Stones,* spent a day with Dolci. The latter said: "I'd expected to find people who were brutal and shiftless. Instead, there's kindness and ignorance. They don't know what they need. The peasants don't know what a dam is. They've never heard of chemical fertilizer."

Levi looked at some of the reports on Dolci's table. One stated that in a handful of houses there were seventeen declared cases of mental illness and epilepsy. Another, that at the start of the banditry in 1943 spacious premises which were being built as a hospital were converted to police barracks, leaving the whole zone without a hospital. In 1951 a 28-bed civic hospital was opened. It had no isolation ward, no delivery room, no child specialist on call. It served about seventy-eight thousand people. There was a maternity center, but it hadn't enough dried milk for all the needy mothers and very many didn't know it existed.

In *Words are Stones,* Levi, who is also a doctor, writes: "We encountered the most elementary problems of a world slavishly confined within the limits set by hunger and disease; and once again, as had happened so many years before,* I was forced against my will to recall old and almost forgotten notions of medicine." He found Dolci "friendly and open . . . with a big, well-formed Nordic head, and lively eyes behind his glasses; cheerful and full of internal energy . . ." Clouds of children called out "Danine! Danine!" as he passed, "as though they were uttering a magic formula." Levi concluded that Dolci's chief quality was the confidence he aroused in others. He was to repeat the words in different circumstances the following year.

Late that summer of 1955 Dolci began to draw in the strings of the inquiry.

Several dealt with the treatment of outlaws in Partinico and in the Papirete Barracks, Palermo; the treatment known as the *cassetta.* One man told Dolci:

When I was arrested they put the mask on me twice. About ten minutes each time. The mask sucked up salt water from the bucket and then they yanked your head back so the water went down your throat. Your stomach swells up like you were pregnant.

* *Christ Stopped at Eboli.*

They beat me nude, on the back, on the legs, all over my
bare body. On the *cassetta* they wrench your genitals. But
it's not only the beatings that are bad, it's the awful cold
of the floor when they throw you down. The floor is soaking
wet, they throw water and salt over you to stop up the bleed-
ing and the swelling. And it's not that the wardens do it
secretly; they do it before their superiors who interrogate
you and make out your statement while it's going on. Butchers!

In the meantime my family—I've three children—got no
assistance from anyone.

"God knows how it sickens me to publicize such distress,"
Dolci wrote, "even though I know it is in defense of the weak, the
ones at the bottom: *but it's up to us to ask forgiveness even from
these people and make amends to them with immediate loving
kindness.*"

He was not unduly confident about obtaining their forgiveness. But he knew it would never come as a result of empty pulpit speeches which spoke of "work and human dignity" and emphasized the doctrine of St. Paul—He who will not work shall not
eat—as though that alone would provide the remedy.

"It isn't that these people don't want to work," he told visitors
over and over. "It's that they don't know *how* to."

He turned to another report. A partial survey of nine hundred families showed nearly half to be destitute—161 of them because the father was, or had been in prison, had joined the outlaws, or had been murdered. He was beginning to understand.
Official theory was that all these irredeemable criminals had
merely *happened* to gather in this one spot. He didn't believe
it. He consulted the case histories of the 161 outlaws in the Madonna quarter. He found there wasn't one man among them he
could classify as a pathological criminal.

Early one morning he pulled back the curtain of the bed-
alcove where he and Vincenzina slept, switched on the light-bulb
over the table, and sat down on the planked ottoman before it,
as he always did at this hour. Below, the peasants were starting to
bump out in the darkness to their fields. The bumping of their

carts over the cobbles rose as tiny shock waves, making the small table rock. He began to write:

"There is a world of condemned among us, condemned to death by us ourselves.

"It sometimes happens that it rises against injustice; then it is put down with the machine gun and the prison.

"It is time to stop siding with the strongest, giving them leave to stifle the hopes of the others, as a cult, in broad daylight.

"I do not believe that we are all so barbarous that we want to go on killing, and let others do murder, like this. I will not believe it. Life, we know only too well, must go on."

The words announced Dolci's stand in Partinico, as they were to announce the despairing town to the world. They became the introduction to *Outlaws*, an arrow of suffering shot into the ears of an obtuse society. It was published by Laterza that year.

Outlaws had begun with a problem, and precise observance of that problem, grown through collective inquiry and understanding, and emerged as a human document binding the crucial facts.

Outlaws soon threatened to become a best seller.

Yet words alone, Dolci now knew, were not enough. Facts, however dramatically displayed, changed nothing. A book was not a toy, a pleasant exercise in rhetoric. It was a tool, an instrument for action. But action, seen from the lost playgrounds of the Partinician alleys in the autumn of 1955, seemed as remote as a Roman teaparty in the Via Veneto.

W

W   XI   W

W

PAUSE
FOR BREATH

From October in 1955 to Easter Day 1956, a period of five months, Dolci's life evolves, in perspective, as a patterned military operation. There is planning, a careful weighing of risk, there is skirmish, retreat, counterattack, and finally, success. But he did not arrange it like that. His instinct had a lot to do with it.

He knew in the autumn of 1955 he would have to act. Individual action was always possible. But individual action was no longer viable. "Why is it in such grave situations it's always left to the individual to intervene on his own initiative?" he had wondered, in *Outlaws*.

"As for 'Christian Brotherhood,' the less said the better ... You find work for one of the sons only to hear the mother complain because the rest of her children are jobless; you help the sick only to get a grumble because you haven't brought the right medicine. And so on all day long, every day of the week. You can't blame them (the first thing they ask for, usually, is work) ..."

Work. Wherever he went, that word. As at Trappeto everything seemed to resolve itself into those four letters.

Patchwork expedients by the state—work depots, housing schemes—had solved nothing. Hand-to-mouth charity by his own team only made things worse. The irrigation scheme was in cold storage. Help from outside? His northern friends were not industrialists and in any case no northern financier who valued his plant would come near West Sicily.

"What do you suggest?" he said to some trade unionists.

"March out and occupy the Sagana fief," they said. This was the antediluvian slogan, heroic and witless, like Polish cavalry charging armored regiments.

He fought for a solution.

He needed support. His own team was minimal—four adults and thirteen children. The only foreseeable backing was political. Here, Partinico was equipped. There were eleven political organizations, four trade unions, and a Catholic Action group. They ranged from the dormant Left to the Right of beyond. He was encouraged by growing dissatisfaction among CDs with their own local administration and canvassed hotly by the Left. But he didn't want to take sides. And he distrusted trade unions.

Party politics riled him. Boycotts, mass rallies, conventional strikes, class warfare did not interest him. They either confused the issue or led to violence, or both; and half the time the peasants didn't even know what the parties stood for. Where the Communists saw right and wrong he spoke of "truth, which is above factions"; where they pounded the class struggle, he talked of "collective responsibility" and "love"; where they spoke of converting the masses and maximum jobs he declared he was not a missionary and didn't believe in political employment agencies.

Work, he said, was not an ultimate. The end was the moral redemption of man. A lasting solution was possible only if the initiative came from below, from the people themselves, and this presupposed a moral and spiritual revival which no colored banner would ever inspire.

His hard moral core was unshakable. The Communists were mystified. Weren't they both on the side of the underdog? Here was a heaven-sent ally, an eloquent spokesman of the poor and a revolutionary to boot, who in the same breath was anti-Capitalist and anti-Communist as well. "The idea of the class struggle ought to have preoccupied him," the Communist writer, Franco Grasso, ruefully records.

Dolci was the Dresden Marxist who would sit on nobody's shelf.

He sympathized. He needed support. He did not wish to

alienate any party. Inevitably, if only because he was a lapsed
Catholic, he would be aligned with the Left whatever he did.
But he felt intuitively that the moment he crossed into one po-
litical camp his hands would be tied.

He was walking on eggs. Ostracized by the Right and wooed
by the Left, he hesitated—and did not commit himself.

November came, and with it no solution. Winter is hard in
a Sicilian community. In Spine Sante there were no fires and too
much rain, earth floors and no drains. Dogs sniffed disappoint-
edly for food scraps. The nonworkers hugged copper lap braziers,
inspected their rising credit with the grocer, and idly consulted
the majestic clots of rubbish which the rains swept past their
calico entrances. Robberies increased. Dolci's neighbor went out
stealing lemons. A man was accused of murdering his brother for
about five dollars. In a nearby street a baby girl of five months
grew seriously ill from undernourishment; the mother sent an
older daughter to Dolci for help, but on the way she stopped to
talk to a friend and forgot her mission. By the time Dolci arrived
it was too late. The child, weighing less than five pounds, died
in convulsions, vomiting her intestines.

Unemployment rose. People came to Number Ten Via Iannello for help, not singly but in droves. There were too many for
Dolci's team to handle.

Winter was only beginning.

By the end of November the situation was taut. Dolci fasted.
On 27 November 1955 he appealed to the press and the main
authorities in Italy. This is the essential part:

> To all:
> I invite everybody who feels a sense of public responsi-
> bility to fast for at least one day to refresh his memory, that
> is, if he has this kind of memory, of what it means to go hun-
> gry....
> If at Trappeto, through the goodwill of friends, private
> people, and the authorities, something has begun . . . here at
> Partinico we have to start from scratch. At least let us:

(1) Send every child to school until the age of 14; transform the present so-called schools,
(2) Help the families of the convicts and the "bandits,"
(3) Give work immediately to the jobless....

Meantime instead of our embracing the "bandits" and seeking their forgiveness, above all by deeds, we shoot at them (and not only here).

Meantime by not building the dam and using the winter waters of the Iato River, up to $7 million goes to waste every year....

Starting tomorrow I shall not eat for one week. And I shall fast a week each year until the dam is built....

We cannot just sit back gaping at this habitual overturning of all our values.

Yours,
DANILO

Outwardly the fast served only to call attention to the problems and bolster local political initiative, and it might be argued that it was thus superfluous. *Outlaws,* published in December 1955, put Partinico squarely in the public eye and Left-wing activity was slowly multiplying of its own accord. However, there were other reasons for the fast. Dolci was brooding a mass action. But the formula was vague. He wanted time—to sound, as well as stir local feeling. Like most men of conscience who, at flashpoint, go their own way whatever the consensus of opinion, he was humble enough—or human enough—to seek confirmation of his motives before the act.

Gronchi and Segni, the Italian President and Prime Minister respectively, and Alessi, the Sicilian Prime Minister, each received a personal note:

Gentlemen,
The action we are undertaking—aware that "the Kingdom of Heaven and its Justice" are not easily brought among mortals—is intended as a serene contribution, the little we can, towards the efforts of all men of goodwill.

On medical orders, toward the end of the 1955 fast and as shown here in 1962, Dolci took a little citrus juice in water or a weak sugar solution to counteract the toxic effects of fasting.

I am sure that you will understand the meaning behind these words.

Affectionately yours. . .

DANILO DOLCI

Dolci fasted in a dark room at the end of Via Iannello. The titleholder was in prison and his wife, who lived with Vincenzina during the fast, was without assistance. Vincenzina sat with him every day. He drank water, let the people talk, listened, and tried to convince everybody of the need for the dam. "It will work wonders," he said. Women said to him, "Child, why do you starve yourself like this?" He replied, mystically: "Exactness and truth melt, and destroy evil."

As publicity mounted, reaction from the Right hardened. An American journalist was informally commissioned by the archpriest to see if Dolci was suffering. The journalist reported back that Dolci could stand and was not yet in a corpse-like condition. The archpriest concluded that the fast was a fake and spread the good news. At night the door was closed—chiefly because of the cold. Behind it, the critics concluded, Dolci was eating cheerfully. The mayor, the local senator, grafting public officials, leading Christian Democrats, landowners paying substandard wages, contractors supposedly constructing public works, joined the anti-Dolci movement. A well-known university don in Palermo, asked by a colleague, Professor Lucio Lombardo-Radice, to join a pro-Dolci committee, said he wanted nothing to do with "that muckraker." The don added: "Delinquents, bandits, madmen are born that way; the remedy is prison, the strait jacket. That's what's needed!" His words echoed in the receptive crannies of conservative minds all over the island.

In Partinico signs of a moral change, a new civilizing force, hesitant and tentative, were reflected in the kaleidoscope of visitors who hovered about the fasting room. Dolci noted an evident desire among the peasants to discuss nonviolent remedies; to turn, for example, to the trade unions, to participate more sanely in the life of the community. He encouraged their talk. He was hopeful.

The fast was a preparation, a necessary respite. It served as a moral brake on a situation which, in late November, was threatening to explode at any moment. It also opened the first crack in the barrel of mistrust towards outsiders.

Towards the end, on medical orders, Dolci took a little citrus juice squeezed into a glass of water to counteract ketonic poisoning. He addressed a second appeal to the nation. His workers explained it to the peasants. It was a plea for basic human rights and ended: "We ask that the dam be built as soon as possible, for the immediate good of all." On 4 December, the last day, thirty peasants joined him and fasted voluntarily. Hundreds filed through the tiny room and signed the appeal. It was sent off covered with crosses. Most of the fifteen hundred who signed were unable to write their names.

On the evening of 4 December Dolci drank a glass of milky coffee and ate some dry biscuits. His mind was clearer.

A few days later he picked up a copy of the Italian Constitution. It was only then that a solution came to him. God—and police reaction—willing, it was the right one. It was time for shock tactics.

☙

☙ XII ☙

☙

THE PLAN
THAT FAILED

THE Italian Constitution is the fruit of the Italian Resistance
movement of the last war. It is, in theory, perhaps the finest democratic code in the world. Article I begins:

Italy is a democratic republic, founded on work.

Article IV states:

*The Republic recognizes the right of all citizens to work
and ensures the conditions necessary to make this right effective.*

*It is the duty of every citizen to follow, according to his abili-
ties and his own choice, such a calling or profession as shall contribute to the material and spiritual progress of the community.*

The solution lay in Article IV. It lay not in breaking the
law, but in *obeying* it. The idea had begun to coat his mind on
the last day of the fast, when Sarriddu said to him dismally: "A
hunger strike of a few days isn't enough by itself." "I know," Dolci
said. "You need a thousand days." "You need a thousand men,"
Sariddu said. From there, to the peasant's suggestion that a thousand of them would protest by lying full length on the railway
track and thereby stop all the trains going to Palermo.

Dolci was intrigued, but he dismissed the idea. It was too
dangerous. And it was passive. He wanted action. "Isn't there
some useful work we can do?" he asked. The peasants told him
that one of the country lanes behind the Madonna quarter, the
Valguarnera track, had become impassable after heavy rain. They

couldn't get their carts through. It was a public road. It was then
that Dolci picked up the Constitution.

Dolci decided on a plan of civil obedience. The state guaranteed the legal right of every citizen to work. He would imple-
ment that guarantee. The people wanted the road repaired. Very
well; they would repair the road. They would hold a "strike-in-
reverse."

The strength of the plan lay in its simplicity and the near-
certainty of arrest. The shock lay in the method. Even if the other side panicked there would be no violence from the demonstrators. This negation of violence—a traditional value dear to
every Sicilian—was the revolutionary aspect. Dolci was sure that
the men had the right qualities. The doubt was in his own mind.
He was not convinced that, alone, he possessed the moral fibre
to rouse these qualities in the others.

On 15 December, ten days after the fast, he led about sixty
unemployed men out to work. In a thin drizzle they began with
picks and shovels to repair the road. They had been working for
fifty minutes, shifting rocks and clearing caved-in verges, when
the police arrived, twenty-eight in all. Inspector La Corte ordered the men to stop working at once. "You're committing an
offense," he declared. "I'll have you all put in prison!" The men
demurred. The inspector began swearing and threatened to order his men to use their clubs. "Enough of machine guns—we
want work!" the men shouted. The inspector promised to find
them work and ordered them home. At that moment Dolci un-
derestimated his own qualities of leadership. He conferred quickly with the men and called off the demonstration. The men obey-
ed the police and went home.

Dolci later said: ". . . it was a grave responsibility to act in
the remote countryside without witnesses, where on one side
were fathers of families and on the other, members of the police
who are not used to strikes . . ."

The real reason was that he was not quite ready to go to
prison.

Dolci's mind, even to those who know him well, has never

*Dolci's former neighbor in Spine Sante, Sariddu, whose sug-
gestions led to the mass fast and strike-in-reverse of 1956.*

appeared logical. It is continually turning in on itself, examin-
ing, re-examining, conducting a private tribunal in the realm of
his own religious truth and moral convictions. This game of chess
he plays, painfully, with himself is the inner spring which re-
leases decisions and actions which at times appear willful, con-
tradictory, and plain damn foolhardy. "He goes along by zigzag,"
an Italian journalist observed. It is frustrating; it is inevitable;
it is Dolci. But in practice he is nearly always consistent.

This time, however, he was not acting consistently. Having
accepted the idea of "disobedience to any police law which con-
tradicts God's law," to be truthful—in his own phrase, to be *exact*

—he was bound to act on that idea. For the first time, according to his own principles, he was guilty of dishonesty. He knew this. And it rankled.

According to his conscience, he was wrong. Tactically, as it turned out, he was right. He intended to obey the Constitution to the letter. The unwillingness of the police—or their inability—to grasp the spirit of the Constitution had demonstrated that this was a crime. He needed now a campaign, with wide publicity, national awareness, and pressure from the top, as well as the bottom. A campaign, not merely a plan. In order to carry out a successful campaign of civil obedience he would have to adopt the rules of civil disobedience.

At last, and only in the face of defeat, did he come to the perfect solution. It was the result of experiment, compromise, and a plan that failed.

ü

ü XIII ü

ü

THE ROAD
TO PRISON

IT was the harshest winter they could remember in that part
of Sicily. A couple of emergency work depots were opened by
the authorities and the Church, but the jobs were parcelled out
by *mafiosi* to a few privileged friends. "I will do everything in my
power to find work for the jobless," the mayor told Dolci. But
two-thirds of the able-bodied male population remained unemployed.

In December 1955 Dolci wrote to Aldo Capitini: "The people are beginning to understand that the act of signing there
(in the fasting room) is tantamount to a pledge to renounce
shooting." He planned his campaign for the last days of January and the first week of February 1956.

One of the premises of civil disobedience is that you give the
enemy all possible warning. You tell him the day, the hour, and
if possible the place. You welcome prison, receive sentence cour-
teously, compliment the judge on his leniency, and, if you are as
generous as Gandhi was, you may even send your adversary—in
Gandhi's case, Smuts—a handmade article which the latter will
then cherish for the rest of his life.

When Dolci's first plan went off half-cocked the police were
disappointed. Ever since the Borgo raid they had been waiting
for a false move.

Dolci was almost ready to oblige. He prepared for a campaign to rouse the nation.

In Partinico he consulted with the families of the unemployed, wrote the text of a television talk he had been asked to give, put on the only respectable jacket he possessed, and went north. In Rome the indefatigable Maria Sacchetti-Fermi embraced him and told him she had founded a national Danilo Dolci Committee. A few days later he was in Turin, and on 13 January he gave his talk from the RAI television studios there. In it he returned to the principle of truth in creed and deed and announced his intentions to the nation. He said:

"In Partinico 2,500 out of 5,100 children do not go to school: they are above all the children of the bandits, the orphans. People say they've bad blood in them. Just for a moment, then, look at the drawings of Matteo, he's one of them (a dozen watercolors of Matteo, aged fourteen, are shown on the screen).

"Not only do they not go to school, the children: they cannot subsist. I would never have believed that suicide might become at times an act of reason. I always thought that to kill yourself you had to have 'a screw loose.' But ever since I began to see children—yes, children—watching me eat through the open door, their eyes starting, their lips drooling, only then did I start to think that to be consistent I should make sure their bellies are full before I take another mouthful myself. Let alone fast for one week in the year! ...

"And when I go back what am I to tell those women who've said to me: 'If you find us work we'll stop being prostitutes'? ...

"Now when I return, if there are no other jobs to be had, while we're waiting for the dam to be built, we shall go to work on the track once again. I'm here to lay down to all of you, that no police charge will ever stop us from working ..."

It was not Government policy to allow sociologists and writers freedom of the air to tell the truth about the south. The talk, toned down only slightly, went out more or less by accident. Dolci heard later that the two political editors who had dared to produce it, Michele Straniero and Furio Colombo, were sacked immediately. They have since become prominent in the Italian cultural world.

Dolci was given a surprise donation by a Turin benefactor.

With the money he bought a car, a prewar Lancia. It had wooden doors and held a busload. Friends who saw him off in Turin said that it wandered sadly down the Corso, pointed towards Milan, like a hearse in search of a funeral. Six days later it reached Rome, via Milan, Padova, Pisa, and Florence. Everywhere Dolci explained his needs to friends, mayors, writers, students. They promised help. Embryo aid-committees sprang up in five centers. In Rome he told Maria Sacchetti-Fermi he was worried. All over the south, from Campania to Sardinia, laborers were demonstrating against feudal conditions. There had been clashes with the police. On the day he spoke in Turin hundreds of southern jobless had demonstrated at Venosa, in Puglia. The police had opened fire, killing a young peasant and wounding six others. It was not difficult to imagine a similar occurrence on the old Valguarnera track outside Partinico.

When Dolci drove back to Partinico he had a passenger with him, a sandy-haired teaching graduate from Gubbio. Goffredo Fofi had just finished his studies. He had read about Dolci in a French review and offered his services in Rome. Dolci's first news on return was that his other young teacher, Ugo Piacentini, a philologist left in charge of the People's University at Trappeto, had been sent away. Piacentini had applied to the Trappeto town council for a change of residence from Savona and been refused, "on the grounds that your residence here is not justified by a remunerative employment or any other adequate reason." Dolci's team was down to three: himself, Carlo, Giovanni. Goffredo was not long out of short trousers.

In any individual yet mass action informed leaders are vital. Without them there can be no self-control.

Dolci telegraphed the authorities, leaving the door open for an eleventh-hour intervention. There was no response. He invited all the trade unions to participate. Two accepted, the middle-of-the-road UIL (Social Democrat) and the Camera del Lavoro. The latter had been kicked out of a moribund state by the refugee-unionist Comparetto who repaid Dolci's hospitality in the hayloft with interest. Comparetto helped to organize the coming action. In Spine Sante, above the bedlam of street criers and donkeys, details were hammered out over bowls of soup and handout suppers in Dolci's upstairs bunkhouse, which was also the dining room. Vincenzina served an average of forty people a night. Professor Lucio Lombardo-Radice came to a meeting, and supper, and went away hungry. Friends and journalists were handed a plate of minestrone and a piece of *mortadella* or goat cheese and called into discussions; those who inquired about the flotillas of children coming and going reported that Dolci did not seem to be at all sure which were his. He appeared calm and unsmiling.

Sariddu's idea of "the Thousand" had blossomed. Monday, 30 January, the anniversary of Gandhi's death, was fixed for a collective peasant hunger strike on Trappeto beach to protest against the continuing fishing abuses. Three days later, if the authorities had not moved, they would return to work on the track again. The fast was a necessary prelude—as much to convince the peasants taking part, as the authorities, that their intentions were honorably peaceful. "There are to be no troublemakers," Dolci said. "Every man must know he's going out to demonstrate in a new spirit; to show that he's got a vast store of riches in his own hands—work." He added, "We'll break our bread with our own hands."

The police were given a week's notice. Posters appeared in Trappeto, Balestrate, and Partinico. Manifestoes put up by the UIL and the Camera del Lavoro contained the text of Article IV of the Constitution and an extract from Dolci's writings: "Not to ensure work for all in accordance with the spirit of the Constitution is to commit murder."

These words and the plan of campaign were published in *L'Ora* and in Italian newspapers. The word "murder" had been carefully chosen.

The police reacted exactly as Dolci hoped they would. They banned the demonstrations.

Dolci was called before the police on 29 January and told

that the proposed mass fast was illegal. "Why?" he asked. The
carabinieri lieutenant said that starving was allowed, but only
individually. Besides, he added, he doubted very much whether
it was lawful for large numbers of people to assemble on a beach.

"When I was a youngster," Dolci said, "I often went swimming on the crowded beaches at Rimini and the Ligurian
Riviera without needing special permission from the police."

"Perhaps," the lieutenant observed, "perhaps there were
police among the bathers."

Dolci said that the people were all in favor of law and order
and reiterated the guarantee of work given in the Constitution.
The officer replied, paternally: "My dear Dolci, my dear Dolci
—all that's just a Utopia."

Dolci was formally asked to call off the fast. He refused.

Next morning, the Monday of the fast, it was raining hard.
Dolci was woken at three-thirty and told that there were some
two hundred police in the Trappeto area, where the fast was to
be held. The village was surrounded. He dressed, climbed into
the old Lancia, and drove to Trappeto. A quick reconnaissance
showed that the police had forbidden the boat captains to go
without food and were holding up traffic on all the access roads,
dispersing new arrivals. A warrant officer, red in the face, was
screaming orders at the top of his voice. Outlying peasants arriving on bicycles were being served tickets because their machines
were "out of order." Because of police concentration Dolci decided it was safest if the fast were held in three different places;
he sent a messenger to Balestrate telling the fishermen there to
fast in their own village, turned the Lancia round, and made
back for Partinico. A police car, jammed with uniforms, tailed
him. He stopped several times to pick up Partinicans who were
already walking out and passed a group of officers standing at the
Partinico turnoff. One of them was Chief Inspector Tommaso
di Giorgi, sent from the Palermo CID to direct operations. He
noted that the police car tailing him had been flagged down by
di Giorgi. Dolci drove on up the hill. A mile and a half outside
Partinico, by the grade crossing, the Lancia ran out of gas.

Everyone jumped out. Dolci ran all the way to the Camera del
Lavoro, arriving just in time to prevent the main body of peasants setting out for Trappeto. Meantime the police car had come
up behind and discovered the abandoned Lancia. It stopped.
There was a hasty conference in the rain. Then the policemen
plunged into the fields on either side of the road and began looking for Dolci among the cauliflowers.

At Trappeto the local fishermen had gathered on the rocky
beach where the police could not get their Jeeps down. Scores
of fishermen stood about, yawning, pondering, and smoking in
the lee of the boats. Starving to them was normal. From the parapet above their womenfolk watched anxiously. The rain continued. Police swarmed the streets in greatcoats and turned-up
collars, patrolled the cliffs, got very wet, and waited for something to happen. Nothing did. A northern visitor was approached by a lieutenant. "What are you doing here?" the officer
said. "I'm a journalist." "There's nothing to be seen here."
"Well, in that case," the journalist said, "why are you here?"
The lieutenant walked away. By afternoon the carabinieri were
reduced to small groups leaning on the houses, banging their
boots round smoking embers to get their feet warm, while fellow
greatcoats combed the cliffs, hunting forlornly for twigs to keep
the fires going.

Hundreds of jobless fasted in the Partinico Camera del
Lavoro. They stood pressed together in the bleak room, their
eyes fixed on a sheet of paper by the window where Mario Fari-
nella, the *L'Ora* correspondent, sat at a rough table writing.
"They brought me an old typewriter," he reported. "I don't
know where they got it from. It's rusted up and soaked from the
rain. 'Here,' the peasant said, holding it in his arms, 'now you
can write your article.' It's dark and I can't read their expressions. There's a baby crying. The women in black shawls are
sitting down, suckling their children . . ."

In Rome, Gronchi, the Head of State, received a telegram.
"We are not fasting today from desperation, out of despair, but
in the hope that we may help Italy to become more civilized . . .

Whoever impedes us is an assassin: we do not pay our taxes so that our country, on sea and land, shall become an evil prison galley in the hands of the powerful. Signed: *one thousand citizens who believe in Article IV of the Constitution.*"

Late that morning the Partinico town council was hastily convened. It was only the second time it had met in thirteen months. Dolci was invited, but on learning that it was intended to distribute soup, declined. "I did not think that this was the right way to solve the problem of unemployment," he said later.

More than a thousand men fasted, for twenty-four hours, in Balestrate, Trappeto, and Partinico. The day passed without incident.

The next day, Tuesday, Dolci launched an appeal in the national press. "Friends of Partinico—The 'bandits' of Partinico wish to become Italian citizens, members of a truly civilized society.

"By fasting and meditating together on Monday we have purified ourselves for Thursday's celebration: work. Nobody can stop us from working together in a quiet orderly manner . . ." He called on everyone, regardless of party or belief: "Let's roll up our sleeves and get out of this abyss of material and spiritual corruption. Unless we pull ourselves out of it, we who are sunk in it and suffer from it, who on earth will do it for us?" 'If one fails, we all fail.'

"We are men of peace," he said. "I am certain that nobody will try to hinder us in this sacred task."

Commenting on Dolci's action, the *Giornale di Sicilia* warned readers of "an exceedingly strange and anachronistic local phenomenon."

On the Wednesday the unemployed gathered in the Camera del Lavoro. Salvatore Termini, union secretary and town councilor, spoke. "Tomorrow let no one ask for money," he said. "We're going out to demonstrate that on our part there's a will to work." The cheers were loud.

At the last minute the UIL pulled out.

That night the first police reinforcements reached Partinico.

When in the early hours Chief Inspector di Giorgi arrived from
Palermo he had four hundred police at his disposal. Shortly before six A.M. Dolci and two hundred jobless made their way out to
the track. They carried work tools only. They had left behind
even the penknives they normally carried to cut bread. Journalists and photographers were on the track already. The lane fell,
muddy and twisting, between caved-in verges to a small stream
which cut across it. The men spread out on both sides of the
stream and began working. Dolci's group was on the town side.
After about twenty minutes seven truckloads of carabinieri arrived. A lieutenant marched down the track and ordered Dolci
to stop working. Dolci took no notice. The lieutenant grabbed
the shovel and gave him over to three constables. Dolci thought
he was under arrest and allowed himself to be led away. Police,
seemingly in combat gear, were pouring on to the track, with
machine guns, clubs, and tear-gas bombs. "I hope you won't do
these people any harm," Dolci said to Inspector La Corte, police
chief of Partinico, offering his hand. La Corte turned away.
Farther on they met Chief Inspector di Giorgi, tall, impeccable
in plain clothes and dark glasses. The latter told the policemen
to release Dolci. Dolci said he would rejoin the others and
promptly doubled back across open country to rejoin the main
body beyond the stream. "Go on working," he said. The police
told him to go away. Dolci grabbed a pick and fell in alongside
the men. "Go on working," he said. All normal access was now
blocked and fresh workers had to arrive across fields and vineyards. Carlo, nearest the stream, was arguing with an officer.
Goffredo's group, isolated from the main body, cut over the top
and joined in lower down. Puffing, di Giorgi came up to Dolci.
He removed his dark glasses and said:

"Signor Dolci, these men must stop working at once. You
must obey the law."

Dolci said, "We're not doing anything against it. You've
told us to stop working and we've heard you. By the Constitution work isn't only a right—it's a duty of us all."

The Chief Inspector burst out laughing. "Signor Dolci,

you mustn't take these things so literally." Several policemen giggled.

"We've come here to do a job of work," Dolci said. "We intend to stay the full eight hours and we don't ask for payment. Whoever prevents us from working is a murderer."

At the sound of the word "murderer" di Giorgi stiffened. He gave an order. Five policemen stepped forward to grab Dolci. The latter sat down on the ground cross-legged, arms folded Gandhi-style. As he was lifted up by his arms and legs his trousers split. "Go on working, go on digging!" he exhorted the others. He was borne away. The five constables had to carry Dolci across the stream and uphill for the best part of a mile to reach the trucks. Dolci did not resist. Every now and then when they were tired they let him down into the mud.

Dolci was arrested at six-thirty a.m. Termini and five others were arrested a few moments later. In spite of police provocation there was no retaliation from the demonstrators—except for Carlo who, wrangling with his guardians, fell into the stream by mistake. He was re-arrested as he climbed out. "Poor Carlo," a colleague said later. "He's the only one of us with a record. The first time he does something really useful for society he lands himself in the jug again."

The police also arrested a photographer and confiscated his movie-camera. They drew up in a line, sounded the advance on a trumpet, and broke up the rest of the demonstration. "Go home," the men were told. The men did not go home. They marched down the main street of Partinico in a silent body and, when blocked by carabinieri, made through the back streets and reassembled at the town hall. There they were promised jobs and were asked to give their names. Those that did so were later charged in court.

Dolci and the six were charged in Partinico on five counts. On the charge sheet Dolci was defined as "a noted political agitator."

Goffredo, the student teacher, was arrested next morning. Di Giorgi and another officer questioned him for two hours, a

piercing light full in his eyes. Goffredo's work had been mainly
with the illiterate. He was jailed for two days. He was then exiled
from Partinico by *foglia di via* for having "no perceptible salary
and no fixed residence."

Two of the six arrested with Dolci were released on bail.
Dolci and the other four—Carlo Zanini, Salvatore Termini, the
union secretary, Ciccio Abbate, a workman, and Ignazio Speciale, a young Communist clerk—were imprisoned in the Ucciardone, Palermo's jail. Dolci was well contented. "If they arrest
us," he'd said to Vincenzina on leaving the house that morning,
"we're home and dry."

Sariddu, describing the events to Vincenzina, said: "What
with the plainclothesman saying to Danilo, 'But these men must
stop working,' and Danilo saying, 'But they won't stop working,' and Danilo's pants splitting and then the trumpet sounding the attack, *Ma-donna*, it was just like a *festa*!"

Chief Inspector di Giorgi wrote out his report. "Public
order has been restored," he said.

❧

❧ XIV ❧

❧

CIRCUS
IN THE HOUSE

NEWS of Dolci's arrest was across Europe and the Atlantic in a few hours. In Italy it was greeted with banner headlines like THEY HAVE ARRESTED DANILO DOLCI (on the Left) and SO-CALLED APOSTLE UNMASKED (on the Right). Liberal intellectuals were indignant at police action; conservatives denounced the intellectuals for daring to be indignant. Reading the newspaper reports, the telegrams, and the Acts of Parliament, it is hard to judge which was the greater—the shock of the intellectuals and the Left or the reaction of the reactionaries on the Right.

Dolci, in prison, received thousands of letters and telegrams from friends and cultural leaders all over Europe. Abbé Pierre sent his blessing. La Pira, the militantly Catholic Mayor of Florence, wired the Home Secretary, Tambroni, to release Dolci, precipitating a crisis in the Florence City Council. Influential men of letters—Moravia, Silone, de Martino, Zavattini, de Sica, the former Prime Minister, Parri, among them—held a protest conference in Rome, declaring: "We consider ourselves in prison with him." When the Italian Radio reported their opinion—that Dolci was moved by Christian principles—the *Vespri d'Italia* said: "This is a deliberate attempt to influence the magistrates." The fascist paper added, "He is simply immoral." In the north student groups got out pro-Dolci leaflets. In Palermo Chief Inspector di Giorgi was promoted to Superintendent. In Partinico the union offices were crammed. Demonstrations continued. The mayor told journalists: "There is noth-

ing abnormal here ... perhaps a little unemployment"—and
was obliged to call in two hundred extra police before he could
hold an emergency meeting of the council.

Responsible journalists found themselves in a dilemma.
"To define Dolci is difficult," *L'Espresso* said. The influential
Rome weekly decided he was not a sociologist, not a missionary,
and not a moralist, concluding rather lamely that he was "a nonviolent man who writes." Curzio Malaparte, the most pungent
journalist of his time, said that Dolci was not a Communist, nor
an anarchist, nor a subversive; he was an idealist, an apostle of
good, a Catholic believer with near-Protestant morals. The
American magazine *Time* was more to the point. "*Dolci* v. *Far
Niente*," it said. Most other critics lost themselves, guessing.
Dolci did not enlighten them for years. He called himself "an
intellectual with a social conscience" and "an integrated Christian,"
which only made the muddle worse.

Government, clerical, and neofascist organs reacted like
small children with guilty consciences who, upbraided for their
misdemeanors, attempt to save face by flinging on their accuser
for not attending Sunday School. The clerical journal *Sicilia
del Popolo* got bogged in the hygienic system of Borgo di Dio
and accused Dolci of running a promiscuous community of free
love. Dolci was criticized for driving a "luxury car"; for refusing
the hand of a rich Milanese girl, and, in the same breath, for
living "comfortably"; for employing Protestants and for writing
books. Christian Democrat politicians reacted as though their
virility were at stake. The Government organ *Giornale d'Italia*
published three articles by Partinico's senator, Santi Savarino:
he attacked Dolci for consorting with Communists, for defam-
ing Partinico, for corrupting the soul of the people, and for belonging to "that intellectual cabal of *useful idiots* which en-
riches the Italian literary fauna." He described Partinico as
"that fine and generous land where I have the honor to be
born." Senator Savarino lives in Rome.

There were strange scenes in the House of Deputies. Opposition members tabled demands for an explanation from

Tambroni. The Communists referred to "the Catholic writer, Danilo Dolci." The Home Secretary did not reply in person. Instead, in a dry bureaucratic voice, an undersecretary, Pugliese, read out an official table of twenty-nine statistics. In stony silence he announced to the last penny how much money had been spent in Partinico and said that the number of unemployed men was only 2467.3. Opposition members pointed out that official figures ignored men out of work for six months of the year.

"Please don't read us a list of sums," the Socialist Musotto said.

The Republican La Malfa observed: "I understand we're now studying plans to build autostradas in Sicily. They haven't got roads yet."

"Periodically," Alicata, for the Communists, said, "a man is called before us to read out in a monotonous voice documents which offend our intelligence. Hon. Pugliese—doesn't it all seem a little grotesque? Don't you see that in the face of reality all these figures, even if exact, are meaningless?"

The Hon. Pugliese did not see. He was at pains to point out that his figures came from the right source.

"Perhaps," Santi, a Socialist, said lightly, "perhaps you asked the Mayor of Partinico for them?"

No, that was not the usual procedure, the undersecretary replied, seriously.

Members tried to define Dolci. They fared no better than the journalists. At one point Musotto produced a copy of *Outlaws* and read from Norberto Bobbio's preface: "The moral and religious figure of Danilo Dolci is, above all, that of one who follows a conscientious line of action." Deputies were baffled.

DEGLI OCHI (Christian Democrat): The Hon. La Malfa said a short while ago that Dolci is backed by Protestants.

PAJETTA (Communist): Could you manage some firsthand information?

DEGLI OCHI: Here the Catholic newspapers say that Danilo Dolci is indeed not a Catholic.

PAJETTA: And is it necessary to put handcuffs on a writer who is
    not a Catholic?

DEGLI OCHI: Oh no ... You know very well that I would never
    dream of consenting to the handcuffing of anyone because
    he is not a Catholic.

The debate ended in uproar, amid the words of the Christian Democrat Sante: "As to the protagonist of this deplorable affair, he erupts into Sicily, into a zone where banditry is minimal ... driven by ideals which have nothing to do with militant Catholicism . . . . I would like to profit from this favorable occasion by inviting the press to inquire into what has been written and above all what has been done by this strange apostle in Partinico (*rude words from Opposition members*) ... with that sense of absolute objectivity of which our journalism is proud. . . ."

In the Senate the Government adopted similar ostrich tactics. There was another debate and another undersecretary read out yet another list of sums.

The official Government account presented Dolci as a common criminal, Communist-inspired, who had flagrantly incited the masses with the object of claiming remuneration from the local authorities. He had been arrested "for abusing and resisting the police who were forced to intervene in order to re-establish public order." To anyone acquainted with the Mafia client system operating between Sicily and Rome it was a familiar pattern of trumpery.

Dolci might have fared worse. As Malaparte wrote in *L'Europeo*, Dolci, like Carnevale, had become dangerous to powerful landowning interests and could count himself lucky to be alive at all.

It is easy to exaggerate the political importance of Dolci's action. But, coming as it did amid a terrible winter, it threw into sharp relief a general situation of unrest in southern Italy. Throughout the south two-fifths of the population was living on one-fifth of the national product and, among the "working" classes, the average daily wage *per capita* would not have sufficed to pay subway fare in most American cities. The Government was spending tens of millions (dollars, not lire) in the south. Its postwar creation, the *Cassa per il Mezzogiorno* (Fund for the South), was building roads, dams, schools, and rehousing settlements from Sassari to the toenail of Italy, and not least in Sicily. But much of the work was wasted. Schools were built without regard for education: absenteeism was rife and hundreds of teachers unemployed. Hospitals were built and never staffed. Rural housing settlements appeared on gaunt hillsides, without water or electricity: the peasants refused to live in them. Dams were planned in areas where rainfall was negligible: when completed they remained empty. Water sluiced through irrigation ducts to benefit only the farms of the privileged. Government prodigality bore no relation to the needs of the people and, in 1956, had scarcely begun to touch the root of southern depression—unemployment. Everywhere, after Venosa, peasants and miners struck, demonstrated, marched behind banners, demanding an end to feudal domination. The Prime Minister, Segni— the protagonist of the sweeping, but dead-letter postwar land reforms—appealed for reason. He tried. But his voice was a reed in the winter winds. Tambroni held the whip hand. The Home Secretary deplored "these protests." The police took him at his word. In Calabria and Sardinia there were clashes and many arrests. In Puglia and East Sicily police routed processions with tear gas, cudgelling and machine gunning laborers to death.

It was all, very largely, the Communist bogey. The ascetic Pius XII gave no lead to a reactionary Church party, and in the key Cardinals of Naples and Palermo—Castaldo and Ruffini— he had two aggressive allies. After eight years of power the Christian Democrats were still suffering from an epidemic of religious McCarthyism which made good Catholic voters think twice about wearing a pink tie, and threatened the fiancées of Left-wing unionists with excommunication if they tried to get as far as the altar. Unemployment was "upsetting." Unemployment meant demonstrations, demonstrations meant marches, and at any moment the red hordes would come pouring into St. Peter's Square. That was roughly the pattern of Government thinking.

Dolci's action fitted snugly into this context. It would have been surprising if the Government had *not* claimed it was Communist-inspired. Conversely, it gave tremendous prestige to both Socialists and Communists whose postwar rise was beginning to have a real impact: welcoming Dolci to the cause of social justice it would have been surprising if they had not boasted the "Catholicism" of their unorthodox ally.

Throughout February Government organs continued their attempts to blacken Dolci's character, thus contributing greatly to the myth of a man they so ardently wished to silence.

In Paris a French journalist heralded *"Le Gandhi de la Sicile."* The phrase travelled. He did indeed have the Gandhi touch. Just as Gandhi had riled the British administration in India so now Dolci in Italy was driving the Government mad.

DOLCI
IN JAIL

In Palermo jail, the Ucciardone, society's public benefactors—
Dolci and the four—were having trouble with bedbugs. They
were in a large cell with forty others, visited daily by the young
Palermo lawyer, Nino Sorgi. Sorgi brought the outside news
and, about the middle of February, a message from DonnaTopa-
zia Alliata, a progressive Sicilian princess, who had worked briefly at Borgo. "Ask Danilo how he is," Donna Topazia said to
Sorgi. "Ask him if he needs anything, will you?" Dolci told the
lawyer, "Tell Donna Topazia the food's quite all right, and I'm
kept interested by talking to the others and listening to their
problems. There's only one thing—it's hard to sleep because of
the bedbugs." The next time Sorgi came he took a bottle of DDT
from his briefcase. "From Donna Topazia," he said. Dolci returned the bottle. The lawyer reported: "Danilo says to thank
you very much, but he won't accept it, you know, because there
are forty others in his cell and if he doesn't have enough for all
of them he won't use it himself." Donna Topazia promptly sent
off a consignment of four gallons of DDT, "hoping finally that
you all may sleep." When she saw Sorgi again he said, "Yes, he's
using it now—and he's really quite happy about it."

The Ucciardone is notorious. During one of the exercise
breaks Dolci saw a prisoner grab another and hold him against
the wall while a third beat him viciously over the head with a
thorny stick. Nobody, neither friends nor warders, interfered.
In the lugubrious Bourbon jail on the city's north outskirts

many inmates existed in perpetual fear of retribution, violence, and inquisitorial torture—not from the warders, some of whom were more afraid than the prisoners, but from the Ucciardone's own internal Mafia. Even today warders ask to be given heavier guard duty rather than patrol the lower sections. Hundreds of prisoners each year are attacked; when questioned about their injuries they invariably say that they fell downstairs. Sentence is passed by a secret tribunal of "lifers" who cow warders by threatening the safety of their families outside, and if necessary —when a prisoner breaks the law of *omertà* (silence)—arrange for the latter's execution inside. Not even Pisciotta—cousin and betrayer of the bandit Giuliano—with all his elaborate precautions, evaded the retributive arm of the Mafia. Pisciotta ate only food prepared by himself or his parents and first tested it on two birds he kept in his cell. He died after drinking a minute cup of his own coffee, dosed with medicine prescribed for a chest complaint which contained enough strychnine to kill a bull.

The grimmest quarter was Section Six. Dolci had scarcely arrived when, from this section, he was sent a plate of bread, olives, and cheese.

Dolci and Co. were interrogated on 3 February, and on 5 February in a public statement affirmed that their actions had been entirely pacific. Application for their release on bail was made the next day.

Demands for Dolci's release mounted. Jean-Paul Sartre devoted a special issue of his review *Temps Modernes* to the strike-in-reverse. Northern Italian university students debated the case. The Turin committee rushed up funds, sent workers, and opened the first social center in Partinico. To do this they rented a house in a hurry, not mentioning Dolci's name. Later, the *mafioso* Frank Coppola was heard to remark, proudly: "What d'you think—in one of my houses I've got a social center!" Gabriella, the adolescent daughter of Maria Sacchetti-Fermi, begged her mother to be allowed to come to Partinico to help out. Gabriella came. So did Franco, the young mechanic. He was then working a precision machine in a Milan factory. He received a wire from Dolci at six one evening. The following morning Franco's boss found the machine idle, with a note on it, and fired Franco on the spot. Franco was already on the train, three-quarters of the way to Sicily.

Dolci spent his days reading, talking, and listening to his companions. One of them had belonged to Giuliano's band. "If I'd known Danilo ten years ago," he said, "I'd never have become a bandit." In the *aria,* the concrete quad where they were exercised twice daily, he met one of the four *mafiosi** imprisoned and awaiting trial for the murder of Carnevale. Carnevale had been "a bit too ambitious," the *mafioso* said. Vincenzina came almost every day, but was able to talk to her husband only through two sets of iron gratings, a four-foot gap between them. Dolci was visited by a delegation of Left-wing deputies. They found him animated and looking forward to an early release. The magistrate set down for the bail hearing was Marcataio, brother of Monsignor Marcataio, an intimate of Cardinal Ruffini. By 18 February, however, after the debate in the House, Dolci apparently was no longer optimistic. He announced:

"From Tuesday next, 21 February—within these walls where our society is now *revenging* itself, and monstrously so, for the evils of everybody, on a few—I will fast, for the time being, for three days."

Tuesday 21 February was the day set down for the bail hearing. There were five charges: illegal assembly; invading public land and altering its condition; refusal to disperse on the orders of the police; abusing the police and violently resisting arrest; and sedition. The magistrate said he had studied the police reports, the "gravity of the offenses" and the "criminal intent" of the accused. In his opinion their release from custody might endanger the public peace. In particular, Dr. Marcataio said, Dolci's behavior, together with his private way of life, gave ample evidence that he was a fellow "with a marked disposition for delinquency."

* Later sentenced to life imprisonment and subsequently, in March 1963, released on appeal, declared "innocent."

Bail was refused.

Dolci was glad of the extra rest in prison. He was allowed all the books he wanted, and made copious notes of conversations with prisoners in an exercise book which he kept under the bed-clothes. The warder in charge of the section knew this and on the nightly cell checks turned a blind eye to Dolci's bunk. "Why is it you never look under my bunk?" Dolci said to him. The warder grinned and muttered in a gravelly voice: "*Io sacciu che rota gira*"—"I know that a wheel rolls." Dolci didn't understand. "In this cell," the warder explained, "there was once a man called Parri." Ferruccio Parri, imprisoned under fascism in the Ucciardone, later became Prime Minister of Italy. The pages of Dolci's notebook were smuggled out every day by Sorgi. The young Palermo lawyer, who was then unknown, gave his services free. In the end he had to sell jewelry and pawn other articles in order to keep his practice going.

Dolci paced the cell, reconstructing and annotating the events on the track, to give a precise account at the coming trial. "It looks bad, Danilo," Sorgi said as the days wore on. Piero Cala-mandrei, the distinguished Florentine lawyer, visited Dolci. He confirmed Sorgi's gloom.

Dolci continued his homework, unperturbed. He wrote every day. His most valuable experience was the encounter with Vincenzo. Vincenzo was a 23-year-old cowherd from the moun-tains behind Castellammare Bay. He had been brought from the Colombaia, another prison. "He was short and squat, and stout," Dolci told me, "and when he ate he ate like a cow. Thun-dering noises. And there were other violent noises he made, bodily sounds ... you know? But there was a lot of likableness in him. He was a man of four thousand years ago. It's not that he *talked*. There'd be a clot of words, and then I'd ask him some-thing, and then half an hour later there'd be another clot of words, and then another clot, and so on. ... Some of his words were Latin, pure Latin. And he couldn't walk properly, 'on shoes,' as we say. Shoes with nailed soles, you understand. He was Nature itself, a primitive natural force I'd never known before."

Clot by clot, Vincenzo's account tumbled out every day for a week.

I always dream of animals—ones out in the fields—because I grew up with animals ever since· I was five. I was born with animals all about me ... not our animals: my father was employed by the year (how many months has a year got?), or by half a year. Either that or they gave him six or eight dollars a month. I don't know how many months a year's got. I don't know if I'm seventeen or nineteen. We could get someone to write to the place where they know about those things ....

When there's no work you eat herbs. Being hungry makes you do queer things. You can't see out of your eyes. You want to kill yourself—all sorts of things. If you've got work you've got everything ....

What are the stars in the sky? I can tell you. You see, the moon is like the sun. I understand the stars: they come out and I see lots of them. It must be something to do with the smoke, it gets into the sky and at night sometimes you can see the stars and sometimes you can't. The moon is made out of sky, the sky is made out of smoke which is made on earth and then goes up there. And sometimes in the mornings you can see the moon too when the sun arrives. The stars move through the night, they're always moving. When day comes they always go in again; the animals go into their stables, and the stars go into their stalls the same way. What the stars are, that's what us men and animals are ....

In the world there are different countries—there are the houses. The world's half a pumpkin. In prison I've had all sorts of strange things: a bed with sheets, covers, mattresses, pillows; whenever did I have these before? I know I was born in the country because they told me so, even my father told me that. I saw houses from a distance, from outside, but I never went inside—what on earth would I have done there? I wasn't the owner. When the police came for

me they got me when I was grazing the cattle and when I
saw them coming I took off . . . .

In prison, at the Colombaia, they gave me a bit of school.
They showed me an egg—"o" for "ovo" they said—and that's
how I learned to say "o." Then they taught me an "o" with
a tiny leg on it, and that was "a." Then they went like a
cow does, "Uuu-uu-hh" and that was "u." Then "e." And
then "i." And that's all . . . .

Of course, there's somebody who rules Italy. Who is it?
Mussolini, I think. It's all the lawyers who do us down, all
the magistrates have a big conspiracy to keep us under. The
wrongdoers, I'd kill the lot of them, I'd set them on fire so
you wouldn't even find their ashes afterwards . . . .

If I could do what I wanted I'd study and learn to write
but I never want to leave my animals. They don't say anything, that's because they haven't got words . . . A cow,
though, if I'm good to it, it gives me fruit, it gives me milk:
I respect it, and it respects me. But Christians don't give me
anything, they only take things from me. I know how to get
on with animals, with cows and sheep and goats; but not
with Christians, I don't know how to present myself. Animals have always been kinder to me than Christians. Some
of the animals come with me wherever I go. I had a kid and
a lamb once that used to follow me, everywhere. If I had
any bread I always gave some to them. They even used to
eat pasta, with sauce on it, that's how friendly they were . . .
They were my best friends, that little kid and the lamb. My
father was either away at the war or in prison or else they
wouldn't let him out of the village, and I hardly ever knew
him; however, I know my mother. My mother and my brothers love me all right. But nobody's ever loved me the way
that kid and that lamb did, not even God. I saw the kid and
the lamb come alive, when they were born, I fed them, they
became part of me, I've never forgotten them, they used to
come with me everywhere. I fed them by holding them up
to the cow's teats, and they used to follow me. They followed me about like puppies . . . Then I sold the kid to
buy some food . . . I bought a kilo of bread, a kilo of fish,
and ate that. And while I was eating I kept thinking of the

kid. Then I didn't eat anything for two days, just thinking about it, and crying. And for the next eight months at work I went on thinking about it, and I still think about it.

In America and Russia there's the same Government as there is here. What's Russia? Russia's a little island. What's China? Is it a sort of grape? I've never heard of it.

Vincenzo was arrested for stealing two bunches of herbs.

... They were on horses and they took me off to the barracks. There they threatened me with a knife, they beat me on the back and kicked me with boots, and they wrote everything down I said—not with a pen though, it was something that went *tin-tin-tin*, who knows what son-of-a-bitching thing it was. Then they made me put a cross on the paper, and they let me go.

Four months later they came back and put me in prison. Then they took me to the Colombaia. Then they tried me and sentenced me to four years and twenty days. They wanted the judge to make it six years. They said, did I want to make an appeal? I was crying so hard I couldn't see through my eyes. And that's why I'm here now, waiting for the appeal, only the landowner whose herbs I took, the one that had me arrested, he never shows up, so I have to go on waiting till he does.

Vincenzo's story in the whole forms a logic of which he alone would have been incapable. On such occasions Dolci, the artist, seeking creation in the expression of shared labor, is at his best. His art is never an abstract thing. More than art, it is his method, his belief, and his way. "Every time we make a discovery like this, a discovery of truth, there's a great joy. And then, in Vincenzo's efforts to express himself, he conquered something himself. And that's what we have to do, not only with the cowherd, but with people."

The story of Vincenzo the cowherd was to open the book which documented Dolci's trial. The trial was to be on 24 March.

On the eve of the trial two Italian lawyers, Achille Battaglia and Federico Comandini, were at Rome airport waiting to board a plane to fly down in Dolci's defense when they heard that the

Rome police had seized a serious review, *Nuovi Argomenti*, containing a sociological account under Dolci's name, and had
charged him with "pornography." The issue in question had
been on sale for months. The intention was obvious. "This is
preposterous!" Battaglia said, in a voice suited to his name. (It
means Battle.) His companion nodded, a little sadly. "Yes, it
does seem to be rather well timed, doesn't it?" At that stage there
was nothing anyone could do about it.

THE TRIAL

THE trial is already a landmark in Italian legal history. It was like something out of Kafka. The police alleged they had been hit, kicked, sworn at, and called murderers and attempted to prove that work tools had been used as weapons. Defense witnesses suggested by Sorgi had either been disallowed or themselves charged. Independent observers had several times to pinch themselves to make sure it was really happening and was not instead some phantasmagoria of the subconscious evolving amid the frocks and gavels of a misty totalitarian state.

Fifty lawyers offered their services in defense free, and intellectuals came from all over Italy to speak on Dolci's behalf. The defense had to be cut to six. It consisted of Battaglia, the top Italian penalist, Calamandrei, the most distinguished civil lawyer in the country, Comandini, and the Sicilian lawyers, Varvaro, Taormina, and Sorgi.

The trial took place in a room of Palermo's old supreme court, Lo Steri, a fourteenth-century building in Piazza Marina from the roof of which three hundred years before it had been the custom to throw down witches to their death. The building also marked the spot where in 1909 the American criminal investigator, Lieutenant Joseph Petrosino, sent in under an assumed name by the New York Police Department to study the liaison between the Sicilian Mafia and its emigrant child in America, The Black Hand (today *Cosa Nostra*), was assassinated by the Mafia Head, Don Vito Cascio Ferro, a few hours after

"I am no anarchist. I am a man who desires that his fellow humans enjoy a minimum of civilized life. . . . What could we do?"—DANILO DOLCI

landing at the port. (After killing Petrosino, Don Vito returned by carriage to an interrupted dinner appointment: he was dining at the time with a Member of Parliament.)

On the opening day of the trial there seemed to be only policemen and poor people. There were two policemen for every three members of the public. Scores were unable to get in. Black-shawled women were jammed round the lawyers' tables, some forced to crouch and peer round policemen's legs in order to maintain a stable position. Journalists had to stand. Visiting lawyers found there were no proper gowns. The presiding judge, Dr. Trainito, flanked by purple-tasselled and white-gloved carabinieri, reached for a bell to call for order, and found there was none. Dolci and Co. arrived in what appeared to be a Red Cross van and were led in between carabinieri, handcuffed and in chains. They were shuffled into place, alongside eighteen other accused, on two benches against a wall. Dolci was squashed on to one end.

"I wish to point out that the defendants are still handcuffed and in chains," Battaglia said. The public prosecutor, Dr. Lo Torto, said that this was thought necessary for the sake of public order. The presiding judge ordered the handcuffs to be removed.

Dolci, who seemed to have lost a little hair in prison, wore a lapel-less tweed jacket over a habitual white expanse of shirt-front, and no tie. He spoke quietly, "The Constitution in Italy is the only law of which nobody need be ashamed," he testified. "I am no anarchist. I am a man who desires that his fellow humans enjoy a minimum of civilized life.

"In the last two years sixteen murders and suicides have been committed in the Partinico area. You know what winter means to the poor. We didn't want to see people go out to steal or commit crimes. But we were being pressed to find some remedy. What could we do? ..." He described the arrest in detail and said that "four or five of them picked me up by my ankles and wrists and carried me face downwards. When they saw they might break something they turned me over on to my back and carried me that way."

"What do you weigh?" the judge asked.

"One hundred and ninety-nine pounds and I am 5 feet 11 inches tall."

"Did the police tear your trousers?" Battaglia said a little later.

"When they lifted me up my trousers split right down, but I'm sure the police didn't do it on purpose."

Standing in a tiny, cleared space below the judges' bench, Dolci was seldom interrupted. Occasionally he gestured, Nordic brows knitting, his right arm and spatulate fingers spreading out in broad evangelic movements. He admitted that he refused to stop working when ordered and urged the men to go on digging. "Your Honor, let me explain my state of mind," he said softly. "If someone ordered me to kill my father or you yourself ... I wouldn't do it because my conscience wouldn't let me: because it is criminal. I consider it is equally a crime against the land and against mankind to stop work. ...

"Let's put our cards down. If they stopped us from working we were going to stay there for the full eight hours, sitting down, with our arms folded. We really had in mind turning the track into a sort of effective employment agency."

"Wouldn't a symbolic half hour have done as well?" the judge said.

"I didn't say the plan was symbolic. We wanted to do a real job of work ... I must make it plain that no one took so much as a penknife along to cut his bread."

"No one is accusing you of being in improper possession of arms."

The judge was mistaken. "The mass, goaded on by Dolci and the leaders, began to shout in tumult, brandishing their instruments, among which were pruning knives," a police witness stated.

The police tried to insert a scurrilous article by Senator Savarino, published in his own paper, the *Giornale d'Italia*, as part of the case for the prosecution; and while Dolci was testifying two officers, waiting to be called as witnesses, slipped in at the back, and eavesdropped. Sorgi bawled them out for violating court procedure. The officers withdrew sheepishly. Constables said in evidence that when they were carrying Dolci he hit or kicked out. Chief Inspector di Giorgi said that Dolci did not hit or kick out. Inspector La Corte said that Dolci "even gave notice of the demonstrations in *L'Ora*" and a few minutes later claimed that the demonstrators had attempted to take the police "by surprise." One constable accusing Abbate of violence, offered to identify him: "I know him because I was the one who escorted him." Without the court's noticing, Speciale quickly changed places with Abbate. The constable promptly identified Speciale. The public roared. The ploy was repeated with another constable who alleged violence. This constable also identified the wrong man. The prosecutor protested at the "indelicacies": at least the defense might ask the judge's permission before switching defendants, he said. "In order to test the reliability of police witnesses," Battaglia replied, "we will repeat the 'indelicacies,' if necessary." By the third day the police case was foundering in a maze of contradictions.

Each night when the accused were handcuffed and taken back to prison a small crowd waited outside to applaud them. Newspapers put out special editions. Foreign journalists multiplied. A group of Italian writers held a press conference in Rome and declared that if Dolci were condemned they would carry on at Partinico in his place. English and Sicilian university students distributing pro-Dolci leaflets were herded into a bar by the Palermo police and the leaflets confiscated.

The defense brought out that there was a film of the entire proceedings which would show there had been no resistance. The photographer in question was unable to help, however. As he was filming the final arrest, he said, "The police grabbed hold of me, tore the camera from my hands and broke it in three pieces. I was thrown to the ground ... At the police station, after the film had been extracted, they returned the camera to me— broken, naturally."

The film was not available in court.

The trial lasted a week. Towards the end a change took place and as, one by one, a gallery of leading Italian intellectuals came forward to testify as character witnesses on Dolci's behalf, the cranky ill-equipped room was transformed into a national tribunal. On one side were the poor and the world of culture and on the other the reactionary forces of law and order, repression and Mafia. Such a collision of forces had never occurred in public.

"Men like Danilo—you need lots of them in Sicily," the novelist Vittorini said. "An old friend of mine, a monk of the Order of the Servants of Mary, introduced him to me. At first I was uneasy about him. I always mistrust the kind of activity where religion and social reform are mixed together. But once I got to know Danilo my reservations disappeared ... As for his Indian-type methods which many people find so upsetting, I find them peculiarly suited to Sicily ... Sicily is very like India. I am Sicilian, Your Honor, I was brought up here. In Sicily you find the same class segregation that exists today in much of India ... In India there are dozens of men like Danilo who are preparing the way for state reforms, and the Government doesn't obstruct them in the least; indeed it helps them."

Vittorini was followed by the philosopher Bobbio and the critic Carocci, by Levi, Lombardo-Radice, Tullio Vinay, Maria Sacchetti-Fermi, and others. They called Dolci naturally by his Christian name. Once the judge slipped up and said "Danilo." Maria Sacchetti-Fermi, a wisp of a woman in a blouse and dark costume, broke down after testifying and embraced Dolci with tears streaming down her face.

"Danilo Dolci's work is the state's work," Levi said. "His prime quality ... is his confidence. It is this confidence which he spreads around him, and which floods his work, which injects hope into the veins of the poor among whom he lives ...

"Danilo Dolci has been accused of abusing the police with words like, 'Whoever stops us from working is an assassin ...' Dolci has used this phrase before. From memory, it is: 'We are living in a world of men condemned to death by us ourselves ...' Yes—as long as men are excluded from the right to ordinary human existence, we are all of us responsible, we are all of us murderers. *All* of us. I am a murderer, and you, too, Your Honor, you are a murderer, and even Danilo Dolci is a murderer. This is the meaning of the phrase that is the *leitmotif* of his book *Outlaws*—it is one of the noblest phrases a man could utter."

Ignazio Silone, too ill to attend, sent a message, saying: "The world of culture is on Danilo's side." The world of authority, however, was not. Dr. Lo Torto, the prosecutor, asked the court to find the prisoners guilty on all counts. "This is a perfectly ordinary case," he said. "I am not here to deny the right to strike, which indeed is sanctioned by the Constitution. But I must point out that a strike means a withdrawal of labor . . . Are we quite certain that Dolci lives up to his pacifist principles? Or doesn't it appear as if Dolci himself by his behavior is the one who stirred up all this tension? Finally, you will note that everyone is agreed that he resisted arrest . . . What more do you need to prove Dolci guilty?"

The defense spoke for nearly two days.

On the final day Calamandrei stood up. Piero Calamandrei was a former Rector of the University of Florence—a spare, tall figure who, striding along in overcoat and scarf, might have been mistaken for a British admiral on furlough. "This isn't an *ordinary* trial at all," he said. "It is an exceptional trial, superlatively extraordinary, absurd. This isn't even a trial: it is an *apology*. A trial in which one seeks to condemn honest men . . . men arrested and sent to the dock under the charge of voluntary observance of the law; with the additional guilt of premeditation! . . .

"Looking back, what will appear to the historian its most significant aspects? His eye will be caught above all by the judgment of the magistrate who, refusing the prisoners bail, affirmed, verbatim, the *marked disposition for delinquency of the above-named defendant*: the *above-named defendant*, for those who may not know, is Danilo Dolci . . . Ah well, the phrase has been written: and in fifty years' time the historian will be able to read it and say to himself: 'Aha! I'm in luck. Here's an interesting case, the trial of a great delinquent, a typical case of *marked disposition for delinquency*.' "

Gazing from behind thick horn-rims with the air of one admonishing small boys, Calamandrei methodically took the police case apart—revealing (with respect) that it was necessary to do so, otherwise the Constitution was a bastard. Several times as he paused, swaying on the points of his shoes, a tense audience crouched at his back seemed about to precipitate him bodily into the arms of the judges. "Do you remember the immortal words of Socrates in the prison of Athens? He speaks of the laws as of living people ... In the more perfect European democracies, the people respect the laws because they participate in them and are proud of them: there is no double interpretation, one for the rich and one for the poor! ... This is the curse of Partinico; but also this has always been the curse of Italy ... for the weak the laws don't count. To get his dues a poor man has to kotow to some important person—or shout his lungs out. But perhaps not even shouting counts, for if he shouts too loud along comes Chief Inspector di Giorgi and takes him off to prison.

"And so along comes Danilo: 'Enough of this curse, enough of this mistrust—and away with violence,' Danilo says. 'The law is a kind of religion. But before the law can work its wonders, you must first of all believe in it.'

"Is he a simpleton? Is he a dreamer?

"Danilo has been compared to Renzo in the famous tavern scene in *The Bethrothed*. You remember? *'Bread, plenty, justice.'* Renzo heard it said by Ferrer, who was a police chief. And Renzo believed it: he, too, began to repeat, 'Bread, plenty, justice.' And he ends up in the hands of the police.

"And so does Danilo. Is he, too, merely a simpleton then? Merely a dreamer? No: Danilo is something more ...

"No, my dear public prosecutor, this is not a 'perfectly ordinary case.' This is not the trial of Danilo Dolci. On that bench are exposed other guilts, other injustices, other crimes. We all know what they are, and so do you.

"Danilo is not on trial here; nor is Partinico; nor is Sicily. It is our country which is on trial ...

"A few days ago I saw in a foreign newspaper this head-

*"This land is like one of the many beautiful little girls you
see in the alleys of its townships. The beauty is often there
beneath the scabs, the raving hair, the wild and tattered rags."*
—DANILO DOLCI

line: '*In Italy he who has faith in the Constitution is denied
bail.*' It isn't true, it isn't true! Your Honors, tell the foreigners
that it isn't true! ... Help us with your judgment, I beseech you,
help the dead who have been sacrificed and help the living to

uphold this Constitution which sets out to give every single Italian citizen equal justice and equal dignity!"

What followed when Calamandrei sat down is described as pandemonium. Calamandrei was not normally an emotional person. He was a civil lawyer, university don, editor; a severe intellectual. When he had finished speaking he buried his face in his hands. He broke down completely. So did almost the entire courtroom. Policemen flushed, the judge had to turn away, men wept openly. When after some minutes the judge had regained control, first of himself and then of the court, the sound of sobbing could still be heard.

The judges' panel went out just before noon. The public waited, hovering in the courtyard outside. Vincenzina remained sitting, hands crossed in her lap. After nearly six hours, when the jury returned, the room was again full. Dr. Trainito galloped through a preamble sixteen pages long. And then, suddenly, it was over. Dolci and the rest were acquitted on the serious charges, involving illegal assembly, disobeying, resisting, and abusing the police; they were found guilty of trespass and inciting to commit an offense and sentenced to fifty days each. They had already served exactly fifty days. They could go home.

On both sides of the Atlantic the verdict was hailed as a victory for Dolci and for nonviolence. But not in Sicily. The judgment was immediately appealed, not only by the defense, but also by the prosecution. In the view of the local authorities, fifty days was too lenient a sentence.

Note: Piero Calamandrei died in 1957.

❦

❦ XVII ❦

❦

DOLCI
MOVES ON

DOLCI denies lifting his technique of nonviolent action from
Gandhi. In a similar way Gandhi denied taking the idea of civil
resistance from Thoreau's famous 1849 essay, *Civil Disobedience.*

Henry Thoreau was a New England rebel and poet. He
fought against Negro slavery. Twenty-four hours in jail for refusing to pay taxes, and thus lend himself to a wrong he condemned, evoked his acute provocative treatise. To be right, Thoreau believed, was more honorable than to be law-abiding.

"As they could not reach me," Thoreau wrote, "they had
resolved to punish my body . . . I saw that the state was half-witted,
that it was timid as a lone woman with her silver spoons, and that
it did not know its friends from its foes, and I lost all my remaining respect for it and pitied it."

Gandhi discovered Thoreau's essay in 1908 when he was
(of course) in prison. He cherished the above extract. He read
the essay several times. He called it "masterly." He began to use
the phrase "*civil disobedience*" "to explain our struggle to the
English readers."

His own code of religious action was *Satyagraha*, which is
very close to Christian communism. Gandhi's biographer, Louis
Fischer, writes: "*Satyagraha* means truth-force or love-force...
Satyagraha is peaceful...The opponent must be 'weaned from
error by patience and sympathy'; weaned, not crushed; converted, not annihilated. *Satyagraha* is the exact opposite of the policy

of an-eye-for-an-eye-for-an-eye-for-an-eye which ends in making everybody blind." Gandhi called it "the vindication of truth not by infliction of suffering on the opponent but on one's self." Gandhi's chief task was to purify India; expulsion of the English would then follow naturally. When in 1921 at Bardoli he called off his first Indian campaign of mass noncooperation—because of mob violence elsewhere—he said: "It is better to be charged with cowardice and weakness than to be guilty of denial of our oath and to sin against God. It is a million times better to *appear* untrue before the world than to *be* untrue to ourselves."

Dolci had already adopted this code when he read Gandhi. In 1953 in a pamphlet issued from Borgo di Dio he declared: "In this world which is an intelligent, organized, and often hypocritical school of murder I will never willfully kill a brother. I shall not live according to my instinct but my spiritual conscience. It is my duty to serve, my place to be with the least, the little ones. I will collaborate with life. . .never with death." He discovered Gandhi and read his *Autobiography* the following year, finding in him "confirmation and enlightenment." More than anything he cherished Gandhi's words, "I do believe that, where there is a choice between cowardice and violence, I would advise violence. . . But I believe that nonviolence is infinitely superior to violence, forgiveness is more manly than punishment."

Dolci was influenced by Gandhi much as the latter was influenced by Thoreau. (Dolci has never read Thoreau's essay.) But by the time each had made his discovery—Gandhi of Thoreau, Dolci of Gandhi—each had vindicated, in word and deed, his own private truth. Each was already a champion, in his separate way, of the private conscience against majority expedience. Thoreau and Gandhi got their original idea of passive resistance from the Hindu gospel, the *Bhagavad Gita*. So did Dolci. Thoreau borrowed from ancient India and repaid the debt with interest. Gandhi took from Thoreau and both refined and perfected the strategy of the mass civil disobedience campaign. Gandhi died, assassinated, in 1948. Since then men have developed forms of passive resistance in many countries—Martin Luther King in the American south, Luthuli and Trevor Huddleston in South Africa, Bertrand Russell and Michael Scott in Britain, Aldo Capitini in Italy.

Dolci did not bring the Gandhian torch out of the East. He did not pioneer the reverse strike. But in 1956 he conceived and conducted the first successful mass civil disobedience campaign on Gandhian lines in the West.* He did so from the most violent corner of peacetime Europe.

The fruits of his action purified a local situation. The tortures in Partinico, in the barracks shed behind the church, stopped; Mancuso and elements of his grafting administration were ousted; Inspector La Corte was transferred; in the next elections protest votes against the Christian Democrat régime soared; Senator Savarino was not re-elected. But Dolci's action went further. It succeeded in welding religious peasants and militant Communists in a nonpolitical protest against social injustice which belittled barriers of class and creed. Partinico's tiny minority voice cried wisdom to the appeal of oppressed masses everywhere. This was the signifiance.

In putting a spark to Christian communism Dolci lit a lamp on the road to solving a universal dilemma: that of finding a formula for the mental health of nations. He anticipated Pope John's revolutionary *Pacem in Terris* encylclical by seven years.

He was thirty-one.

On Easter Saturday, 1956, the day after the trial ended, Franco Grasso, the writer, was standing in a Palermo suburb holding a copy of *L'Ora*. On the front page was a picture of Dolci leaving prison. "A woman asked me for the newspaper," Grasso

* Students of nonviolence may feel that the Norwegian resistance by the clergy and teachers to the occupying Nazis in the last war destroys the claim. But the Norwegian action was anonymous and loose; the thousands who boycotted Nazi decrees responded to their private consciences, they were not led.

Francis Deák's long and successful Gandhi-type resistance in Hungary to the Austrian hegemony (1850-67) does invalidate the claim, if Hungary is considered part of Western Europe.

writes, "kissed Dolci's image, passionately, over and over again, and then asked me to take her to him to be 'recommended for a favor,' on behalf of her son. On the same page was a large photograph of Pius XII, giving his [Easter] blessing; it received no part of her effusions. . .."

Dolci came out of prison a bit dishevelled, but clean-shaven, as usual.

In the photograph he is muffled in coat and beret and carries a huge bundle of newspapers, a pair of boots, and a kitbag of clothes. He is surrounded by a shoal of well-wishers. He appears bewildered, like a mariner stepping ashore from a wreck.

From prison he went to the quay, saw off Calamandrei and others on the nine o'clock boat, then drove to Partinico where hundreds had waited up in the square and were already fêting the return of Termini, Speciale, and Abbate. Carlo Zanini, because of his previous record, was the only one not released immediately. Children presented each with a red carnation. It was after midnight when Dolci, stumbling through the feeble lighting and mud of Spine Sante, regained his family. His two-year-old daughter Libera had put a branch of peach blossom on the table. He sat down to a bowl of soup, and *companaggio*, and presently Vincenzina handed him a bundle of proofs. They were the proofs of all the poems he had kept, including the only poems he had written in Sicilian. While he was in prison a friend, Giuseppe Ricca, had gathered them together for a Milan publisher. (*Poesie*, the collected poems, appeared in April). Spine Sante neighbors came in and out with a bluster of greetings, and one or two of them said: "But why on earth did they arrest you, Danilo?"

Dolci had come to a peak of popularity. He did not see himself as a bringer of miracles. "I'm no magician," he said. He was a working man, even a plodder. His task was moral as well as practical, to tend seeds of hope already planted, to purify. He went on his detergent way: "To the press: . . . Throughout Italy we are systematically assassins. There is no guarantee of work for all; there is no real freedom of thought, of expression, of action; there is no provision for the invalids and the children of convicts; no education for all. There is talk of reforms, of revolution, of God; yet the maid still waits at table and then goes into the kitchen and eats her meal alone; civil servants still pay taxes towards the upkeep of the brothels; prisoners are treated as if society were waging a vendetta against them. (I shall always remember those convicts serving ten or twenty or thirty years—their pained eager eyes watching intently through the bars two cats copulating in the garden below, while the prison radio blared out a boxing match; and, high on the outside wall, one could read the hypocritical carved words: *Omnia vincit amor.*)

"Better in prison with these victims than out there 'free,' if privileged. If we're not careful we'll soon see political banishment revived, and then a little later they'll light the faggots again for those who seek the truth, the 'heretics,' while the prefects look on with candles in their hands. . ."

Yet he did not believe, with Gandhi, that "we must widen the prison gates and enter them as a bridegroom enters the bride's chambers." For Gandhi, going to prison was a necessary therapeutic to rousing a nation for liberty. Dolci had no such faith in the medicinal value of Italian prisons. He was prepared to go to prison again himself, but he was not prepared to call for the same sacrifice from a people whose daily life was dominated by the fear of prison. The impact of his campaign did not blind him to the fact that his aims were still mistrusted by the peasants. Another reformer might have capitalized on his success and plunged into a mass civil resistance movement. Politically the moment could not have been riper. Dolci did not believe in short cuts. And he was not for political games. His ideas were unchanged, but evolving. "Let us multiply and deepen our studies, from below," he continued, "realizing man's potential and the land's—so that the achievement of an intelligent plan for full employment may be based on sane economics. . . The idea of yeast isn't enough to make the bread rise; you need the yeast itself, and in the flour.

"The tomorrow we long for is coming, even if today it appears only too far off."

From this a cogent pattern of thought emerges. He feels a responsibility for all—almost on a cosmic scale. He is stirred to action. He remains optimistic. He is impatient to do good. Full employment and moral reform are still the platforms. The tools are love (or truth), nonviolence, sacrifice—and courage. The courage to go on denouncing social evil and apathy, go on implanting this idea of resistance to evil in the minds of a suffering people. Terms like "from below," "planning for full employment" and "sane economics" are used together, germinally and clearly, for the first time. His inspiration remains profoundly Christian, universal brotherhood is still the *modus operandi*, but Nomadelphia and Borgo di Dio are far behind.

Dolci put aside cosmic thoughts and came back to reality. In the Ucciardone he had secured from fellow prisoners descriptions of police tortures carried out in Palermo's Papirete Barracks, near the flea market. They are reminiscent of those used by the Nazis or the French in Algiers. Gavin Maxwell, in *The Ten Pains of Death*, was to add to this evidence. The brutalities described are on similar, but more elaborate lines to the *cassetta* treatment used in Partinico: cigarettes ground out on bare flesh, sadistic beatings, electric current applied to men's genitals. These statements he included in the book which grew out of the strike-in-reverse. It was commissioned by the distinguished publisher, Einaudi, and appeared that summer as *Article Four on Trial*. The tortures, which were never denied, later stopped.

It was late spring 1956. Dolci looked round him. In Partinico the scum had been whipped off the cesspool, but the waters were still troubled underneath. Dolci's diary records:

> 9 April: Another young man has been stabbed through the heart in Partinico tonight. He was only seventeen. An old woman, who saw it happen, died on the spot from fright.

23 April: Another woman was murdered in Via della Madonna: she was only nineteen.

5 May: Another man has been murdered, the fourth in a month.

29 May: The body of a youth has been found in an advanced state of decomposition in the watertank of a house.

7 June: Someone has been shot in the head, but it looks as if he has escaped serious injury.

Opposition had not lessened. Franco went into a tobacconist for some cigarettes. A clerk he knew was chatting to the proprietor. Recognizing Franco the man hurriedly crossed himself and went out.

"There's a lot to be done, Franco," Dolci said. It was typical of the man that, having put down his pen ostensibly to gather in the threads where he had left off, he should pick it up again almost immediately. Dolci asked his colleagues for their advice—as he always did. They advised him to consolidate the work in Partinico, expand the tiny social center financed from Turin, press for the dam on the Iato—after all, that was one of the reasons for coming to Partinico, wasn't it? If not, they said, the peasants would be left buoyed up but in limbo, and eventually feel resentment. Dolci listened, and then went his own way—as he always did.

His task, as he saw it, was still to expose. It was not enough to throw a little mud; you had to throw an awful lot, and go on throwing, until some of it stuck.

The question then was not "What next?" but "Where next?" In fact, Dolci did not even ask himself the question. He already knew the answer. Palermo.

ĩ

ĩ XVIII ĩ

ĩ

INQUIRY
IN PALERMO

PAUL DE MUSSET, brother of the poet Alfred, describes Palermo as a courtesan whose sultry charms so seduced the Carthaginian, Arab, and Saracen invaders that they left her beauty intact. "The happy city," he says. Likewise Garibaldi, the last conqueror, fell captive at Palermo's feet: beyond closing the convents and blowing up a few Bourbon arsenals he didn't knock the old lady about very much. Tourists also find the Sicilian capital enticing. There is a fragrance of musk and the Orient. Arab steeds pad the soft black streets. Behind the portrait gargoyles of the Cathedral and the mosaics of the Palatine Chapel, arabesque dirges of hawkers sweep the people's markets, and under wrought-iron balconies young girls, beautiful at thirteen, gaze rapidly before turning their backs on the eye of the intruder. Above the bay where Nelson moored is Mt. Pellegrino, bearing the shrine of St. Rosalia, the only Sicilian saint in the calendar. Goethe called the headland "The most beautiful promontory in the world." Below, the city floods the plain, spilling flakes of white farmhouses into a shell of lush green vegetation. The shell rises to an orifice of ocher mountains. Looking back on Palermo from the Norman cathedral of Monreale, the gateway to these mountains, the tourist sighs in the heat, and smells camomile and, gazing on the banded apron at his feet—ocher, green, white, and the rainbow blues of the blue-ribbed Tyrrhenian Sea—tends to conclude that Goethe was right, and that sights like the Bay of Naples are vastly overrated.

This is about all the tourist sees. But not far from the broad thoroughfare of Via della Libertà and the chic opulence of Via Ruggiero Settimo, just behind the imposing *palazzi* and the romanesque church fronts, there is another Palermo, a maze of tiny *rioni*, sectors, dank-smelling little *casbahs*, where thousands live in conditions rivalling Asiatic squalor. These are not border slums—they are banked up in the heart of the city, acres of them. If you walk the two or three hundred yards in a straight line from the great Cathedral to the Palace of Justice, you pass through the middle of one of the worst of them, the Capo. They are not like Neapolitan slums—there is something secretive about them, grim and undeclared; after nightfall when the cries of the wandering vendors and the bundles of secondhand American clothing have gone away they wear a curfew look, and the memory of Arab mosques and veils hangs close.

In 1956 more than a hundred thousand people, or a fifth of the city's population, were living in these slums. Some were nothing more than holes in the ground, grottoes. About ten thousand people were living in grottoes.

There was no regular work for these people. In Milan half the population was "active"; in Palermo, a quarter.

In 1860 Garibaldi smelled these zones. He ordered an immediate investigation. Nothing happened. Almost a century later the situation was unchanged—if anything it was worse, because the overcrowding was greater. Cardinal Ruffini's lavish Church aid and Christmas messages had not affected the reality, or the civic conscience. In 1954 the authorities did look at them. The City Council in an official report, said: "Families at most have one or two rooms without the most elementary benefits of hygiene, without lavatory, kitchen, water, and even sometimes artificial light, without air and without sunlight, where humidity, cold, dust, and the stink of drains and refuse is appalling. These conditions, plus the overcrowding and the consequent promiscuity, have led to a state of physical and moral degradation which can be described without exaggeration as utterly terrifying."

The report was unanimously approved by the Sicilian Regional Assembly. Nothing happened. The City Council had a

deficit of over eleven million dollars. The Department of Public
Works was studying plans to build autostradas.

Dolci saw his task clearly. To leave Trappeto and Partinico
with skeleton crews and expose Palermo to the world. The task
was greater than it seems. For he chose not the city alone, but the
province as well. To do this he first toured the interior in the
old Lancia, selecting some of the tragic spots—Alia, Vicari, Bisaquino, San Giuseppe Iato, Villalba. He sent in volunteers, student sociologists and teachers from the north, to sift and document and make the statistical interviews; he did the longer story
interviews himself. He worked the city with Gino Orlando.

Gino was an itinerant barber. He is the apotheosis of Dolci's
theory that a moral outcast, given work and treated as a human
being, is able to pull himself out of the gutter by his own boot-
straps. Gino, the illegitimate son of a *spiccia-faccende* (a kind of
street copyist) and a municipal clerk, began life as a pickpocket.
By the time he was seventeen he had known brothels, the contraband trade, and prison; at eighteen, reform school, but he was
caught kissing the mayor's daughter behind the bushes and expelled; at twenty he was exiled. Then someone took an interest
in him and gave him useful work. He began to follow politics
and became a trade unionist, leading peasants in the postwar
land reforms to occupy the fiefs in defiance of the Mafia. He did
not return to crime. When Dolci met Gino in 1955, he encountered a man who was still living precariously, but who had not
been crushed by a nine-year wait at the Labor Exchange for a
regular job—a middle-aged man with a limp and an unusual
sensibility, a man with a positive attitude to life.

Gino was Dolci's passport to Palermo. He knew every alley
and every courtyard, he knew the police and he knew the *cioco-
lattari*, the stool pigeons. He knew where to find a young workman reduced to a paralytic beggar after being flogged by rawhide
whips in prison, or an artisan's son who lived as a turkey-raffler
doing conjuring tricks at eleven A.M. on Thursdays with a ten-
thousand-lire note pinned to his lapel. He knew the forty-seven
legal activities by which the hungry fifth scraped an existence,

and all the illegal ones. The pair of them worked together fifteen hours a day. With his quick, limping gait Gino covered half the city, from organ-grinders' corner in the Kalsa to the flooded basements of Cortile lo Cicero, Dolci bustling alongside in sandals, open shirt, and beret, asking endless questions.

"Work?" Gino said. "What urge can there be for these people to look for proper work when they know that industry doesn't exist?"

Gino found the subjects and introduced them to Dolci. Dolci, with his flair for gaining a person's confidence and eliciting information, then made the interviews. He wrote everything down in longhand, interviewing each subject two or three times. "This is *their* inquiry," he told Gino. From time to time, there were conferences in Partinico when the team came together from the outlying villages. There was no loafing, except on occasional Sundays when they would pile a score of Spine Sante children into the Lancia and take them to the beach; the volunteers went too, as much for their own recuperation as the children's. They worked openly and carefully, and for the most part unmolested. Once when he returned to Palermo from documenting a fief at Tudìa, Turrumé, and Arcia, near Villalba—where fifty families lived all the year round in straw shacks—Dolci received word from Sorgi, the lawyer, warning him not to return there. A group of *mafiosi* had called at Sorgi's office to threaten Dolci by proxy. Dolci did go back. Nothing happened. They worked mostly under a psychological strain, the thought of police obstruction nibbling constantly at their minds. The Partinico police watched volunteers carefully, stalking them especially over residence permits. When Lawrence and Maddalena Rayner—he was English, she Italian—came from Rome to help with the inquiry, and filled in their original residence as England, a plainclothesman asked Dolci to explain.

"Signor Dolci," he said, "I need to know which pass they crossed to enter France from England." Dolci explained that between England and France there was a channel. "Look, Dolci," the officer said, "I know very well that you're not one of us. But you

must also respect my position—I have to earn my keep. Now will
you please tell me *which pass they crossed?*"

The Palermo inquiry lasted the summer. Dolci's workers went
round the villages and talked to over five hundred day laborers in
the *piazze*, in the cafés, in the trade union offices. In general
these men found work on two days out of seven. The rest of the
time they stood about with their hands in their pockets or tried to
keep afloat by gathering wild vegetables or snails or breaking up
iron crosses taken from the cemeteries in order to sell them. Dolci
calculated that 120,000 to 140,000 people in the province lived
like this, by work which was not work. For Palermo city the
figures were only slightly better.

Dolci's permanent core was Giovanni, Franco, Alberto
L'Abbate, a young Florentine sociologist, and Goffredo the student
teacher. Geoffredo, though banished for his part in the reverse
strike, had returned to Partinico just the same and remained,
enclosed in Spine Sante, teaching the illiterate. When Dolci proposed—or, as Goffredo says, "imposed"—the Palermo inquiry, he
volunteered to go in first and break the ground, setting up a base
from which Dolci might operate later. Dolci chose a quarter bi-
sected by the railroad, a big courtyard a stone's throw from the
seat of the Sicilian Regional Parliament. Of it he wrote: "130
families live in 118 rooms, plus five cubbyholes. Only one family has a lavatory. The other families cook, eat, sleep, and defecate
in their one room." "Decent" folk, he added, relieved themselves
on the railway line. *Average* number of persons per room: 4.2.
"There are five sordid two-storied and three-storied houses in
the last stages of dilapidation and a few squalid huts and shacks.
The walls sweat with damp and the rooms are live with scorpions,
fleas, and cockroaches . . ."

This was Cortile Cascino.

Perhaps it wasn't surprising that the Palermitans generally
had achieved a certain indifference to the plight of their hungry
fifth. A university professor and a Communist member of the
City Council said that until Dolci's inquiry was published later

he didn't know that Cortile Cascino existed. He lived just round the corner.

Goffredo went in alone. He was eighteen at the time. "It was a case of going there and doing whatever it was possible to do for these people," he says. "I rented a shack for $9.80 a month. Danilo had no money. I lived on $16.80 a month which Lucio Lombardo-Radice gave me and with whatever the people of the Cortile could spare. I ate with them, every evening a different family. Simple pasta, every night pasta. We ate artichokes in artichoke time and tomatoes the whole summer long. Meat, once in four months.

"Cortile today is pretty bad—then it was a cesspool. There was a kind of lake in the middle where the kids used to play, naked; I can't describe what was in that lake . . . My shed was on the edge of it, alongside the railway line. There wasn't a child above eight who didn't go out to work in a shop or a mechanic's yard or a bakery. Most of them had never seen a school. I taught them to read and write, and also their fathers, from seven in the morning until nearly midnight. It was chaotic. Imprisoned in that shed, people coming and going, the continual racket. I became jittery; then stomach trouble—I used to slip into Partinico on weekends for treatment.

"Each week there was a frightful row, people got hurt every time. The people were in such despair these strifes broke out over nothing—two kids playing and arguing, the mother of one intervenes, slaps one, screams at the other; the other mother steps in, then her husband, then the husband of the first woman, the neighbors making up the chorus . . . and away it went.

"I was usually called in as peacemaker.

"Living like that though, I got to thinking like them. I learned their *argot* and became one of them. I looked like them, and smelled it. There was one terrible row, half the courtyard swarmed in, and I——I suddenly forgot myself and bored in too. I went berserk. I remember picking up a woman by the hair and swinging her . . .

"The police were too frightened to come near the place.

The only time I saw the police that year, they came in a bundle of twelve, at midnight, to arrest one man. It was the only way.

"They planted an informer, a semi-drunkard called Nenne. We all knew him. I used to tell him my movements, to save him trouble, 'Hey, Nenne,' I'd say, 'I'm going to Partinico tomorrow,' or, 'You know Danilo's coming on Monday?' It was all part of the system.

"My shack was also the first-aid center. There was a woman giving penicillin injections, the kind where you mix the liquid with the powder, and the poor child she was injecting was yowling its ears off. The woman was mixing together *nothing*. She was injecting pure powder. I got so angry I grabbed the needle and tried myself. I found I did it much better. From then on I became the nurse. I did two hours' nursing every morning, and then the schooling. I had something like 120 children coming for lessons every day.

"I had no toilet, no water. We washed at the fountain and relieved ourselves on the railroad track. Every time we did that we risked being fined five dollars. I had to be thoroughly deloused when I finally left. My father came down once from the north. He scarcely recognized me. He almost ran out of the place. My father's a demolition expert."

Altogether Goffredo spent two years in Cortile Cascino. He then abandoned teaching and became a qualified social worker; he has just published a study on emigration. He was the first of scores on whom Dolci was to have a positive formative influence.

When Dolci first came to the courtyard the people took him for a priest, because of the beret. They crowded round as if he were a new species. Goffredo told him that to keep alive the boys resorted to stealing, the girls to prostitution. Heterosexual and homosexual prostitution were flourishing. Life expectancy was around thirty-five. Goffredo showed him a room where eight people slept in one bed. "We sleep four at the top and four at the bottom," the wife said. "My uncle, my husband, my sister, myself, and four children. We keep the door open to breathe better."

That summer a baby boy died, the little blood he had being sucked out of him by rats while the mother was at the fountain doing the washing. Dolci knew that when the inquiry was
over he would return to fast among these people.

He worked through autumn on the reports and consigned
the book to Einaudi. On 17 December he lay down in Goffredo's
shack and initiated a group hunger strike as "a warning to all."
Fifteen people fasted for eight days—five in Palermo, Dolci and
Goffredo in Cortile Cascino, Franco, Alberto, and Francesco
Lanzaroni in Capo; Mauro Gobbini and Giovanni Mottura at
Bisaquino; Grazia Fresca and Carlo Ravasini at Alia; others at
Vicari and S. Giuseppe Iato; and a Catholic group from southern France at Partinico. It was a collective protest at the destitution of an entire province, from the feudal terror of Bisaquino
and the landslides of Alia to the pollution of the capital, where
Mafia continued to strangle living conditions and there was a
murder on an average every five days to prove it. By itself the
protest achieved nothing, affected nobody, except Goffredo who
got cramp and acidosis on the final day and had to be given sugar
injections. The authorities saw it as a gigantic bluff. Dolci saw
it as a halfway house, a link in a chain of pressurizing events, with
the eventual goal of "work—work for all." "All" by now was a
key word. He was like a machine—he gave himself no rest and
he determined that the authorities should have none either. The
gadfly was determined not to be swatted.

When the fast was over and he went home to Partinico for
Christmas, he was reasonably satisfied. He already had the ma-
terial for the next round in his hands—the advance copies of the
book which a representative of Einaudi had brought to Cortile
Cascino during the fast. In Italy it appeared as *Inchiesta a Palermo*
(Inquiry in Palermo); in the United States as *Report from Palermo*.

Somebody compared him to an eagle—watching, swooping,
sometimes missing the mark, but always there, hovering. Dolci
laughed. "This isn't an eagle's work," he said. "This is the labor
of an ox."

There were visitors to Partinico that Christmas. They were

the quiet vegetarian kind. They were a group of French and Italian-born pacifists, all in homespun, from Lanza del Vasto's work-and-prayer colony in the south of France. They had volunteered to join the fast and stayed over for Christmas. Lanza himself is vividly remembered. In height he topped Dolci, a venerable prophet's figure with a lean brown face and a twiney snow-white beard. He wore sandals, carried a staff, and kept warm beneath a thick woollen jerkin of unbleached homespun. Even to-day, at 63, fanaticism has not spoiled him; he remains a gentle, if slightly crazy patriarch, one of the more lovable of Catholic anarchists. On Christmas Eve he handed Dolci a contribution for his work. "Why don't you give it to the people?" Dolci said. He called Sariddu. Sariddu found himself holding ten crisp ten-thousand-lire notes. "For the people," Lanza said. By morning Sariddu, his wife, and a few neighbors had prepared food parcels for the forty Spine Sante families most in need, with enough money left over to throw a *festa* for the whole quarter.

A hundred thousand lire ($168) would have kept a qualified teacher or nurse in Partinico for six months. Dolci badly needed qualified workers. A colleague chided him for his recklessness. "Get away with you," Dolci said. "It's Christmas."

All the same he knew it was a last fling. The days of charitable gestures were almost over.

W

W XIX W

W

CONGRESS
ON A SHOESTRING

Report from Palermo was Dolci's Christmas message for
1956. *Figaro Littéraire* hailed it. *The Times Literary Supplement*
called it "not only a literary but also a sociological masterpiece."
Yet when it appeared in Italy many broad-minded Catholics
were offended. The Partinico archpriest warned his flock to "beware of the wolf in sheep's clothing" and higher ecclesiastical
authorities trusted that the police would not be too long in taking action. Even the Left wondered. A Communist deputy said
to Dolci, "My word, you've been clever, digging up all that misery." Dolci was upset. "I've never denied that the beautiful exists," he said. "I merely say that this *also* exists. If you go to a doctor with a bad stomach ulcer it doesn't help your condition to
be told what lovely big brown eyes you have."

The Protestant pastor, Tullio Vinay, said later: "Why is it
that the Food and Agricultural Organization, which has its
world headquarters in Rome, cannot work in Italy? Because the
Italian Government continues to shut its eyes to reality, it won't
admit it has an underdeveloped zone on its own doorstep. It's
this *stupid* sense of patriotism of ours. Italians do not like to
hear a diagnosis of their situation."

Vinay's words were illustrated about this time by a film, a
television documentary made by Stephen Peet in western Sicily
and based on just those conditions which Dolci had revealed.
When the film was transmitted by the BBC, the Italian television
authorities had a fit. Peet, using a 16-mm. camera, made the film

as a tourist—and smuggled it out in his assistant's underwear.
The explosion occurred at a European Broadcasting Meeting at
Cannes, when the Comptroller of Italian Television, in the words
of an eye-witness, "went nearly apoplectic with rage that the
BBC had had the gumption to put this thing out." About the
same time, in London, Peet was asked to call at an address in
Victoria. It turned out to be a branch of the Italian State Tourist
Department. It was late one afternoon. The manager and his
secretary, both Italians, were sitting at their desks. Peet introduced
himself. The manager looked up and said, "Did *you* make the film
about Sicily?" Peet admitted it. "What would you think if an
Italian came over here and made that kind of film about England?"
Peet said nothing. The manager continued in a loud voice: "Would
that be right? Would it? Eh?" Peet let him get it off his chest.
When he had finished the manager got up, put on his coat, and
bade the secretary goodnight. At the door he grabbed Peet by the
hand and shook it hard. "Well done!" he said. "May God go with
you. There should be a film like that made about Italy every week."
With that he departed.

The revelation of the lives of the Palermitan poor was a
surprise packet all round. Why was this? In 1957 Italy was still,
both in the educational and social research fields, in the dol-
drums; there was yet no School of Sociology. Had Dolci merely
catalogued the poor, as professional sociologists did, it would
have raised storm enough. But Dolci, the amateur, went further. Norberto Bobbio says of *Outlaws:* "Rather than an inquiry it is a body of witness . . . These people are witnesses who
cry scandal." *Report from Palermo* calls up a whole army of
witness—peasants and prostitutes, cardsharps, women fish-salters
leech-doctors, beggars, *mafiosi*, witches, snailgarnerers, cowherds,
money-changers, and platoons of others. They fall in with their
sackcloth morals and bar-alley slang, crying "work—not charity,"
and catalogue themselves by request. Dolci spared no details. The
book did for the Sicilians what Mayhew, in the 1850s, did for the
London poor. Between the lines, *Report from Palermo* was the
heaviest indictment of Mafia–Government collusion and of

"*I've never denied that the beautiful exists. I merely say that this* also *exists. If you go to the doctor with a bad stomach ulcer it doesn't help your condition to be told what lovely big brown eyes you have.*"—DANILO DOLCI

Church apathy then published. It was a human documentary with the lid off.

It was also a much more homogeneous study than *Outlaws*. World authorities like the psychologist Erich Fromm and the economist Gunnar Myrdal welcomed it as a valuable contribution to social science. Aldous Huxley, in a preface to the English and American editions, said: "A new Gandhi, a modern St. Francis needs to be equipped with much more than compassion and seraphic love. He needs a degree in one of the sciences and a nodding acquaintance with a dozen disciplines beyond the pale of his own special field. It is only by making the best of both worlds—the world of the head no less than the world of the heart, that the twentieth-century saint can hope to be effective. Danilo Dolci is one of these modern Franciscans-with-a degree." Huxley was wrong about the degree, but his was an accurate interpretation of what an informed public outside Italy thought and felt. Translations were prepared in six languages. *Report from Palermo* received a Viareggio Prize, Italy's most coveted literary award. Then the Rome chief of police let fall the charge he had been holding over Dolci's head since the eve of the reverse strike trial in 1956. On 27 June 1957, Dolci appeared in Rome charged with publishing obscene matter.

In the first part of the book, *The Witnesses,* are thirty-one personal stories. On almost every page Dolci's reportage touched guilty or squeamish consciences:

> Once upon a time the *parrini* (priests) came along on Shanks' mare to beg for charity; nowadays they do their alms-collecting on Lambrettas or in up-to-date Fiats.

> Some people leave their cars in the street and pay men to sleep in them. It comes cheaper than a garage.

> Do we go to mass? 'Course we do—we're all Catholics, every one of us. Religion's going to mass on Sundays and the big Feast Days. Before we begin gutting the fish we always cross ourselves ... Most people vote CD because if they vote CD they're voting for Our Lord.

Since I've been to prison I've let my beard grow. When I come out I shan't be able to hawk scrap iron—I can't pay back the money I borrowed, so I've no cash for a permit. I shall have to go on practicing magic ...

"If He's really up there, why doesn't He send us work?" I say to myself.

What's the Mafia got to do with coffins? Coffin-making's one of the very few industries there are in Palermo; it may not be large, but it's very profitable and the competition's fierce. This year four or five coffin-makers were murdered. The industry's controlled by the Mafia of the wholesale markets ... The cigarettes (contraband) are often hidden in coffins ....

If we haven't enough leeches we send for the barber who opens a vein in the sick person's wrist and lets out a stream of blood. We hardly ever call in the doctor; it costs too much.

The police had singled out the story of Gino Orlando. They objected to a pungent factual six-line description of Gino's visit to a licensed brothel, with three other youngsters, at the age of twelve. Dolci was charged, not with Einaudi, the publisher of the book, but with Carocci, the publisher of *Nuovi Argomenti*, the serious review in which Gino's account first appeared.

Once again eminent lawyers came to Dolci's defense. A book wasn't dirty in itself, it had no smell, Dolci said. "The aim was not to work scandal. The aim was to give a voice to those who offered—and were denied—their useful labor; and to pose a problem." Dolci claimed that the work was a scientific study which only scientifically qualified men could judge; and that the harsh realism was dictated by the needs of the argument and the whole tenor of the investigation.

A large public was turned away. The entire case was held *in camera*. The judges refused to hear evidence from men of letters and from sociologists and other experts. Dolci's plea was rejected. The passage was alleged to be injurious to public decency and, with Carocci, he was sentenced to two months' imprisonment.

They did not go to jail. An appeal, and bail, were allowed and a year later the judgment was reversed and they were exonerated. It did not matter. The original sentence stuck in the Italian mind.

From "habitual delinquent" in 1956 Dolci thus graduated to "pornographer" in 1957. He was thoroughly branded.

"The obscenity laws in Italy are pretty strict in theory," *The Observer* in England commented, "but in practice passages like these get by so long as they are written by nice safe novelists without social consciences."

Dolci is a man of ideas. He takes them seriously. Words and thoughts and ideas are the stuffing of his work. He has no time for small talk; in fact, he has none. Sometimes ideas obsess him. It can be frightening or it can be embarrassing. Chatting with him, I have thrown an idea up, banteringly, and been horrified to find it immediately seized on, like gold dust, and examined under the weighing glass of those inscrutable rimless spectacles; and then when I explained it was in jest he was momentarily offended. So it was, during a recess in the Rome trial, when a friend suggested he should organize a meeting of experts to discuss the implications of his various inquiries: he seized on the idea and made it his own, and began immediately to put it into operation. Dolci is a big man, and he likes big ideas. He did not organize a *riunione*, a meeting. "We'll have a *convegno*," a congress, he said. And thus a few months later in Palermo there came about the Congress for Full Employment.

"Really, we think that Italy and in particular Sicily have already had a stomachful of study conferences," the *Cittadino Siciliano* said; "but Danilo apparently hasn't noticed this." It was quite a friendly comment for the neofascist press. The congress was to be a form of inquiry, of pressure and resolution, by experts. There was the usual pre-inquiry dustup in Partinico among the group, some of whom thought Dolci was becoming "study mad." But Dolci by now had hold of his idea, like a mastiff. The critics had to give way, or depart. Before long some of them departed, Giovanni and Goffredo among them. Others, with visions of the workhouse looming, mentioned that a congress would cost money. What would they live on afterwards? "Never mind," Dolci said. "Something will turn up." In the moments of fiscal stress which have occurred throughout his life, rather more commonly than the seasons, he has usually said this. He has usually been right.

He announced the congress in July 1957, months in advance. "The problem of full employment will never be solved if it is never posed," he said. "In Italy just over a billion dollars are spent each year on the police and the army, all carefully thought out and planned in advance. Yet in Italy there does not exist one single study center for full employment." He warned that if an awareness of the problem had not registered on the public conscience by the end of the congress, three days later he and Franco would begin a fast, and go on fasting until public opinion was thoroughly roused. What was the man up to with his Utopia of "*full* employment"? people wondered. In fact, the term was practically unknown in Italy. Italians had never got past a dream of *maximum* employment.

The congress was preceded by four months' work. It was organized from Spine Sante, in the bedroom-cum-night-school-cum-writing-room halfway up the stairs where Dolci worked and slept, and in the communal bunkroom upstairs where almost everyone else slept, and it took place in one of Palermo's more grandiose *palazzi*. It was floated on the art of Carlo Levi, the Viareggio Prize, the Lancia, a few pawned articles, the patronage of public figures and statesmen like the former Prime Minister, Parri, and the goodwill of a considerable body of international experts from Scandinavia to Brazil who sent messages of support. Levi (painter as well as writer) did the posters, and the Lancia—bought for $420, sold for $84—paid for their production. The Viareggio Prize, worth $1,680, paid for the congress. It took place on the first three days of November and was attended by leading Italian sociologists, economists, and town planners.

By the end of 1954, the Socialist Giolitti told the gathering, the national economy had lifted itself out of the depths of the war, beaten inflation, and taken on new life. Meantime a Parliamentary Commission had revealed that a million and a half southerners were completely out of work and a further four million able to find jobs for only six months of the year, a fourth of the southern population was living in real poverty, and a sixth was illiterate. Then, he said, Government experts had presented the Vanoni Plan which, it was stated, would resolve *everything*. But the plan had never been used, "except by the ruling classes for their Sunday speeches." If anything the situation in 1957 was worse than in 1954 when the Vanoni Plan was presented. A message from the Swedish economist Gunnar Myrdal said: "Full employment is essentially a matter of organization." But the congress found that in Italy the problem had first to do with a Government's faculty of hearing. After digesting and deliberating fifteen papers presented by specialists, and a basinful of facts collected by Dolci's team in ten communes, it found that the people themselves were not aware of their problems, did not know how they could be solved—nor did the planners. "The politicians don't know," roared the chairman, Bruno Zevi, a lively Rome architect, "because they don't *want* to know!" It found that official projects failed in practice because there was no interaction between the planners at the top and the people at the bottom. They were completely out of gear.

The congress restated fundamentals. It called for experts to band together and study a flexible coordinated policy which would make full use of the resources of the people. It urged research groups in the towns and in the villages. It brought the terms *full employment* and the newfangled *pianificazione*— "planning for the planners," someone called it—into common usage and gave them a sharp new dimension. It posed a gigantic problem.

If the Government was aware of the need to tackle the problem, it gave no sign. All the principal authorities were invited to the congress. None came.

On the evening of 6 November, three days after the conference ended, Dolci and Franco kept their promise and stopped eating. They fasted in Cortile Cascino, in a gray, stagnant room that was never deserted, in a cardboard-cutout shack papered on the inside with Levi's posters and on the outside with the perennial crisscross of poor people's washing. On 14 November, the eighth day, a Sicilian journalist wrote: "The children of the Cortile have made friends with this huge hungering man who speaks their own language .... Yesterday morning scores came to see a comic film of Charlot, the first film of their life. As soon as it gets dark the men come. It is a ritual. They can't all get in at once, and wait their turn, standing outside until late." The fast spoke directly to the people. Through them Dolci asked the authorities the simple ancient question, "Why do you spend money on that which is not bread?" There was no reply. After ten days, friends began to fear for their health. Franco, lacking oxygen, had just enough strength to get up and open the window. He thought he was going to die. On the following day, Sunday 17 November, Levi and the German political historian, Robert Jungk, visited them and told them it was time to stop the fast. It had already stirred sluggish consciences, they said. Dolci said he had received no such official assurances. That night, still fasting, the pair were taken by car to Palermo's vast hall of oratory, the Politeama, where an audience of thousands heard Levi make an appeal for liberty and equality worthy of John Stuart Mill. Ever since the publication of *Christ Stopped at Eboli* Levi has had a fabled reputation with a big section of the Italian public. With the Sicilian veteran, Girolamo Li Causi, he represents that very special brand of Italian Communist, born of the Resistance, who is no more Communist than George Orwell was; in his unbending socialism and his sensitivity to the high-pressure tactics of fascism Levi is, in fact, about the nearest equivalent to an Italian Orwell. His appeal to a Sicilian audience, despite a rather shaggy exterior and a front line of yellowed teeth, eaten away by Tuscan cigars, is strong. He understands low-keyed oratory and when he stood up in the Politeama and accused the authorities point-blank he was given an ovation. He talked, not of slums, but of "concentration camps of misery." On unemployment he said: "This army of jobless is the fruit of all the deficiencies, the mistakes, the favoritisms of our nation's history. It's natural that the authorities don't want to dirty their hands over it, that they have but a single reaction to the pressure of facts: silence. This silence is the essential stock-in-trade of that archaic organization which you all know well, the silence of the Mafia."

After the speech the silence, from the official press, continued. Dolci and Franco returned to Cortile Cascino and went on fasting. They refused to take anything more than the juice of half an orange, squeezed into a tumbler of water daily, which the doctor ordered. They were both exhausted. They broke the fast on 19 November, at noon on the thirteenth day, when Dolci was finally persuaded that there had been a sufficient impact on the public conscience. The long protest was rewarded. A few days later the Palermo authorities announced an eighty-four-million-dollar plan for slum clearance. The plan included the tearing down of Cortile Cascino and a neighboring slum in rather worse repair called Hole of Death, and the rehousing of the twelve hundred inhabitants in new low-rent flats.

It was, people said, a complete capitulation; a victory for the poor. The long chain reaction, which had begun with an inquiry in Palermo eighteen months before, was over.

Dolci did not think so. A program of public works, as far as he was concerned, had nothing to do with a policy for full employment. Slum reform had nothing to do with a reform in slum thinking. The problem that the congress had posed was still there. He talked it over with a reduced band of tired helpers. There was that letdown feeling which comes after giving birth to something you don't quite expect, and which remains there, sitting up gawkily and leering at you. Dolci was in a quandary. In his mind he turned over the litter of his six years in Sicily:

three major inquiries, four books, two trials, one stretch in jail, six fasts. He had come full circle, the "triangle of hunger" was complete—Trappeto–Partinico–Palermo; probing–exposing–starving; inquiry–book–fast. He had done it three times. He had performed a kind of sociological hat trick. For what?

At Trappeto little had changed. In Borgo di Dio he had founded a white elephant. Much of the money for which he had fasted had been spent on a "People's University" which was now empty. True, a kindergarten was still functioning, the village had had a face-lift, but the Mafia still ran the seas and every month more fishermen went away to the north for work. In Partinico the authorities were seeing to the drains; in Palermo, to the slums—or so they said. But unemployment? Everything as before. He was convinced of one thing: of the need to remain in Partinico—because of the dam. Partinico was the nerve center for the whole scheme.

But it was all too chancy, too uncoordinated. There was a need to put things "under expert management," as the TV advertisements said. Everything pointed ultimately to the overwhelming need for experts to plan *with the people;* and everything pointed, immediately, away from the Government's being the agency to do it. "Research groups," the conference had said ...

Dolci is one of those people, like Shelley, for whom the miseries of the world remain miseries, and will not let them rest. I do not know if the thought sequence I have described went on quite in this way. Nobody does. As one of the team says, "Danilo disappeared for three days." For the third time in his life Dolci went into a kind of coma, muttering to himself, thinking aloud, talking to nobody, staring at meals. He came out of it in rather poorer shape than he had emerged from the fast, but he came out of it resolved. The Government obviously had no intention of tackling the problem of full employment. In that case, he would. Simply that.

He was no longer fighting a lone spiritual battle; technological as well as cultural aid was assured—the conference had indicated that. The conference had also said "organization," "planning," "study groups." Very well. He would provide the study groups. He would become an organizer *and* a planner.

"There is something un-Italian about this selfless reckless champion of the underdog," *The Observer* noted in a profile earlier that year. Reckless was the word.

Dolci had no money. The conference had taken everything, including some of the Turin committee's grant intended for the social center. Funds were so low that workers were reduced to cutting the wires in their house to save the electricity bill. To found even a skeleton study scheme he needed about fifteen million lire.

"Something will turn up," he had said. It was December 1957. He told the others of his decision. There was no charity from Via Iannello that Christmas; dinner was sackcloth and hashes. Dolci put out no Christmas message. He seemed weighed down, hunched into himself, like a shepherd in a snowdrift waiting to take his flock over the mountains in search of new pastures, peering bleakly at the lowering ridges for a passage that might carry them safely through.

New Year came, and the clouds lifted. On 1 January 1958 Radio Moscow announced that "peace partisan" Dolci had won the Lenin (formerly Stalin) Peace Prize. It praised the "incisive vigor" with which he had depicted the conditions in Sicily and invited him to Russia to receive the prize. The announcer added that it was worth about sixteen million lire.

Dolci heard the news on the radio, like everyone else. He took off his spectacles, blinked and said, "Good—it will be very useful."

He was quite unprepared for the fresh storm it unleashed. The Communists exulted, claiming him for their own. Friends, however, told him he could not possibly accept. The voice of the Social Democrats, *La Giustizia*, called on him to reject an award which "comes from the executioners of the workers in Hungary."

Dolci didn't even hesitate. The prize had no conditions attached. "I'll always accept from anywhere gifts that help my mission of good works," he said. He accepted the $26,600 prize gratefully, and promptly announced his plan to found a chain of study centers for full employment in western Sicily.

It was the third and most momentous turning point in his life. He marched boldly into the mountains.

From time to time, plotting a path across the salient peaks of Dolci's career, I have had recourse to the singular document mentioned in the preface, which a colleague has subtitled "Gullible's Troubles, a Guide for Innocents." This is the confidential police report on Dolci presented to me by the offices of Cardinal Ruffini. Page three deals with the Congress for Full Employment. In the opinion of the police and, evidently, of Cardinal Ruffini, the congress was a "complete flop" and changed nothing. They are wrong. The congress did change something. It changed Dolci.

PART THREE

Often there are those moments, dark, dark, when you work . . . alone with God; those moments when everybody betrays. Those are the dark painful times. Those are the times when life is carried forward.

—DANILO DOLCI

XX

PRIZEWINNER
WITHOUT A PASSPORT

THE change that came over Dolci after the Lenin Prize was that he made the sacrifice of not living with the people any longer. He withdrew, into an office. Inevitably this led to misunderstanding and bitterness, especially among the saint-worshippers.

Dolci is a man whose normal, natural way is that of listening, encouraging, imparting, the way of individual charity. But it is equally important for him to do things. In order to do the things he now wished to do he began to pull round himself a mantle of bureaucracy which he asked for but really did not want. This did not happen immediately. When it did, it all but stifled him. This man, born essentially to be a free agent, found himself constricted by the beast of his own creation. He became more detached, to the point where it appeared he had forgotten the peasant. Yet, given his temperament, which is basically incompatible with any organization, the wonder is not that he became more detached in these years, but that he survived them at all. Any normal man would have been broken before the end of 1959. Between 1958 and 1961 Dolci went to court twice, wrote two more books and dozens of pamphlets, held a congress which rocked Italy, attended hundreds of meetings, worked a minimum of fourteen hours a day, and, when available, gave Vincenzina two more children. He also visited three continents, and lectured and presented papers all over Europe.

It is easy to apportion blame in these years, but more realistic to see them in perspective as experimentally necessary to

Dolci's inner education and to try to imagine the cumulative
effect of Government repression on the mind of a man forced to
live on the bleak comfort of his own wits.

On 16 January 1958, after the news of the Lenin Prize,
Dolci made a speech in Palermo in which he said: "I am not a
Communist. I accept this prize and am profoundly thankful.
Some people will say, 'Here's another useful idiot playing the
Communist game.' On all sides I've been asked for an explanation. I really believe in the need for peace—that is, in the nonviolent struggle and revolution, clean in method and without
compromise. I've seen that you can murder people by shooting
them, but also by neglecting them. I've decided to choose—not
to follow any particular trends, even if they've been suggested
to me as a virtue or a necessary discipline. I know this new way
might be dangerous, that there's a risk of presumptuousness or
isolation. But I also know this: an apple, when it matures, becomes ripe either for eating or for wasting away until from the
seeds are brought forth fresh fruit; if you sow apples you can't
expect to reap carrots; if someone has pneumonia you don't
cure him by beating him. I know many people say, 'Oh, he's ingenuous, a dreamer, he doesn't understand that what really
counts in the end is force.' *I'd* say that he who hasn't yet understood that the discovery of truth is the strongest force of all, he's
the ingenuous one, he's the dreamer. I believe that men will
collaborate better as their thoughts, with the help of scientific
analysis, are shorn of all rhetoric, superstition, complexes, dog-
mas of all kinds. Reality is complex. To understand it men have
tried Christianity, liberalism, Gandhism, socialism. There's
some truth in all these solutions. We're all mendicants of
truth."

He told Sasha Moorsom, of the BBC: "I'll take money from
the Devil or the Pope. I'm not fussy where it comes from."

Criticism of him did not diminish. Socialists who had previously supported him were incensed. (In 1957 Nenni, head of
the Socialist party, had refused to accept the same prize, be-

Dolci at his desk in Partinico—a man whose normal, natural way is that of listening, encouraging, imparting, the way of individual charity.

cause of Budapest.) Old friends were bitterly upset, especially the novelist Ignazio Silone.

Dolci said he would go to Moscow to receive the prize and make a speech there on nonviolence, "if they will give me the passport." He was not allowed to go to Moscow. He travelled nonetheless. He went out and asked questions. He went to Italy, Switzerland, France, England, Scandinavia. The headings of a series of newspaper articles he published on return give the tone of his inquiries: *"How Sweden Seeks To Give Work to*

All." *"In Norway Unemployment Rather than Unknown Is Inconceivable." "A Century of English Initiative Towards Conquering Unemployment."* He noted that the Swedish wore their well-being uneasily and that the English were worried by the American recession; and wondered if overdeveloped countries like these did not perhaps suffer from a worse moral evil than did Sicily.

He lectured. He put Sicily's case squarely. In England he told of trained Sicilian teachers "in plenty" and of absenteeism from schools of well over fifty per cent; and was misreported as describing a town of sixteen thousand people attended by a single agricultural expert who had difficulty in getting gas for his car and by 237 armed police (he cited 97 police). In France he met Abbé Pierre, Pastor Trocmé, Sartre, and others, and told journalists, when asked what the local churches and the Mafia did to help: "It is very likely in the backward areas that the Government authority, the religious authority, the judicial authority, and the Mafia are one and the same thing." Jean Steinmann,* a young Catholic theologian, of Notre Dame, who had met Dolci before, said: "The man no longer hesitates"; the Paris weekly *L'Express* compared him to "a surgeon operating in emergency." In Stockholm Dolci was reported to have said that "the Italian Government offers Sicily the single contribution of the police force" and, according to *Aftonbladet,* that "In Palermo the tourists walk the main streets whereas the police forbid the slum inhabitants to do so ... When an epidemic breaks out the police isolate these quarters and allow people to die in misery." Italy, he said, was too proud to accept foreign experts for its underdeveloped south and the foreign aid it did receive it often squandered. If there was so much misery then in the south, he was asked, "Why does Italy spend so many millions each year buying foreign soccer stars?" Dolci said he didn't know.

He spoke fearlessly and with some restraint. He exagger-

* Author of *Pour ou Contre Danilo Dolci* (Cerf, 1959).

ated about freedom of circulation in Palermo, but otherwise told the basic truth. He was not always accurately reported.

Everywhere he appealed for experts to come to his aid.

He returned to Partinico towards the end of April. He had just time to write the series of articles and to prepare his case in time for the appeal against the 1956 reverse strike sentence. The appeal was set down in Palermo for 2 May.

On 30 April a police officer called at his house in Spine Sante and asked to see his passport. The officer said he wanted to inspect the visa entries. Dolci handed him the passport. The officer put it in his pocket and walked away. The next day, 1 May —the eve of the appeal—the Italian Home Secretary, Tambroni, announced that he had withdrawn Dolci's passport because "he has defamed Italy abroad."

It was the second time the Government had attempted to prejudice Dolci in the eyes of a jury immediately before a court case.

Tambroni was deluged with telegrams of protest. Leading foreign newspapers critized his action heavily. At this time the 1958 national elections were under way and Left-wing parties were increasing in favor. *The Manchester Guardian* commented: "The action of Signor Tambroni in withdrawing the passport suggests that the strain of the electoral campaign is beginning to wear down the Government's nerves."

In the words of the influential Milan weekly, *Corriere della Sera*, Tambroni "came a cropper." But having fallen down, the Home Secretary made no move to adjust his position. He was backed up at once by the Siena police who charged Dolci with insulting public institutions and spreading false reports likely to disturb public order. Dolci had addressed students in Siena on 22 April.

Sixty French writers, editors, and poets wrote to the Italian press, calling on Tambroni to restore the passport—among them Cocteau, Sartre, Mauriac, Daniélou, Lacroix, and Gabriel Marcel. The protest of so many noted Frenchmen, many of them fervent Catholics, shook the Italian Catholic press. According

to the Jesuit *Civiltà Cattolica*, the quasi-official Vatican periodi-
cal, the appeal was "astounding." Another Catholic journal, *Il
Quotidiano*, said the French writers were "out of touch," because they had obviously not read the things the Vatican mouthpiece, *L'Osservatore Romano*, had said about Dolci.

Dolci offered documentary proof, published in book form,
that what he had exposed was true; and said that in common
with Gandhi he believed there was strength in truthful reports.
He challenged the Home Secretary to refute his facts by expert
opinion. Tambroni did not respond.

In court Dolci's counsel, Battaglia and Comandini, refused
to proceed with the reverse strike appeal until the matter of the
passport was settled. The presiding judge, Dr. Francesco Re, a
rickety old man with sleepy eyes, half closed behind myopic
spectacles, said he did not think the court could consider the request, as the authorities had allowed, by this stage, only another
half hour before the next case came on.

"What?" Battaglia interrupted. "With eighteen defense
lawyers yet to speak?"

Altogether, two hours had been allowed for the appeal, involving Dolci and the twenty-two others convicted of lawless
occupation of Government land and sedition, the time normally taken (in a Sicilian court) to dispatch a common case of
chicken theft. The sitting took place in Palermo's new Palace of
Justice, a speckled structure in marbled blocks and vast colon-
nades, built at a cost of two million eight hundred dollars and
sited imposingly between the slums of the Capo and the spires
of the Cathedral. International correspondents heard Battaglia
and Comandini, who again gave their services free, press their
plea:

BATTAGLIA: We can't accept this—this unjust and infamous ac-
    cusation.
COMANADINI: Dolci has the right to defend himself.
CROWN PROSECUTOR: The passport has nothing to do with it.
COMANDINI: This concerns an official statement of the Minister.

CROWN PROSECUTOR: But we came here to try Dolci, not the Home Secretary.

COMANDINI: I demand the right to produce documentary evidence to show that the Home Secretary (*turning to the other lawyers*) ... how shall I put it? (*the lawyers smile*)— Yes, that the Home Secretary is a liar.

The court was in a quandary. Unwittingly, the prosecutor gave it a piece of sound advice. "We must not allow a tiny incident in Partinico to develop into a national episode," he said. The court, after several adjournments, and hesitations, took the hint. The appeal was postponed until the autumn—well after the elections.

The appeal was eventually heard in November 1958. This time Dolci was sentenced to eight months' imprisonment. But an amnesty and another appeal—to Cassation, the highest court —were allowed. The eight months' sentence was not quashed for another four years. In the meantime the court reserved the right to enforce it at any time.

The Siena police let the charge of insult drop.

Dolci walked out from the abortive appeal in May 1958 with no passport and wondering who the enemy was—the Law, the Internal Affairs, the Police, or the Mafia. According to at least two newspapers, Dolci's arch enemy was now none of these, but one man—Cardinal Ruffini, Archbishop of Palermo.

Tambroni's action in withdrawing the passport was taken on the advice of Cardinal Ruffini. Telling me this quite voluntarily, His Eminence's secretary, Monsignor Longhi, added with relish: "And the Government was right to punish Dolci!"

XXI

CROPS AND FAILURES

In some ways Tambroni's was a fortuitous blunder. It acted as a clarion call to philanthropists and informed observers all over Europe. In Switzerland two emigré sons of rich Sicilian landowners began a subscription effort. Elsewhere friends sought recruits. Danilo Dolci Committees were formed. These foreign committees, which became the human and financial cornerstone of many of his new activities, took some time to shake down. And as they had to keep pace with a man called Dolci, and as everything Dolci did was both urgent and unorthodox, it is not surprising that some of them came about in a similar way.

In 1958 a Dutch languages student, Bianca Dony, and a 25-year-old French journalist, Alain Godon, were in Paris working with Abbé Pierre, the French worker-priest, when they heard of the passport seizure and decided, over a cigarette, to visit Dolci in Partinico. They hitchhiked down. Dolci explained the area, the study centers he had begun to set up, arranged accommodation, took them round. Godon went back to France. Bianca went home to the Hague. There she decided to send Dolci a contribution. She thought of sending about $300. To get the money she wrote a newspaper article and asked two journalist-friends to do the same. She says: "The articles appeared. And nearly $2,000 arrived, like that. Then my trouble started. I thought: 'Never send money, not this much money, to an Italian—not even a northern Italian.' So I kept it. And every day, another journalist came and asked for an interview. 'How is it down there?' And,

Bianca Dony

'What are they doing to this man?' And so on. More articles.
And in a short time this two thousand dollars had doubled. I
was upset. I didn't want to get involved; I was too busy with my
own studies. These journalists asked, 'What are you doing with
this money? Is there a committee? Has it a bank account?' And,
of course, I must have said yes. Yes, yes, I said. It was getting beyond me. And then—I ask you. There it was in all the papers:
committee, bank account, secretary, Sicilian Gandhi and all."

At that stage there was a girl of nineteen, holding an "account"
(a suitcase, stuffed with checks and guilders, under her bed) for

a man who knew nothing whatever about it. Thus the Dutch
Danilo Dolci Committee was founded.

Bianca eventually called in friends qualified to form a regular committee and became the secretary. Godon, who returned to
Sicily, was the first of several workers it supported.

By 1959 there were Dolci Committees in England, France,
Holland, Switzerland (two committees), Norway, Sweden, and
North Italy (various). Germany and Belgium followed later.
Most were founded or actively supported by men with international reputations in the humanist sciences—Waller and Kuenstler
in England, Friedmann and Rochefort in France, Trocmé in
Switzerland, Myrdal in Sweden, Jungk in Germany, Van Lier in
Holland. In Italy Dolci continued to be supported by intellectual
groups and occasional Catholic rebels, like the "saintly" Mayor
of Florence, La Pira. But no official body recognized him. No
Dolci Committee was founded in Sicily. Even Italian Communists were becoming wary of the reformer who was making
such good friends of the capitalists abroad. Dolci had previously
been asked, three times, to go into Parliament—once by the
Socialists and twice by the Communists. "Thanks," he said,
"but our work is different." In 1958 the Sicilian regional secretary
of the Communist party said, while praising his humanitarian out-
look: "We do not agree with Dolci's vision of the world."

Dolci had become an irretrievable rebel on a limb, held up
entirely by voluntary groups outside Sicily. His "vision" had not
yet become clear. It was submerged beneath an onrush of volunteers.

They were agrotechnicians, teachers, social workers, nurses,
and an assortment of students on vacation and ex-journalists.
The more enthusiastic ones didn't bother to apply through the
committees. They simply bought train tickets for the thousand-
mile-plus journey to Partinico and arrived. Some hitchhiked.
One bicycled. Later, "a young Englishman arrived, wearing a
Scottish kilt and without any money." After a week he was lent
the necessary ten thousand lire for his journey home.

Dolci moved, reluctantly, from his base in Spine Sante to a

Eduard Wätjen

bigger ramshackle building at the other end of town. It was known as the Center. It stood at the end of a blunt alley, Via Capua, in the wine-sellers' quarter and from its gloomy second story look-ed onto open country towards the hills of Montelepre. Rather, it would have looked onto open country had not an ancient ecclesiastical decree forbidden the tenants to use the only win-dows which commanded a view. Until the Lenin Prize was cash-ed, they couldn't afford even a duplicator. Led by Pasquale Malpede, a former rural mayor in Salerno province and the first administrator, the recruits marched in bearing planks, bricks, old light bulbs, and hundredweights of blank paper. Office equipment included two typewriters (one of them rusty), a rubber stamp, and an instrument for punching holes which someone had acquired in the Palermo flea market. A small band of farmers and artisans—Ciccio the peasant, Peppino the cartwrecker, Giuseppe the wine-seller, Pino the mechanic, Salvatore and Dionisio the potters—promptly opened a bank of unlimited credit to all Dolci workers, procured furniture at bedrock prices, enlisted errand boys, presented wine, *objets d'art,* and other home comforts at no price at all.

Franco had now returned, for good, and became Dolci's general factotum and secretary. He was followed by a handsome blond German in his forties, Eduard Wätjen. Eduard was Dolci's first mature adviser. He wore khaki and corduroys and was a philosopher of the celestial kind. He was not always practical, but he gave everybody courage. Eduard had been a key man in the German underground. After helping to organize the *putsch* against Hitler he had escaped execution, smuggled himself out, and ended the war as vice-consul in Basel. He went to America, observed the growth of the materialist image, and left again in horror. Back in West Germany he was asked to stand for the new Federal Parliament, decided against politics, returned to Switzerland, and devoted himself to abstract painting and the young Karl Marx. He became interested in philosophy as an aid to science and development work in the corners of Europe, came to Partinico and, realizing the potential significance of Dolci's work for southern Europe, stayed. Like everybody else at Partinico he did several jobs. He advised, arbitrated, translated, worked on the expansion program, and unscrambled the workers' private problems. He is still the Center's soul-doctor.

Apart from Eduard and one or two others, Dolci did not quite get the élite, the experts he wanted. Nor could he go out again and look for them. The Home Secretary still had his passport. Following his old maxim, "There's good in everybody," he tended to take on almost anyone. Many recruits were guided more by inspiration than experience, and the committees who sent them, most of whom had no idea of real conditions, can hardly be blamed for sometimes sending unsuitable material.

Dolci told newcomers they were going out to work in unyielding ground, amid a peculiarly introspective mass misery where no spirit of cooperative enterprise existed and where "it is almost an article of faith that a man must keep himself to himself at any cost." They would each be in one of five zones, into which he had divided a big slice of West Sicily—an area of 430,000 inhabitants, containing only four people with degrees in agriculture, no competent authority on education or sociology, and with an average of a murder every five days. Each worker would be a "moral reference point." Each center, built round an agrotechnician and a welfare group, would try to stimulate local employment, to encourage a consciousness towards self-help rather than provide an outside stimulus which would cease if the center should close. This was the basic dogma. Political propaganda of any kind was banned. Charity was out. Violence was to be disowned, also "falsehood, opportunism, fanaticism, dogmatism, and above all waste." He outlined a series of projects, "in no sense intended to replace or oppose existing public services, but rather to inspire them to work with greater efficiency." His main advice was, "Go slow."

To those who realized the importance of proceeding quietly, it made sense. But to the majority it was all rather woolly, like a tactical commando exercise over unmapped territory in the dark. It was going to be rough, on typist's wages. Many were short-term volunteers and, like Dolci himself when he came to Trappeto, anxious to get things *done*. It was going to be difficult to "go slow." It was also going to be lonely.

After a shakedown in Partinico the workers were deposited in the field.

Dolci had selected three villages fairly close together—Trappeto (Italian-financed), Roccamena (Swedish), and Corleone (Swiss)—ringing Partinico; and two farther afield—Menfi (British) and Cammarata (Dutch and Norwegian), both in Agrigento province. These were the guinea-pig centers, the spokes of a radial plan to study full employment for the west of the island.

The workers settled in openly and conspicuously—it was impossible, amid police interrogation and folksy peasant curiosity, any other way. Roccamena center was two tumbledown rooms and an irresponsible lavatory. Menfi, a villa. In Cammarata a young Dutchwoman, an animal specialist, worked alone from above a butcher's shop. Roccamena, where the peasants traditionally burned manure rather than use it to fertilize a barren soil, had been chosen for its extreme backwardness. Corleone, because of an unbelievable rate of death by violence and because of the extent of *omertà*, the code of silence which surrounds any Mafia crime. Cammarata, the most remote center, because of a history of landslides and pagan superstition—a third of one sample of peasants interviewed said that soil erosion and landfalls were due to "magic spells." Menfi was chosen as a classic example of water wastage.

Dolci had sited his centers carefully, but few will ever thank him for selecting Corleone. It happened apparently by accident. Michele Mandiello, an enterprising agronomist, was with Dolci at the time and recalls: "It was to be either Bisaquino or Corleone. We drove into Bisaquino and went into the *trattoria*. They said we could eat there. We were both starving. 'What've you got?' Danilo asked. 'What've you *brought*?' the proprietor shouted back. Danilo looked at me, strangely, and we got back into the car and drove on to Corleone." Corleone at least had a kind of restaurant. (In the eating houses of the interior it is still normal for patrons to take along their own food to be cooked.)

Corleone (population, sixteen thousand) is probably the most violent and sinister town in the peacetime world. It is a living graveyard. The town is dominated by a shaggy spectacular rock, on top of which sits the jail, and a hundred yards or so due east by the church which is as big as a cathedral. These two edifices, the jail and the church, glower at each other across the heights; in between are the houses, dusty hovels, clustered

Children waiting for the Center at Corleone to open

grayly about a maze of serpentine alleys. The people wear the habit of mourning, perpetually, and in the soul of this habit repose the essence and the apotheosis of *omertà*. Mafia draws strength from *omertà*. *Omertà* means manliness or self-control, and the idea of keeping oneself strictly to oneself in every circumstance; it implies refusal to help established authority and is native to the Sicilian's character by the time he is ten years old. Thus, surrounding any Mafia crime, there is a blank wall of silence. A policeman's job becomes impossible. Eye-witnesses who are persuaded to give evidence invariably state they were looking the other way when the shot was fired; neighbors of the criminal, that they saw him peaceably sunning himself on his balcony when the crime was committed. Since 1944 more men have died unnatural deaths in Corleone (153 of them between 1944 and 1948) than the number of Corleonesi killed at the front in both world wars. Despite the presence of 97 police, hardly any of these crimes have been solved. The social reformer similarly finds himself surrounded by a conspiracy of silence. Many people have been asked to work in Corleone for Dolci, and declined, myself included. Among the first to volunteer were young women—Swiss, French, German—and it is the women who have stuck. The men, the agrarians and the teachers, have continued to change rapidly.

All the centers were in Mafia communities, all sick with chronic unemployment. Of the five, including Trappeto, only two had a cinema, one a sports ground, and in no case did the church show an active interest in anything but souls.

The secretary of the Swedish Committee, Ingrid Reinius Larsson, visited Roccamena in 1959. She called on the priest to pay her respects and asked how many children went to school or received various kinds of help. The answer was, "These are questions for my conscience and God alone."

It is hard to communicate the experience of working in a Mafia community. It is beyond frustration. After the first qualified reception, cordial, homely, overwhelmingly hospitable, you become intangibly sorted into a dozen different compartments, all of them wrong, and the object of sinuous tugging opinion—a curiosity amid an intensely curious people. The villagers remain childlike, helpful and amazingly unreliable; acceptance is possible, but only on their terms; normal values of truth and justice, normal sensitivities vanish. The conventions are *other*. The chief conventions are apathy and mistrust. They are not hidden conventions; they are stated. For anyone trying to accomplish anything even remotely connected with "change," no

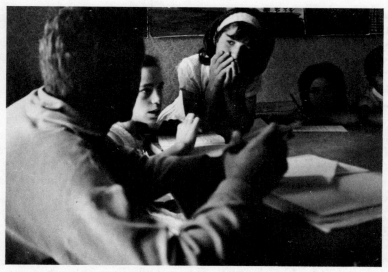

In a school at one of the Dolci centers

matter how busy he may keep himself, they make for an intensely lonely existence. To this day, the feeling no Dolci worker in the field has been able to overcome is the feeling of deep isolation.

Volunteers lived almost exclusively on a basic diet of raw onions, tomatoes, bread—sometimes soaked in oil—and pasta. The work consumed them and rarely did they last as long as six months.

Teams began discussion groups, sewing classes, courses for illiterates, theatre activities—anything to break down the wall and get close to the people. Dolci's *doposcuole* (after-school) came into being. These *doposcuole* were free-expression classes for children of all ages, and became so popular that in three centers enrolling had to be restricted until more teachers were available. (Today more than five hundred children, normally denied a reasonable education, benefit from them.) Nurses had to combat not only antediluvian cures imposed by quacks, but ostracism by the local doctors themselves. Agronomists encouraged the use of new methods and fertilizers, sowed demonstration plots, planned model farms, called in local authorities, and studied extension projects. Aurelio Finelli, a Neapolitan technician who worked for a time at Cammarata, describes the terrain: "It takes courage—it can be actually dangerous—to go off into the countryside after heavy rains. I've seen with my own eyes peasants transporting sacks of grain get as far as they can with the mule and then off load the stuff on to their own backs and stagger on for a mile and a half, knee-deep in the mud." In Palermo a sociologist continued Goffredo's work in Cortile Cascino and began a rag cooperative. Dolci's old writing room in Spine Sante became a dispensary. Within a fortnight of its conversion it was clinic, first-aid station, crèche, and maternity post, and two nurses were worked off their feet. Sometimes peasants brought along their mules for an injection.

Considering the language barrier (most workers had only a smattering of Italian on arrival), the enervating heat, the diet, the ill health (the trots, plus complications—almost everyone was affected), the fact that no reliable doctor was on hand, that escape to a relaxed atmosphere was impossible, given the inevitable clash of temperament (the technicians, who were paid, tended to look down on the volunteers, who were not), and the fact that nobody *quite* had Dolci's combination of God-given confidence, unquenchable enthusiasm, and ox-like constitution—it was a brave start.

Dolci visited and encouraged; at Partinico he collated, advised, chaired endless meetings, took VIPs round, lamented the lack of interpreters, drew up schedule after program schedule and—a big bone of contention—diverted workers to collect data for his sixth book in Italian, *Waste*. He worried about the dam for the Iato River. Unemployment had eased only slightly, and for the wrong reason—emigration. Every week more jobless men asked his workers to help them fill in labor permit forms for North Italy, Germany, Switzerland, Belgium, France. Everywhere the men were emigrating in a neurosis of despair. He feared that planning for the dam had got bogged down, but could do little about it. He, too, was becoming bogged down—by the bureaucracy of his Center. Almost every weekend there were meetings. They became increasingly theoretical. Capitini speaks of Dolci's "passionate thirst for order." Newcomers discovered that his favorite word was "exactness" and that besides orderliness he was a stickler for punctuality, annotating, scheduling, and measuring. It marked his interview technique with peasants—no phrase was ever omitted—and it marked his administrative method: no detail too small, no fact too insignificant for consideration. He was not helped by an adminstration, trying hard in five languages, which was devotedly inefficient. Pasquale did his best, but he was really a soil specialist. Thousands of facts and graphs and analyses piled up on reject doors which had become tables and on long planks laid on bricks which had become bookshelves. Peasants who entered timorously through the cardboard doors, seeking advice perhaps for footrot or mule-lameness or bovine gestation, thought they had stumbled into a paper factory by mistake. Workers, reporting for these general meetings, found they had an odd poetic flavor; they seemed to bear no relation to the immediate problems they were facing in their villages. Arriving tired and sometimes irritable they were asked to comment on schedules labelled "method of approach" and "nature of action," which they did, only to find that their advice was seldom heeded. They were puzzled. All they wanted was a bath.

The tendency to introspection is an occupational hazard of shoestring humanitarianism. Dolci's expanding Center, which had a four-year teething period, was not an exception. After a time workers found the meetings had a languorous therapeutic value. No other escape from isolation being possible, they came to accept them almost with relief.

Introspection is also part of outcast living. Paradoxically, it is one of the cogs which keeps renegade group machinery going. And it now became conditioned by factors outside anybody's control. It was a time when the Italian political Right was beginning to shiver. Rumblings everywhere foretold a coming swing leftward. Prime Minister Segni's Internal Affairs Department was unnaturally testy about social experiments such as those which Dolci's guinea pigs were now implanting.

Tambroni's war began quietly enough. On 20 July 1958 a press release from Sicily stated:

> The Italian authorities refused to allow a Swedish economist to speak yesterday in the small farming community of Roccamena, some thirty miles inland. The economist, Gunnar Adler-Karlsson, who has a scholarship from the Swedish Royal Academy of Science, was invited by friends to talk on "Aspects of Social Life in Sweden" after showing some U.S. Information Service films. At first the authorities claimed that this was not the moment for such a talk, because of the "international tension" in the Middle East. Later, the police commissioner in Palermo explained that "being a tourist Mr. Adler-Karlsson did not have the right to address either public or private gatherings. . ." According to the commissioner, "A tourist may only be a tourist, and may not study or participate in any other cultural activity whatsoever without special permission."

There was no lasting objection to Mr. Adler-Karlsson showing the American films.

Mr. Adler-Karlsson had been conducting an economic survey for Dolci in Roccamena.

Foreigners are required in Italy to take out a residence permit after three days. It is normally renewed every three months. For some reason the police insist on inscribing all visitors as "tourists," whether they are on holiday or not.

The police had begun making small difficulties for the workers, chafing them with long harangues, pistols evident, and, occasionally, veiled threats. In Sardinia a group of university lecturers, including Capitini, came under individual police scrutiny when they announced active support of Dolci's program. Mention of the name Dolci, Capitini says, was now enough to give policemen "the trots," while in Rome the Home Secretary's dossier, "Danilo Dolci Movement," was full to bursting. An enlightened Englishwoman, Daphne Phelps, who ran her villa at Taormina as a guesthouse for friends, entered Tambroni's black book after Dolci had stayed there a night. "Miss Phelps, you don't know," a policeman said to her, "but that man is dangerous!"

In Roccamena a peasant who attended the center's weekly agrarian meetings, was invited to the police station and asked: "What are they doing at these farmers' discussions? Are they spies?" Offered payment, for information, the peasant said, "I am not a rat," and left.

At the end of 1958 Dolci had some thirty workers, engaged on as many minor projects. In Roccamena the local people were coming to see them—nurses like the Swiss-German girl, Meta Berchtold, and the French journalist-teacher, Alain Godon—as good capable people. Literacy classes, house-to-house visits, practical agricultural advice, had started to instil a little hope.

But this was too much progress for one small farming community of 3,371 souls.

Meta's permit was due to expire in the summer of 1959. On 6 February it was cancelled and she was told to leave Italy within two days. Godon, applying to renew his permit, was given a week to get out. He refused to go. He was asked to sign a statement that he was "undesirable." He refused to sign and went to Rome. From there he was expelled, abusively, by *foglia di via* (the device had been officially annulled two years before). Inquiring about the expulsions, the lawyer Nino Sorgi was told they were by order of the Home Secretary.

Two Swiss welfare workers, laden with equipment for Partinico, were stopped in a train at the Italian border, arrested, and locked in a room at Bardonecchia. Their passports were in order. After three hours they were put on another train and turned back.

In the Senate a spokesman for Tambroni said the expulsions were necessary because Dolci was a defamer and an undesirable, and therefore anyone coming to Italy to work for him was in the same category. Pressed, he said: "They didn't have the right papers."

At this time the BBC transmitted a sixty-minute radio documentary, championing Dolci and his work, prepared by Gavin Maxwell and Sasha Moorsom. It was outspoken, but truthful. The Italian Government protested hotly to the Foreign Office for the "false and tendentious accusations." In the program Aldous Huxley compared the slums of Palermo to those of Cairo or Calcutta and described Dolci as "the ideal twentieth-century saint." The Rome political weekly *Il Mondo* said that in all probability Mr. Huxley had now entered Tambroni's black list.

In a paper later delivered at Basel, Dolci wrote: "It takes great wisdom to give the best of oneself in creative work (to give without loss, to grasp the flame without coming to harm—but oh, how difficult!)."

Other short-term volunteers went home; some were recalled by worried parents. Dolci was left with mostly Italians. He was boxed in, his source of supply cut. Even consignments of powdered milk arriving for his clinics were held up by Customs.

In London the British Committee, advertising for a social assistant for Menfi, was besieged with requests. But all the committees could risk sending was sympathy because of Tambrani's ban.

Dolci continued to rise at four, with the peasants, pull on an old cream sweater, walk through the darkened streets from Spine Sante to Via Capua, and work through the dawn hours on the chapters of *Waste*. He wrote: "This land is like one of the many beautiful little girls you see in the alleys of its townships. The beauty is often there beneath the scabs, the raving hair, the wild and tattered rags: and already you can picture what an appearance of graphic and noble intelligence a good upbringing would give to those features. . ." By the time Franco arrived at eight-thirty he would have done three to four hours' work and, after a sortie to the corner bar by the baker's for breakfast—a glass of milk and a roll—be ready to start his normal activity dedicated to that upbringing.

Some relief did appear. It came in the form of two houses and a person.

The first house was Daphne Phelps' spacious villa, high on Taormina cliff. Miss Phelps is a Yorkshire woman and the island's least-known benefactor. She has the interest of the Sicilians at heart and, as unofficial head of Taormina's English-speaking colony, is sometimes referred to as the Squire of Sicily. She inherited the house from her uncle Robert Kitson, a painter, and has been living in Sicily longer than Dolci. She, too—being a rich woman and, in the words of a friend, "a natural target for lots of little dark men on the make"—is somewhat embattled; and periodically has trouble with five different kinds of local police and the local taxcollector. To escape death duties and taxes, which promised bankruptcy, she turned the place into a lodging house (select, friends only) and, hearing of Dolci's plight, offered his workers a week's rest, free, in time of need. The care and attention she and her cook lavished on the early volunteers averted more breakdowns than the committees will ever know.

The second house was a nest of bedrooms, laid end to end, above Giuseppe's wineshop and almost alongside the Partinico Center. It was baptized the House of Volunteers and served as a dormitory for new recruits, discussion center, canteen, and general visitors' club. Sometimes visiting professors were installed there. Among other things it had been the local brothel. It is said that the first visitor was an English journalist. He had just drawn the shutters and turned the lights on when a man banged loudly on the door below. The journalist opened his window, leaned out, and said, in his best Italian, "What d'you want?" There was a pause, and then a Sicilian voice said: "Holy Mother—*men!*" and vanished. It was not a delightful place, but it was an improvement on the only hotel, which *was* a brothel. It had a bathroom which—besides affording a useful view of the

police barracks—had a bath. When Giuseppe remembered to
turn on the water pump, the bath worked. A cook was engaged.
Giuseppe's cloudy wine was eighteen cents a quart, meals fifteen
cents, and a bed was seventy-five cents a month, the price of
laundering the sheets. It was a haven.

The person was Pasqualino (Pasquale Marchese). He was
Sicilian. He was essentially a bringer of light and laughter, a
morale booster, at a time when the Center's run-down body,
blocked in most channels, was in dire need of a laxative. He
was a little man who smoked Alpha cigarettes, who could never
be found and yet who achieved a prodigious amount of work.
He burst on the scene in the spring of 1959, bearing his dearest
possession, a duplicating machine, and with it proceeded to
churn out thousands of words monthly to Dolci subscribers all
over Europe. He was an expert on Sicilian language, unscrambled the difficult dialectic interviews for *Waste*, and worked for
an initial wage of eight dollars and a half a month. When off-
duty he compiled a Sicilian dictionary, a volume of popular
peasant poetry, and, in odd corners of his two-room dwelling,
enough pieces of traditional wood carving—from dismantled
mule barrows—to rebuild an entire cart. His intense love of
Sicily, his chaotic cheerfulness, and his table, endeared him to
all the foreigners, especially the English, and he worked tire-
lessly for Dolci for three and a half years. His talent had flower-
ed shortly before, in his early twenties, when he became the
youngest newspaper editor on the island. At Sciacca he wrote,
edited, proofread, accounted, distributed, and sold his own paper,
probably the first—and last—independent newspaper south of
Rome. It was known for a remarkable horoscope. Pasqualino
composed his horoscope with care from the horoscope of another
paper, a well-known national journal, which he cut into
pieces and shuffled together again more or less blindly, according to whim. Readers swore that Pasqualino's horoscope was
infallible. He was a Genuine. He was intellectual, poet, anti-
quarian, raconteur, historian. Like many others he was under-

valued, and spent most of his time at the Center turning the handle of the duplicating machine. When he left, in rather sad circumstances, it was a double loss, for he took his duplicating machine with him.

The year 1959 ended in a flurry of question marks. The Rome Government called for tenders for the Iato dam. It got none. A policeman called at Spine Sante and returned Dolci his passport. No explanation. Dolci had been invited to present a paper at the 14th *Rencontres Internationales* in Geneva, a world forum for science, humanism, and sociology. He was now able to go. Open police persecution of Dolci's band now ceased. The change in official attitude was due, it is reliably stated, to intervention by the Italian Prime Minister; Segni found that the unfavorable reaction created abroad was damaging Italy's international reputation.

Troubles continued nonetheless.

Dolci had managed to attract a new group of Italian social workers, to compensate earlier losses, led by a woman consultant, Gisella di Iuvalta. While he was in Geneva she closed down two centers and recalled the social workers to Partinico; on his return Dolci was presented with an ultimatum. The ultimatum was discussed at a seminar at Trappeto lasting, it is said, twenty-eight days. He was told that his way of combining social and agrarian work in separate centers was wrong and that documentary inquiries raised false hopes among the people; he was asked to concentrate the welfare services in Partinico and cede a measure of policy control or Gisella and friends would leave. They left. Among others who went with them were Goffredo Fofi and the sociologist Alberto L'Abbate, the two veterans of Cortile Cascino. The Dutch Committee also withdrew its workers and closed down at Cammarata. The schism had a sequel. Goffedo, Gisella, Alberto, and others sabotaged funds from one of the north Italian committees and, with the money, began doing social work in Calabria—in opposition, as it were, to Dolci. Nowadays, Goffredo, one of the leaders of the coup, tells the story against themselves and admits that most of the muddle they campaigned against at Partinico is well overcome.

Dolci had lost the Cammarata center and a base in Palermo, a committee, most of his social workers and agronomists, and two other centers were closed. His regular team was down to five—Franco, Eduard, Pasqualino, and two agriculturalists, Pasquale and Michele. Dolci has summed up his empirical philosophy in this way: "It is to extract the truth from my own experience." Experience now told him it was time to stop patchwork volunteering.

He was not deterred. He needed long-term specialists. He would go out and get them. Luckily, now that the ban on foreigners was lifted, some were already on the way.

In a few months things were back to normal. In spring 1960 subscribers abroad learned, in *Notes for Friends,* that

at Roccamena
The peasants' meetings continue weekly .... The main topic of discussion has been the construction of a dam on the River Bruca...(Andrea Ferretti).

at Corleone
At first little Francesco used to work with a dour, closed expression, never asking questions. Now he arrives looking confident, grinning from ear to ear. (Cécile Goy).

Enthusiasm for the [dressmaking] class has grown so that every day more mothers bring their daughters along to see if they might join. One woman brought her own chair to make quite sure that her daughter was accepted. (Verena Wolfensberger).

at Menfi
... 39 experimental plots are now sown...about a fourth of an acre each on an average, enough to enable us to successfully demonstrate new crops and different techniques of cultivation to smallholders who know absolutely nothing about them...(Michele Mandiello).

at Trappeto and Partinico

William and Pino have been doing the cropping chart;
Hans has nearly finished the playground; Annie is supervising a group of girls who are sewing dresses and making
puppets for the theater which Hans and the boys are building from old crates. . . .

Gianfranco, Franco, and Pino are making final revisions
to the book [*Waste*]. . . .Elaine is looking after the youngsters, advising on hygiene, and giving injections. Gerrit has
taken on the film showings and, with Pasquale, is trying to
convince the peasants about the importance of the dam.
Elsa does house visits and also the cooking. . . . (Anna Alasia).

A course has been started for illiterate boys aged from ten
to fifteen. . . . They work as cowherds and day laborers.
Several are getting on well and can already write their own
names. (Lorenzo and Paola Barbera).

There was also an item about Silvio, who was making notes
on parasites and preparing for a conference to be held at a town
called Palma di Montechiaro.

XXII

THE GREAT SMELL

In February–March 1960 Dolci lectured in Switzerland, France, Sweden, and England. He was troubled by a heart complaint and mentioned it privately. Publicly he said he was "not tired, just a little weary."

He told audiences of a Sicilian girl who had become engaged to a young man of a well-endowed family. They became intimate. Then, after pressure from his parents, he left her. Before long the girl's friends, relatives, and neighbors approached her, one by one, saying: "How is it you haven't killed him? Here you are, your reputation's done for, and yet you haven't killed him?" It was the girl's father who bought her the revolver. After a month or so of this advice she shot the young man three times in the heart and killed him.

It was not an isolated instance, he explained. Nor was the girl antisocial. She had been compelled to kill in order to remain accepted, within the social framework of her village.

"Our work is complex," he said, "and irrational. The problem is not one of money, but of men. Experts are needed who can see the problem objectively and precisely. Its solution lies in an awareness and an exactness of action. It's as if a crane were trying to lift a very heavy weight. If a button has to be pressed in a certain spot, it's pointless to press here—or there; it must be pressed *here*, and only then can the crane lift the load. If you put even the greatest pressure on the wrong spot nothing happens."

The tour was a big success. In Paris he was fêted. In London one meeting drew fifteen hundred, and in Oxford so many turned up to a lecture chamber in the town hall that the meeting had to be moved to the main hall. The 224-pound reformer with the 48-inch waist, who travelled second-class with no luggage, drew crowds everywhere. His careful social inquiries sometimes led officials to consider him naïve and innocent, and a Lancashire employment officer said: "I shouldn't think things will work out as he hopes, but things will nevertheless work out a lot better than they would without him."

On Dolci's last day in Britain Stephen Peet's documentary, *Murder by Neglect,* showing Dolci's work, was sceened on BBC television. Audiences who knew the island through a Byronic haze of temples, Taormina, and *tarantelle* danced amid orange blossom, were disturbed—among other things by the sight of a twelve-year-old boy searching for his unemployed father until he discovered, accidentally, that his father had been arrested a week before for stealing to feed the family; and by the sight of a family of eleven, living with their mule, in one room in a town called Palma di Montechiaro.

On tour Dolci, a serious man, without noticeable sense of humor, is dogged by tragicomedy. The one hitch on this tour was the seat of his trousers, which split, while he was lunching near Tottenham Court Road. He was due to speak that night and had brought no spare pair. Peet, who was there at the time, scoured London for a pair of ready-made dark trousers, waist 48 inch. Shopkeepers laughed at the thought. Desperate, Peet rang Moss Bros. "Yes, sir," a voice said, "how many pairs would you like?" The English Committee bought the trousers, and the coat to match. It was the first suit Dolci had owned since leaving home in 1949.

In Partinico some of the experts he needed were already settling in. Dolci arrived back in his new Moss Bros. suit, but instead of getting down to work with them, he made a characteristic swerve. For three weeks he was lost in a maze of consultation, statistics, and sorties by car, far and near, in the company of a thin, bespectacled doctor named Silvio Pampiglione. Then he collected statistics, colleagues, and all the motor transport available and bundled them all off to the distant town of Palma di Montechiaro for a congress.

Today at a distance of four years the value of this gathering is still hotly disputed. Many who were there cannot remember where they lodged or how any work at all was accomplished. It was that sort of congress.

Palma di Montechiaro is a seaside town of little more than twenty thousand inhabitants. It lies on the Mediterranean coast between Agrigento and Licata and faces, or more properly leans towards, Africa. It is the town of *The Leopard*, Lampedusa's masterpiece about the Sicilian aristocracy taken at the point of decline. Lampedusa does not describe what Dr. Pampiglione found there.

Pampiglione is a Roman doctor, with a scientific bias for vermin. He is lecturer of parasitology at the University of Rome. In 1959 he offered his services to Dolci and the latter suggested Palma. Pampiglione spent some months in Palma and made a remarkable report. He asked for a congress. Dolci, who had other things on his mind, shelved the idea. He felt it wrong to scatter his resources any farther afield; the admonishments of the Trappeto seminar had taught him that conferences were apt to leave villagers high and dry and, unless followed up by practical social work, greatly disgruntled. He went abroad. Returning, he found that in the meantime Pampiglione had been promised considerable backing for a conference, and changed his mind. He threw his weight behind the idea and on 27 April 1960, supported by pressmen, regional deputies, and half the Italian sociological and cultural world, drove down to take the unsuspecting town by storm.

Until that day Palma had never seen foreigners at close quarters. Sicilian motorists pass through the village rapidly, if possible with their eyes closed. It does not have the quaint wedding-cake bulge of the typical poor southern village. Its poverty is spectacular. The cavernous streets are scored by serpentines of black feces and other matter, and a veil of chalky dust pollutes the air. From the main road the whole plaster town tilts downwards, as though arrested in a macabre lunge towards the sea. Once I drove through with a woman companion. She looked once, and screamed. She did not speak again until we were some distance outside the township.

Kathleen Nott, the critic and writer, arrived for the opening of the congress. It was a hot spring morning. She says: "My first impression was a frightful smell about a mile up the road which nearly killed us [Daphne Phelps and an English accountant were with her]. A smell of non-drains. We'd hardly stepped down when the people began climbing all over us like flies— 'Send us a suit of clothes?' or, 'Please, a box of toys for little Giannina?' They thought we were Americans. They can't tell the difference anyway. I got stranded alone and was flat on my back beneath people most of the time. The only place I know of at all comparable is Calcutta.

"It was meant to be a sort of Dotheboy's Hall situation— 'cleen windows,' you know. We were told that 84 per cent of the population had no lavs and then to go out and smell for ourselves. I thought I'd be driven completely out of my mind. I couldn't stand more than a morning first of all, and escaped to Agrigento. Most of us thought it was a great mistake to hold the conference *there*. And yet it was a brilliant idea, even if it was madly distracting."

Mistake or not, it lasted three days.

The congress was held in the cinema, second only to the cathedral in status. It was opened by the President of the Regional Government and blessed by the Archbishop of Agrigento. The President arrived two hours late—he had been spending this time, it was said, praying with the archbishop. The cinema was jammed with Palma folk who rushed it in droves the moment the doors opened. Perhaps fifty per cent understood what it was all about. Many were old women in black headshawls, bent nearly double. They sat there, bowed and silent. They thought it was a kind of vaudeville. Those who could not get in massed in the square and listened to the discussions over loudspeakers. Proceedings were broadcast all over the town by a public-address system which did not break down, so that passing motorists carried reports up the coast of a freak election contest. The neofascists had put it round that the visitors would distribute twenty million lire. Delegates emerging from the cinema for air were pounded on, pawed, grabbed, begged from, and followed wherever they went.

Yet the congress succeeded.

Simultaneous translation was contrived in three languages. Sufficient carabinieri were rallied as a bodyguard to impress the President. And appetites were satisfied by a small body of nuns who prepared meals in a nearby convent. "Curious, this congress," the Sicilian writer Sciascia notes, after breakfasting on coffee and spiced almond cakes in the refectory, in company with priests, cardiganed students, regional deputies, armed policemen, and white fluttering nuns, unobtrusively but actively hawking their handicraft on the side.

Chaos distresses most people. It inspires Dolci. The miracle of his last-minute tactical improvization was such that the congress itself never got out of hand. Overall it produced exactly the effect of horrific revulsion on the thinking outside population that he desired. It was perfectly consistent with his expressionistic way of rousing people's consciences.

Palma was splashed across every major newspaper in Italy.

Visitors did not enjoy Palma. They felt it was terrible. But they have never forgotten it. Nor have the Sicilian authorities who for the first time, and to their credit, sat down alongside Dolci at a congress from which they themselves could emerge only as scapegoats. (They have never sat down at a public table with him since.) For the first time Dolci was seen in a responsible scientific *cadre* by his opponents.

The speakers appeared on a stark platform, casting long scalloped shadows. Pampiglione stood up, lean, square-jawed, wearing black-rimmed hexagonal spectacles. He carried a black satchel. In it was the report. Even today in cold print it has an air of crisis. It is the only statistical report I know which is at once repellent and compassionate. With Dolci's first book, *Act Quickly (and Well)*, it should be compulsory reading in all western schools.

It told the conference that conditions had not materially altered since 1639, when the first census was taken; that 90 per cent of the houses were without water and 86 per cent without lavatories; that from 267 children examined three-quarters had tapeworms, and from 235 people of all ages almost 50 per cent had dwarf tapeworms or other varieties; that the *average* was five people to a room; that in the heart of the town, 3,404 people shared their rooms with 5,085 animals—mules, donkeys, horses, goats, cows, calves, dogs, cats, ferrets, and backyard animals "of all descriptions"—and eight varieties of bugs and insects. The report added that:

> illiteracy was 64 per cent;
> only one house, of 600 seen, was free of rats and mice;
> of 100 women taken at random little more than half their
>   total births (827 pregnancies) had survived;
> infectious diseases were rampant;
> there had been a hospital—in 1666.

Pampiglione had studied 600 families, person to person. "However," he said, "there is no reason to suppose, from official figures available, that conditions in Palma di Montechiaro ... differ greatly from those existing in other west Sicilian communities."

The mayor, the prefect, the local bishop, the archbishop, the Sicilian President, and other officials, listened to it all, and were moved. The same, many of them, who a few years before had denounced Dolci for daring to suggest that Sicilian villages were destitute.

Dolci and Pampiglione, in contrast to everybody else, made quiet, controlled speeches. "Nobody could have doubted which was Dolci," Kathleen Nott says, writing in *Commentary*. "An exceptionally tall, big-boned, youngish man with a round, pale, mild countenance and dressed in what looked like a black soutane ... I did not really take in his clothing; it was like some rather abstract stage direction to express a dedicated, even a consecrated personality."

It was, in fact, the Moss Bros. suit.

He spoke about waste, his perennial theme, and explained what he was trying to do at Partinico and the other centers. For Palma he proposed nothing. He merely stated. Afterwards people came up and asked what he intended *doing* about Palma. He replied, "Go and look at this place." The evasion infuriated many people, and, prodded by a situation which she felt to be a direct incitement to violence, Miss Nott was moved to say, in her frank, hearty way: "What would you do if you landed yourself in a revolutionary situation where nonviolence was impractical?" Dolci said he didn't understand. Daphne Phelps, whose Italian was fluent, repeated the question. He said he still didn't understand. Miss Nott demurred. Finally, Dolci said, "Go and look at this place yourself." "I now see," she writes, "that Dolci could not have answered me in any other way. To have given an answer one way or the other about the future, as it might be determined by his opponents, would be doing a kind of violence to that present which he is trying to initiate. Though to outsiders Dolci can appear somewhat mysterious, I believe myself that this is only because he is so obvious, so naïvely honest, and so consistent."

In the light of the feeble excuses which have been made for Palma, and places like it, it is revealing to compare Dolci's sincere humanism with a fairly typical Italian political attitude. Girolamo Li Causi, the father-figure of Sicilian Communism, later said to me: "We Communists should be ashamed. We once had Palma in our hands, but we did nothing to rid it of its misery."

Dolci has always believed that if you solve people's economic problems for them you don't solve all their problems; and that it is just as important that fifty men should get together

and lay their own drain as it is that they should enjoy the benefits of sewerage.

He hoped the Sicilians would do something about Palma
themselves. This they are now doing—after some delay, naturally.

Nobody expected that anything would really happen during the congress. Surprisingly, on the last day, something did. A
cable arrived from Holland offering $16,800 a year for five years.
It was addressed to a Dutch Franciscan delegate, Father Salvinus
Duynstee. Duynstee, a sociologist-priest, announced he would
begin social work in Palma immediately. After the congress he
set up a busy welfare center.

Dolci also received offers of money, from Germany and
northern Italy.

He returned to Partinico and incorporated Pampiglione's
report, worm for worm, in the last section of *Waste*. The book
is a scientific, humane, and deeply moving account of mass exploitation. With the Mexican studies of Oscar Lewis, it gives
a new dimension to the art of social documentary and makes
most other sociological studies seem museum pieces by compari-
son. Pampiglione's report is a terrifying chapter, like all the
rest.

Dolci left Palma as he found it. For some time he had to
live down the mutterings of newly acquired colleagues, on Lampedusa's theme of "change everything in order to change nothing." (*The Leopard* is self-prescribed reading for Dolci recruits.) In this period, until 1962, nearly all Dolci's new chillun
got wings. They wanted him to fly in many different directions;
whether he went, or not, it still provoked criticism. His simple
stubbornness caused him to back very few of their ideas. Pampiglione's was an exception. Dolci says: "I once made a list of
all the things people wanted me to do with the Center—historical
studies, chicken-raising experiments, folk high schools . . . by the
time I reached thirty, I gave up. If I'd listened to them where would
I be now?"

After Palma, Sicilians coined their most unloving label for

him, "*il professionista della miseria.*" Dolci seldom replies to these taunts.

By accident *The Times Literary Supplement* demolishes this one for him. It notes that the Palma *exposé* puts Lampedusa's "wonderful elegy on the old Sicilian nobility ... into some perspective."

It is worth adding that Lampedusa's words, "change everything in order to change nothing," are really the maxim of Church and Mafia in Palma di Montechiaro—as Visconti discovered when he attempted, without success, to film *The Leopard* there in 1962, and as Father Duynstee was soon to discover when he began his welfare center, to his sadness and eventual exile in 1963.

Dolci wished the Dutch priest well and turned resolutely to his more complex, more durable ideas of change. He had some difficulty in communicating these ideas, clearly and forcibly, to his new specialists. But they made an immediate impression on one woman who had arrived a month or so before.

XXIII

A PLACE
BY THE SEA

"For years we've been searching for community development officers and adult educationalists for Western Sicily," Dolci told a peace conference in Basel later in 1960. "In Italy these people don't exist. I don't believe there are any in Germany, nor have we managed to find any in Switzerland or France. In England we have found one person; and she is working down there now, submerged beneath the tens of thousands of people."

The person was Ilys Booker, a Canadian woman from Winnipeg. She came to England in 1954, on holiday, joined the Council of Social Service in London as a development officer on the new housing estates, and never went back to Canada. She came to Menfi for the British Committee in February 1960. She was forty.

Explaining Dolci's work to *Manchester Guardian* readers, Professor Waller had written, almost apologetically: "The British have undertaken to do what they can in a place by the sea, Menfi, between Selinunte and Agrigento." Nobody expected that Ilys, a single woman, would be able to do very much. Ilys is a modest, quiet-toned woman with her hair, graying a little, tied in a bun. She has a wry Canadian accent and a man-sized chuckle, neither of which prevents her from merging unobtrusively into her surroundings. When she came to Sicily she spoke no Italian, had never worked in an underdeveloped area, and knew little of Sicilian values. But she did know that Dolci's slow

Ilys Booker

way towards self-help was the only permanent, the only valid
approach to the Sicilian problem.

Menfi was the least backward center, a small flat town of
thirteen thousand inhabitants, gridded into squares and straight
alleys, neat and almost sewered, with globules of color from
flowerpots over courtyards and gleaming pans visible in the
kitchens of houses which did not appear to be on the verge of
collapse. The houses wore paint, the streets a little bitumen.
The center was closed up when she arrived. There was only
Michele, the southern Italian technician, and a lively social

worker, Gianfranco, who left a week later against his will. Gianfranco was removed by a posse of two friends, his father, mother,
and two uncles, to the safety of North Italy, on the strength of
a doctor's certificate stating he was "mental." For money, Ilys
discovered, you could get a Sicilian doctor to agree to anything.

Waller gave her a similar insight. (Ross Waller is Professor
of Adult Education at Manchester University and was one of
the first to proclaim Dolci's importance to the English-speaking
world. He is chairman of the Dolci Trust in Britain.) He wrote
to Ilys: "We were at Partinico at New Year with all the volunteers. I expounded with fervor the principles of self-help and
local development and finished with the question, 'Now, are
we to believe that the Sicilians won't help themselves?' Silence.
Then a serious-looking man I didn't know said thoughtfully,
'Yes, I think they will, if they are paid just a little bit for doing
it.' "

Ilys did not reopen the previous center, a terraced villa
near the carabinieri barracks. None of the early volunteers had
understood the need to go in quietly; people had stopped sending their children to its *doposcuola* when workers appeared
with questionnaires for *Waste* ("We were afraid of all these
questions," the melon man told her); Menfi had been scandalized by mixed sleeping, terrace parties, and an Englishwoman
who spent part of her time leaning over the balcony blowing
kisses to the carabinieri. "One feels a bit guilty that we sent you
out there," Robin Dixon, the trust secretary, wrote. Ilys replied:
"My method is one of slow, slow, slow contact." She refused to
impose.

She took rooms in the Street of All Goodness on the other
side of town, quietly opened a small center in yet another quarter, Via Mazzini, and went there every day with Michele's niece,
Aurora. For weeks she did nothing but go there with Aurora,
absorb the language and the customs, and talk to a few women.
Later, when they said, "Are you going to have a *doposcuola?*"
she began helping the children with their homework: on the
first day seven children came; on the second, 26; on the third,

35; on the fourth, 43 ... Then the mothers said, "You must
teach us to sew." Ilys pretended to. In the first half hour the
women realized they sewed much better than she did, but they
never accepted the fact, on the traditional assumption that the
foreigner is always more capable. "It becomes apparent," she
noted, "that there is a deeply rooted habit of thinking enthusiastically, going hand-in-hand with a fantastic resignation and
absolute belief in their own powerlessness."

In her small house she did her own chores, never went out
at night, slowed her pace to the timeless rhythm of her neighbors. She wrote endlessly to Waller and Dixon. "An unmarried
woman, without her family, living alone in the town is considered immoral just on the strength of combined circumstances," she wrote. It was three months before the quarter
round All Goodness Street accepted the fact that she was not a
dangerous, loose woman. People took her automatically to be
an Evangelist, and she wondered, as she walked about that first
spring, why the mothers—all of whom knew her—suddenly began to snatch their children out of her path. Then she heard
that the archpriest's sermon had included the passage: "Don't
let your children fall under the shadow of the foreigners."

"It is inconceivable to the Sicilian that anyone would work
without political or religious motives," she reported.

She also observed: "In an agricultural economy eggs are
imported from Israel, potatoes, onions, beans, and milk from
Italy, meat from Yugoslavia and Holland. . . . Large numbers
of unemployed men stand about day in and out, waiting to be
called for work. They give the impression it is a holiday, as indeed it is, an almost perpetual holiday."

Ilys received a Swiss social assistant, and rejected Partinico's
offer of "a nice young Englishman" who would be glad to help
for two months. "And when I asked what he could do, they said
he was handy at all sorts of things, and could unblock drains."
All through she had one hand tied to the erratic apron strings
of Partinico, where for the first time amid the *bêtises* and petty
rivalries which commonly bedevil community development

"*Large numbers of unemployed men stand about day in and out, waiting to be called for work. They give the impression it is a holiday, as indeed it is, an almost perpetual holiday.*"—ILYS BOOKER

work, Dolci was beginning to wince. As Partinico's growing
pains mounted, Ilys felt as much for Dolci as anyone. "I feel that
poor Danilo gets dragged hither and yon by all those enthusiastic
workers . . . and he tries to be agreeable to all until the force of
their will gets to be too much for him and he closes down trans-
mission and it's not possible to communicate." Waller wrote back,
in April 1960: "He is a truly great man. That doesn't mean he is a
good organizer or administrator; that he isn't and never will be.
But his spirit matters a lot." "Part of the trouble is his own damn-
able modesty," Ilys replied. "He refuses to 'give orders.' "

Most of Partinico's problems, in miniature, came her way.
She had to conciliate Michele, who was beset by irrigation worries. Some years before, the Government had built a dam, but
neglected to tell the peasants how it worked. As a result three-
quarters of the water flowed straight into the sea. Michele la-
bored amid the illogical spectacle of the rich man's fields profit-
ing by a system intended to water the poor man's dead soil; and
when he began to explain the meaning of secondary and terti-
ary channels some farmers actually complained that the modern
canal system *ran across their land*. One or two progressive peasants deliberately misled the ignorant over irrigating experimental crops. Michele encouraged soil conservation and gave away
poplar saplings. The peasants didn't believe "those long thin
sticks" were really trees and were surprised when they later produced leaves. They grew cereals only on land flogged bare by
centuries of misuse. But as they saw the miracle of irrigation
flower on Michele's 61 demonstration plots, they began to experiment; with each new crop a little mistrust vanished.

Ilys took on three young British social workers, John
Ogden, Philip Reidford, and Janet Rees. She put them through
the same apprenticeship she had undergone herself. Janet lived
with Ilys, the boys elsewhere. They ate at her house and left
every evening before nine. It was months before either Janet or
Ilys was able to walk the town with the boys without causing
raised eyebrows. Partinico chafed Ilys' excessive caution. "I preferred to err this way," she says. Once she and John took Nina,

the first Sicilian teacher to help, to buy some books in Palermo. Nina was seen by a Menfi lawyer sitting in the railway station bar with John—Ilys was at the newsstand twenty yards away. The lawyer thought they were on a *scappata* (weekend spree, sex implied) and reported to Nina's father. "Half the town jumped to the same conclusion as the lawyer."

The boys moved about the town, chatting, listening, assessing problems, drinking endless cups of black coffee, and filled in the four-months-long summer break with creative activities for the children who normally ran the streets wild. John listed thirteen major problems in Menfi. One was sex taboos. Inevitably he was involved in an almost daily conversation with peasants which went like this: "In London how d'you enjoy yourself?" "Oh, take a girl out—a meal, a film, go to a concert." "Then what d'you do?" "Usually take her home, eat something, you know, talk——" "Then what do you do?" "I usually go home." "You never *do* her?" "No." "Why not?" "We're not married." "And you call that enjoying yourself?"

Ilys tried several times to meet the archpriest. He avoided an encounter. Requests to use church stages for dramatic activities for the children were refused. A progressive young priest conceded Janet an interview for an hour. She explained Dolci's story and aims carefully. He said: "But even though the Church might agree you are doing good work it must condemn you because this work comes under the aegis of one who has moved away from the skirt of the mother."

Some three hundred school-aged children had not had a day's education and half of Menfi's 85 qualified teachers were unemployed. From its hobby-like beginnings Ilys built up a thriving *doposcuola*. But the local schools director would not cooperate. He told her it was against the law to start a completely free after-school schoolroom, and local teachers, aching for jobs, were afraid to join her in case they were penalized. "It's naïve in the extreme for people to think that if we make friendly visits to the priest and so on ... that they will smile and let us get on with things," she wrote.

Summer was the real enemy. Sicilian heat is not unlike African. It hangs about the streets like a vapor. Summer meant occasional relief at Porto Palo beach, but it also meant flies and a flow of visitors from Partinico. Only some committees appreciated that the Partinico headquarters was not a travel agency— "Last week we counted twenty unexpected arrivals in four days," the normally placid administrator, Eyvind Hytten, told the English committee. "Every one represents, in addition to the trouble of finding rooms, at least some half hour of explanation of the work, and at times several hours. ... Please tell your friends ... to eliminate persons who come here in order to look with awe at Danilo, and who back out with disgust when they learn he does not sit the day long half-naked on a carpet, distributing bread and nice words to starving children." About half the hero-worshippers got dysentery, and the English-speaking ones, imagining Menfi as a kind of seaside spa, filtered down to Ilys' doorstep. Most were of the pestiferous kind. Cranks, beards, women artists, dilettantes, photographers, philanthropists, and incompatible vegetarians in outrageous dress. Several fell sick on her. She fed them all—in August 1961 she cooked two hundred meals above normal—all, that is, except an Englishman in his seventies who came on a bicycle and, against advice, braved the local restaurant. He used sign language to order a cup of tea and a poached egg. The waiter brought the tea and an egg in its shell. "Poached," the old man said, imitating the action of cracking the egg. Whereupon the waiter cracked it straight into the cup of tea.

Ilys circularized Partinico and points abroad: "Women, please do not wear shorts or slacks and please do not wear bikinis on Porto Palo; men, please do not wear shorts."

She was made occasional chairman of the Partinico meetings, fretted at their drawn-out wastage, and told Waller: "I'd give a lot to be a Cheshire cat and just disappear and leave my smile behind ..."

Menfi's saving grace was its semiautonomy. It was the only center responsible directly to its committee abroad and paid directly by it. Other centers had their money channelled through Partinico. Menfi workers were thus envied—their salaries arrived regularly. Even so budgeting was painful. Ilys reported: "Phil brought a list the other day—'Monthly: stamps $2.66, coffees $2.24, stationery 16¢, toothpaste 32¢, soap 17¢, razor blades 48¢, haircut 25¢, cigarettes and matches $8.72. Total, $15.' He asks if it is possible to have a little more than the $9.80 a month." The *doposcuola* went on growing. Two Sicilian teachers joined it—they were paid just a little bit for doing so. For a long time it was a school for manners, an uphill battle in a society which encouraged children to yell all day long, tear toys limb from limb, capture lame birds in order to strangle or torture them, while adults stood and laughed. Ilys and the three all got dysentery. Philip got jaundice. The doctor came and, without getting out of his car, said Philip was to eat nothing. He drove off, saying he was going hunting and would be back later.

Gradually they became accepted. Adults asked for English lessons. People began to ask for help of all kinds. John found it difficult not to sympathize with their fatalism. A family he knew well called him in—the father, unemployed for two years; six children—a fourteen-year-old shepherd, a girl of eleven, children of eight, six, three, and a babe-in-arms; the mother, ill with pulmonary trouble; the girl ran the house, the eight-year-old had not been to school because there was no money for books, the six-year-old wanted to go but couldn't because of a scalp infection.

"You know there's ECA (the municipal social security office)," John told the father.

"Yes, I've been there."

"What did they do?"

"They gave me ten pounds of pasta."

John secured chits from ECA for medical aid, explained countless forms to the family, and, after long delay, ended up with medicine for the mother, books for the boy, treatment for the child's scalp infection, and shoes for another child.

When I called on Ilys in January 1961 there were 110 children attending the *doposcuola*, many lining up for an hour before the doors were opened, and five exhausted teachers sweating out two shifts daily. "At first they couldn't fathom our quiet methods, our willingness to explain, couldn't understand why we didn't beat them," John said. "Now ki.ls who used to be truant are brought along every day by their parents."

"After fifteen months," Ilys wrote, "the women are becoming more friendly, but it will take many more months before we could embark on community center activities; fifteen months serve only to make people more accustomed to foreigners. It doesn't compel them to take action. ... The *doposcuola* seems to have a much more profound influence than the elementary school. It 'awakens' the children, people say to us. This supports what I have always believed, that if one works towards developing awareness, people see it and feel it, and after a year they are now expressing it. ...."

Ilys went on as she had begun, quietly, keeping her team together, mustering goodwill, plugging away at the silent saboteurs—ignorance, apathy, suspicion, fatalism. Then, because she was also working closely with Partinico, factors outside her control intervened. Sicily is the original European home of intrigue and it was perhaps natural that, with a dozen high-powered individualists on his staff, including two or three anarchists, some of it should rub off on to Dolci's organization at Partinico. Workers flared up—a series of minor suppurating schisms—and the insidious unnamable quality which tinges the Sicilian atmosphere began to sap everyone's will, including Ilys'. In May 1961 she told London, "Whoever comes to Menfi should be aware that odd situations develop in a sense outside Danilo himself." In June she took to her bed, exhausted. "I'm no good at intrigue," she said. In August she left, a tired but not a despairing woman. "I have high hopes for Menfi—five years of continuous slow work would change a lot."

When Ilys left Menfi after eighteen months she reported "no practical or visible results." She left, however, something more. "Our business as educators," Dolci had said, "is to get people to recognize their own problems; by raising questions we cause these problems to exist for the people so they may begin to seek ways of solving them. . . . We prepare the ground for change."

Her tedious preparatory approach laid the basis not for a social agency, but for a pilot community development project. As a result, durable changes of attitude are now taking place in Menfi. "Dolci" and "progress" are no longer synonymous with "subversion." Local body hindrances are of the past, even the church is vaguely cooperative. The *doposcuola* is officially recognized and has a staff of nine teachers, all Sicilian. Peasants who in 1960 would not use manure because "it dirties the land" are now producing tobacco. Farmers who once said "we were born to be wretched" and "the Government has abandoned us," and whose ideas of solving their problems were either "emigrate to Venezuela" or "leave them to God," have formed a two-hundred-plus-member cooperative to stimulate production and marketing of new crops. The measure of confidence Ilys' successors, Harry and Winnie Jamieson, were able to instil is directly related to the calm unflappable policy of the woman before them. Ilys improved on Dolci's maxim, "go slow," and went slower than anyone.

In its diminutive way Menfi is as good a piece of extra-colonial development as the British have achieved anywhere for many a long day.

✿ XXIV ✿

IN DANILOLAND

DOLCI's Center at Partinico was never really planned. It grew through a maze of debits and devoted servants, both godless and god-given, by check and by hazard and by expedience, by the frailty of indecisions and the strength of mistakes forgotten, and above all by the sublimation of an enormous will to serve. It is really an extension of Dolci's personality. There have been casualties all along the way. But in the lonely world of the reformer it is not unknown that the qualities which make him great in battle—self-confidence, courage, refusal to compromise— are the very ones to balk him in times of lull.

I first met Dolci after Palma, in the winter of 1960. It was a time for Italy of industrial boom and of strikes in every trade and profession, of a victory against neofascism in the north and a hardening of ecclesiastical arteries in the south, of mounting pressure from the Left and half-baked Government reforms at the center. The tourist budget was jolly. In Sicily anti-Mafia propaganda was rising and the tourist rate was starting to slump, urban poor were mortgaging themselves into the grave with television on the installment plan, and peasants were abandoning the land. The Center was expanding.

Dolci was preparing for a trip to America and about to embark on a series of tape-recorded conversations with peasants, the theme of *Conversations*, his next book. I was curious to meet a man who was only then becoming controversial in a European sense. I had to wait a few minutes to see him. The Center had a frayed look. Police needling was by no means ended, and a continuing series of Mafia murders in Borgetto, a mile up the road, did not make for relaxation. Until recently Dolci had refused any salary or personal expenses and specialists were told, "I hope we shall manage to keep you living in these months." The building was draughty and smelled of grain, must, and rat poison. It was thin and angular, and whenever a truck went down the main street it wobbled. A scene of humanitarian chaos hit you the moment you came up the stairs. The walls and every inch of flat space were covered with files, papers, maps, graphs, and charts. People came and went from a series of partitioned cubbyholes. The men wore old clothes, the women seemed not to have known makeup for weeks. There was a buzz of tense conversation, a feel of improvization, and a strong emphasis on manual labor. One felt instantly an unseen driving force. Amid a catharsis of foreign tongues and tension one felt strangely welcome. A door opened and I caught sight of a blond man in khaki and a skullcap poring over notes and muttering to himself in German. Later, over lunch, when he expounded to a new female recruit the folly of wearing trousers, even by dark, in a Sicilian community, I knew it must be Eduard. A thin, silk-voiced Italian introduced himself as Teresio the demographer. He had a bundle of maps under one arm and a roll of loose spaghetti under the other and invited me to supper. He said Dolci was with a Dutch photographer from Milan. He introduced Marius Hammer, a Swiss economist, and Birgitta, a Swedish girl, who was sorting leaflets. She was preparing a musical program for the *doposcuola*, she said, and had been asked to teach English to Sicilian adults, but was having difficulty learning Italian. She mentioned that Vicky had tripped over a body on the way to work the day before. Vicky was Josephine Bawtree, from Oxfordshire, who had given up a $60-a-week job with the United Nations to become liaison officer. A hand appeared from behind a door and hung a notice on a nail. The notice said, "Duplicating. Go away. Pasqualino." A peasant with a black moustache wandered in and said he was Ciccio; he had a message for Eyvind,

Pasqualino Marchese

he said, about the well. He was followed up the stairs by a lean
Australian journalist called Lonnie. She took orders for lunch,
and said if I wanted sheets to see Piero. I explained that I was
not the new volunteer. Lonnie said the Center was invigorating
after the BBC, but that Partinico was hell for a single woman.
If I was going back to England, she said, would I please send
her a consignment of DDT. "There are two things in Sicily you
never understand," she said lightly. "One is the Mafia, and the
other is the Center." Later, when I became involved in it, I real-

ized that the confusion was more apparent than real; and also that a certain amount was necessary to Dolci.

A door opened and Dolci stood there. He blocked the doorframe. He was wearing the milky homespun sweater Lanza del Vasto had given him. One cuff was frayed and a button missing from the neckline. There was a friendly bear-like confidence in his greeting, and when he sat down, spreading his massive arms on the desk like tree-trunks, he spoke with a gentle authority. It was a serene, groomed presence—the close-clipped fingernails, the impeccably shaven oval features, the precise notes he made of all my questions—in almost clinical contrast to his unruly surroundings. The room had a minimum of comfort, the only concession to the twentieth century being a tiny watch which he disinterred from a mass of papers and consulted before sitting down. Workers slipped in and out, urgently, as we talked. He spoke in gusts, calm, equable statements; and the current of his personality came across the desk in minor shock waves. We talked, as I remember, mostly about folk music; in fifteen minutes he gave me more valuable information about peasant life than I would have got from a month in Palermo. Once, when I asked about his beliefs, he jumped up and charged down the corridor to show me Einstein's declaration on human rights—it placarded a whole wall. "That," he said, "is my religion." Several things he did indicated that he was not altogether at ease amid the encroaching civilization of his Center; that he was not really a desk man. And yet, paradoxically, he was the groomed one—it was the wild thing. Or so it seemed. I remember he said, almost formally: "Everywhere you'll see poverty, suffering, ignorance. We're engaged, we're committed, and therefore we have to take account of the political means by which these evils can be remedied. We belong to the world of politics, but not to the world of party politics. Nevertheless, we believe the mass of people needs in its own interests to move Left, that is towards social and economic progress."

My main impression was of extreme gentleness and of a man utterly in control of his emotions.

Gerrit Huizer

That night there was a gathering at his home. Dolci had moved from Spine Sante to a modest apartment on the Corso, by Nightingale Street. A talented staff stood about, pressed into the small dining room, drank wine, discussed the various studies, sang spirituals, and, when Gerrit, the bearded cooperativist, presented a Dutch version of "Old Macdonald Had a Farm," sat on the floor with Dolci's children and clapped vociferously for more. Dolci's safety valve was a lean-to upright piano on which he played Bach and Schumann's *Scenes from Childhood* with a subdued pensive touch. Everybody went home early.

Partinico by now accepted foreigners, almost gratefully, yet
commented thoughtfully on almost everything they did. Partinicans never quite believed, for example, that Elsa was Gerrit's
wife: they said the couple *couldn't* be married, because they
went on picnics together. Some lived in the House of Volunteers, the rest in solitary rooms over muddied streets. Michael
Faber, the English economist, converted an empty flour mill
for his family. A Norwegian professor of moral philosophy,
Eyvind Hytten, who had given up a teaching post at Stockholm
University to become the new administrator, lived with his
wife Kerstin and two children in an abandoned farmhouse. It
was reached by gum boots and muddy cart tracks. Kerstin drew
all her water from a well. I visited Eyvind often, and later worked with him. His frail, candid features seemed incongruous amid
the devious channels of a high-powered action group. "It's like
walking on eggs," he said. "There are more snags inherent in
the work than you'd think possible. People say our whole system
of financing the work by voluntary aid is irresponsible—but then
the whole damn organization is irresponsible in a certain way.
There are always hangers-on. Many come in search—not because
they've found—and with different talents. Most have different
ideas. Naturally many go away again. We're bound to experiment. And it would be ingenuous to pretend that an initiative
like ours must develop automatically, without obstacles and
times of stagnation." Eyvind accepted the task cheerfully. His
boyish appearance masked a shrewd Nordic maturity and loy-
alty which were to temper despair and keep the whole organization from sliding over a cliff.

Soon the Center had moved uptown to an even bigger
building, a rambling white arsenal with walls a yard thick towards the Alcamo end of the Corso where Garibaldi had marched in. In May 1961 Dolci had a total staff of sixty-one.

The most valuable work done at this time was a socioeconomic study by Faber, Doglio, and others. Michael Faber
was a young Oxford economist who had been forced to leave a

university teaching post in Southern Rhodesia after opposing
the Government's racial policy. Carlo Doglio was an urbanistic
consultant responsible for the Olivetti community development
project at Ivrea. They typified an élite of gifted, sometimes
brilliant planners the Center attracted at this time. There were
also men like the Sicilian Giuseppe Ganduscio, a former union
leader in Ribera who had been forced to leave Sicily because
of threats from the Mafia. He sold his factory in Florence and
returned to work for Dolci, only to fall victim to cancer from
which he died in 1963. Vincenzo Borruso, the Sicilian student
who had worked at Borgo in 1954, returned to become the center's permanent doctor. A Canadian veterinary, Frank Manol-
son, arrived unexpectedly from Paris in a T-shirt and a battered
Volkswagen and began a rabbit-breeding experiment to raise
the meat consumption of peasant families whose average intake
was less than a third that of the national average.

The year began with the eternal worry over money—there
were no funds to pay half the salaries. By May the monthly debt
was $3,360 and rising. By July the Center was receiving only a
third of the money it said it was spending each month. Dolci
does not waste money; he uses it. Pre-1962, his cavalier attitude
toward it infected Center policy, though he was doubtless encouraged by the lack of a qualified treasurer. Even today the
Center hasn't *quite* discovered the need for one. The Center is
unique.

It was a strange world. You worked too long and ate too
little, and the water at Ciammarita beach was not refreshing
because there was too much salt in it. You had no privacy, worked
to no discipline, save what you imposed yourself, you had no
criteria because the conditions were new, and, apart from Dolci's
figures, which were accurate but limited, no statistics were worth
counting on. You found yourself swinging between exhilara-
tion and despair, and wondered how much *longer* the local Sicilians
would go on feeling abandoned, because Dolci no longer distributed old clothes in the weekends. You swore often, drank
too much heavy wine, and were comforted by the thought that

if you fell seriously ill the nearest good hospital was in Rome. You witnessed more quarrels, heard more screams, saw more mawkishness in a week than you had known in a lifetime. You began to lose your sense of humor. Perhaps you were becoming insensitive too. You created small frictions, unknowingly, among friends, and you tried to relax. But you couldn't relax, because of the noise, and because that sharp shouting Sicilian dialect was starting to annoy you. In six months you aged six years. A sort of blankness descended and you found yourself funnelled into a vortex of town double-talk and compromise which you never accepted, but never wholly rejected either because compromise often saved time, and time, somehow, seemed important. Sometimes you found yourself believing, along with Gandhi, that it was the reformer and not society who was anxious for the reforms. Gradually you found yourself becoming involved in a love–hate relationship with the place, and knew that when you left there would be deep nostalgia for this curious organization and these smelly streets. You wondered how in hell you had become embroiled in what was really a pacifist outfit, and then you remembered that behind it all was the inspiration of this plodding, moonfaced man who had such an unshakable belief in the basic goodness of human beings. You supposed that that was what kept him going. He neither smoked nor swore, and seldom drank, and worked harder than any three of you together. You waited for him to crack but he never did. He seemed to grow younger with the days. When you arrived you quickly recovered from his habit of calling you instantly by your Christian name; attunement to his use of the royal "we" and his habit of ignoring your private world and occasional love affairs took a little longer.

Above all, you realized in the summer of 1961, there were now too many individualists at the Center, when there was really room for only one, and that was Dolci, and sooner or later someone would have to go. But Dolci had a curious habit of retiring from open conflict and you were not quite certain how it would come about.

Thurber, in an autobiographical sketch, tells of an English teacher he suffered called Miss Groby. Miss Groby had a fetish for "the Container for the Thing Contained." It nearly drove James Thurber mad. Dolci has a comparable weakness—he invests some words with a quality of magic which the words alone do not possess—and in that summer of 1961 this had much the same effect on his team. It has to do with authoritarianism. Dolci dislikes discipline. Most pacifists do. Dolci dislikes the word and the act. He has always rebelled against authority, whether that of his father, of Don Zeno, the Church, or the State. He talks most of his father's "heavy hand." I have the impression that Dolci the reformer was born deep in youth, with the beatings he received from his father. When he pulled a cumbersome organization round his shoulders and lined it with ideas and personalities he realized that, to work in a group, discipline was necessary; but he shied at using the word. Instead of "discipline" he preferred "coordinate" (his title is Coordinator), instead of "control," "verify". . .words which did not have the ring of regimentation or fascism. He imposed the words but neglected to impose the actions they represented. In routine matters this is not serious, it is merely confusing. A volunteer, for example, told the Center would "contribute towards expenses" was never sure if this meant he would have his train fare refunded or merely enable him to get his shoes repaired free. But, as policy in time of internal stress, it evades a very real problem. For while you may easily verify a clan of unruly guests in your house, it doesn't necessarily follow that you have effectively controlled them or set your house in order.

It was the paralyzing effect of this Indian word-magic which split the Center.

While Dolci was in America early in 1961 a splinter group, Italian, vaguely anarchical, and Communist-aligned, grew up within the organization and consolidated itself on his return. It had a name and held its own meetings. Its influence proliferated, Faber's study was impeded, tempers became frayed. Instead of taking disciplinary action Dolci attempted to "co-

Michael Faber

ordinate." "Danilo is quite aware of a difficult situation," Ilys wrote, "but he won't order anyone off the premises....He's in a proper bloody mess." Meetings grew taut, outside pressure groups were involved; in the end nobody knew who was allied to what. Dolci appeared preoccupied. He seemed, in Ilys' words, "to be going round some curious bend." Part of the trouble was the insidious atmosphere of Partinico itself; almost everybody had become a little Sicilianized by it. Eventually, Dolci, with the help of Eyvind and Eduard, shrugged the group off, but not before the various side effects had undermined loyalties.

The Communist clique left, but the wound healed slowly. A procession of leave-takers followed over the next months—Ilys, Gerrit, Michael, Marius, Frank, Pasqualino. Some would have gone anyway, but at least three losses were conditioned by Dolci's ambivalence and his peculiar numbness in the face of the original crisis. "He will not impose himself on other people's personalities and activities—it is a disabling and not uncommon aspect of the pacifist complex," Waller had written prophetically in February 1960, eighteen months before.

Several times in conversation, remembering people who had served him, Dolci told me he had failed to "valorize them properly." By valorize he meant extract the best and channel it thriftily. He remembered them sharply, poignantly, little bits of guilt appearing out of the subconscious. He did not own to wastage. The one time I taxed him on it he said: "If I hadn't had the will to go on serving the area—I'm stubborn, you know —I'd have been all over the place. I know, I've been accused of being false. How many times! Because I tried not to destroy relationships with people, not send them away, and at the same time remain true to the needs of the zone and that which convinced me."

In that same summer of discontent Dolci announced his intention of going to Russia in the autumn. The trip was to be largely at the Soviet Government's expense. But coming on top of a trip to America—where prospects of a new committee and more funds were bright—it was likely to jeopardize the American feeling, and his colleagues advised him to postpone the visit to Russia. "But I'm not a Communist," Dolci said. "We know that, Danilo," they said, "but the Americans don't." They pressed him hard. He would not be budged. He went to Russia in the autumn.

If these things show an extraordinary *naïveté*, they also reveal a deep simplicity.

It is one of his greatest strengths. Dolci is a very simple man. He has made some extraordinary mistakes. Mistakes become stepping-stones. He casts off trouble like a skin and carries on. "I think this is one of the secrets why he has gone on for such a long time," Eyvind says. "He has this ability to just wipe out the past, just go on. This fantastic ability to forget, to forget good things and also bad things, to have neither bad conscience for what he did not achieve nor pride for what he actually did achieve."

Dolci also has the ability to draw people from the ends of the earth, use them, exploit them to the full, even exhaust them; he may tread on them, disillusion them, even forget their existence; but in the end the extraordinary leavening effect he exerts on the Italian intellectual world works its changes on them too. In the end he does change them. And usually they remain grateful to him. Many of those who left during the troubles of 1961-2 have written to tell me this.

Lamberto Borghi, an outstanding Italian educationalist and one of Dolci's first colleagues, has said: "Danilo is a man of power; there is a great original energy in what he has done, and it is greatly worth while to be associated with him, frustrating as it may sometimes seem. . . ."

Years before, at Trappeto, he had written a poem in Sicilian in which he said: "I must be that which I have never been." He had wanted to be a planner, an organizer, and was not. But if the rupture of 1961 showed he was not a planner it also showed, more significantly, that he was not a politician. More and more, I believe, as the world wears on and into the Orwell era, what it will need most are simple men, not politicians. Saints, if you like—but the human kind.

ʚ

ʚ XXV ʚ

ʚ

PRELUDE
TO A FAST

DOLCI has a demon in him. It is irrational and instinctive, and capable of lying dormant for long periods. When it is roused it has the voice of authority. People listen.

All the same it goes about its task methodically.

Dolci emerged from the rupture unscathed, his beliefs unimpaired, his passion for energizing and doing things undimmed. It is fairly clear that by 1962 he felt he was becoming chained to a desk. It irked him, administrative decisions bored him. Like Spartacus, the Thracian revolutionary, he was more acted upon than acting, and not always convincing. He was losing touch with the people.

A main reason for his coming to Partinico was the projected dam for the Iato River. It was the hinge of his plan for full employment—the project Faber and Co., and now Doglio, were studying. This depended on a chain of three irrigation dams, in areas where Dolci had sited his centers. One of these dams, on the Carboi River near Menfi, was built and in Mafia hands— hence the wastage and Michele's daily educational battle at Menfi. Proposals for the other two, the Iato and the Bruca, were mysteriously blocked.

In 1961 the Iato had been just another source of disagreement at the Center. One group declared the project technically unsound. Dolci barely listened. He had not invented the dam. Technically it was out of his grip. He was concerned with the moral issue. He had been morally involved for a long time.

Suddenly the issue came sharply into focus. Dolci decided to fast.

Once again there was division in the ranks. He was told his decision was badly timed, was undiplomatic.

Dolci had always believed that truth and acts of faith carry with them the seeds of their own best propaganda. Against the advice of his colleagues he carried on. He was convinced that he was right.

Had the thousands of acres of woods which once covered Sicily been spared by the early invaders, artificial lakes might not have become a matter of life and death to Sicilian agriculture. Water is a basic problem of all Italian life. In Sicily, the peasants say, "Water is another God."

Water is also important to the Mafia. It is a traditional lifeline. In 1962 Mafia controlled water supplies, selling the precious liquid by the hour at rates no peasant or sharecropper could afford. It controlled its "right" by syndicates, and defended it when necessary by force. Something as large as a $16,800,000 irrigation dam threatened to take control right out of Mafia hands and struck at the very core of one of its most ancient monopolies.

This partly explained the history of Iato.

Iato went back to 1948 when the Italian Government voted money for an irrigation project in Partinico. Dolci did not know this when he came to Trappeto in 1952 and broached a modest scheme using a forty horsepower pump. His scheme had grown to a $89,600 irrigation plan by the time he discovered, at Regional offices in Palermo, that preliminary plans for a full-scale dam already existed. He moved to Partinico, began an educational campaign, and, on frequent trips to the capital, was assured plans were "progressing." At the end of 1955, when two-thirds of the male population was out of work and there was still no executive plan, he fasted; 1,500 peasants signed an appeal asking for speedy action. Few understood then what a dam would mean. In 1956 the Region set aside $3,360,000 for initial surveys. Rome sent reassurances. "I was ingenuous enough then to accept the Minister's promises," Dolci says, "and for eighteen months or so I let things slide." "Slide" is typically Dolcian. In these eighteen months or so he went to prison, wrote two books, fasted twice, and held a congress.

A word is needed to explain what happens to public works in Sicily. Many are called for. Few serve—in any efficient sense. Since 1948 Sicily has had political and fiscal autonomy; but Regional public works agencies, like ERAS, the land-reform branch, are responsible ultimately to a parent finance body in Rome, the *Cassa per il Mezzogiorno* (Fund for the South), for special tasks. Dams enter this category. Usually the chain of command is such that between ERAS and the *Cassa* there is scope for deep incomprehension. No one can say accurately how much corruption devours public works departments in Palermo; but recently a regional deputy gave a fair guide. "They offered me public works," the deputy related. " 'No thanks,' I said. 'If I go there one of two things happens: I either become *mafioso* or I become a corpse.' " By 1955 the Mafia had influential friends lodged in all the furrows of public administration in Palermo. Government contracts were a prime source of profit—it could lift them or bury them, more or less at leisure.

In 1956 Dolci's correspondence on the dam weighed more than forty pounds. The following year the executive plans were finished, and finally, in 1959, the *Cassa* called for construction tenders. No Sicilian firm tendered. The *Cassa* called for tenders twice. There was no response in Sicily. The Mafia had let it be known it considered the dam "a bad thing." At this stage Dolci began to reawaken the fag ends of hope among the peasants— those who had not emigrated—and sent in his own technicians to check the surveys. Where technical advice failed, the bearded charm of Gerrit the Dutchman helped to conquer. But it was a tedious peasant-to-peasant drag. Then in 1960 a big Roman firm, Vianini, took up the contract. At this time nearly all major industry in Sicily was concentrated on the east of the island, away from Mafia intimidation.

The Mafia had two weapons at its disposal, fear and violence. It chose the former—fear of noncompensation. Peasants whose land would be flooded had a very real and justifiable fear of being paid "late and badly," as experience at Menfi showed. Menfi farmers, whose land had been expropriated for the Carboi reservoir, were not only still awaiting compensation but actually paying taxes on land and houses which had been under water for five years. The Mafia so indoctrinated the Partinico farmers that all ERAS' efforts at negotiation failed.

The dam was bigger than anything existing in West Sicily. It would flood a wide valley of vineyards five miles south of Partinico, ironically the best land in the area, but irrigate 25,000 acres of barren plains. Dolci's men calculated that it would increase agricultural fertility by 225 per cent, create between three and four thousand new jobs, raise income entering the zone by $1,400,000 a year, and encourage small-scale industry and processing factories, then nonexistent. Ten communes would benefit.

It was now 1961. In Partinico Mafia interests were controlled by a syndicate of big landowners, headed by a man called Centineo. It had its own technicians and its own lawyers. Its headquarters were a stone's throw from the Center. Dolci, unaware of the depth of Mafia infiltration, was in correspondence with Giulio Pastore, the Minister in charge of the *Cassa*. Dolci exhorted urgency. Pastore said there would be no further delays. Vianini sent down its top technicians.

A game of cat-and-mouse began, with four groups of specialists in the area—the ERAS technicians, Dolci's, the Mafia's, and Vianini's.

Left-wing unionists began campaigning for the dam. Dolci intensified his campaign. Construction materials arrived at Palermo harbor and airport. All seemed well.

Newspapers carried reports that work had begun.

In July Dolci announced his visit to Russia.

In August the Mafia produced its second weapon and opened fire.

At this time a series of water projects ringed Palermo province. The Mafia first attacked a dam on the Scansano River behind Palermo, being built to provide drinking water for the capital, causing damages of $1,400,000 in a night. Elsewhere workers' yards and quarters were destroyed. Engineers were frightened off. One had his car burned. A tugboat was damaged.

It then set its sights on Iato. On 12 August the house of a popular dam supporter and leading Socialist, Fiorino, was razed by fire, and his vines and fruit trees destroyed. Fiorino's land adjoined a property of Centineo's. Dolci warned Pastore of the explosive local situation. There were rallies, mass protests, investigations, assurances from the Regional President. A six-hundred-ton vessel which had arrived from France to drain the mouth of the Iato was damaged by a plastic bomb. Five watchmen were needed at all times to guard major equipment at Palermo. Intimidations, anonymous letters, threats, continued.

The war of nerves had the desired effect. Quietly, ERAS and Vianini withdrew their personnel. Concessionary contractors withdrew men and materials. Vianini later said they had found it "too difficult to continue."

By spring 1962, when the dam should have been half built, all activity had ceased. Not a pick had been lifted, not a stone turned.

Dolci was then in a Swiss clinic, on doctor's orders. He was overweight and bothered by recurring heart trouble.

In April 1962 the Italian Senate, after years of prevarication, agreed to set up a Commission of Inquiry into the Mafia; and the Home Secretary, Taviani, made history by becoming the first Cabinet Minister to deplore publicly the secret society. Previously it had rarely been mentioned by Government benchers, let alone discussed. However, having said that Mafia was a bad thing, Taviani then did about the Commission exactly what Pastore was doing about the news that his $16,800,000 dam had been muzzled—nothing.

Incredible as it seems, at the beginning of August 1962, fifteen years after it was first projected, only a handful of people had any idea what had become of the dam for the River Iato. Cataldo, the Mayor of Partinico, for example, told journalists he thought it was "well under way." The Mafia and politicians with vested interests knew. The firm of Vianini knew. ERAS and the *Cassa* knew. Presumably Pastore also knew, as Vianini were claiming $672,000 damages.

In a statement made about this time Pastore says there was "some delay." This was due, he explained, to a "unilateral modification in the agreements already taken as regards expropriation." It was, as Eyvind said, "an exquisitely political problem." One suspects that Pastore, who is a reasonable but not an inspired man, was in a delicate situation.

Dolci discovered it was a total Mafia situation in June. Returning from Switzerland he called at the *Cassa* and was told privately (not by Pastore) that the Mafia had threatened to throw bombs if Vianini's technicians even attempted to lay the foundations. He decided then to act, but kept his counsel for two months. In this period he appeared at the Court of Cassation, where the reverse strike sentence was finally quashed—though he was not completely exonerated: he was ordered to pay considerable costs resulting from the original trial. So far he has refused to pay any costs. He went to India, delivered a paper to an antinuclear-arms convention, and returned to cope with eve-of-publication alterations to a new book, *Conversations*, and a backlog of correspondence, meetings, VIPs to show round, and the usual flow of summer visitors, most of whom wanted to present, personally, a small check towards the work. One Sunday he took Vincenzina and the children to the beach. A visitor commented that he was working too hard. "No, no, it's quite normal," Franco said. "In the old days you'd never catch him taking Sunday off." Dolci then left for a world peace congress in Moscow (he completed his speech on the plane) and was away nine days. Immediately on his return from Moscow he announced he would fast for ten days in September. He had not fasted for five years. To Pastore, he called it "a protest and a warning," but it amounted to a nonviolent ultimatum to the Mafia. It was then the end of July.

Gaspare Centineo, president of the Partinico syndicate formed ostensibly to protect the interests of the farmers whose land would be flooded, was a wholesale merchant in fruit and vegetables. He was thirty-seven, Dolci's age, tallish for a Sicilian, elegantly dressed, with an overbearing manner and a bulking aggressive stare. Partinicans regarded him as Santo Fleres' probable successor, and referred to him as *"uno che sa scacciare le mosche"*—one who has a way of removing opposition.

When Dolci and Franco called to see Centineo on the night of 26 July at his warehouse, the syndicate headquarters, they noticed on the walls photographic maps of the flooding zone, prepared by ERAS, the same maps which the Center had tried repeatedly to obtain without avail; and a letter from the *Cassa* to a CD deputy in Rome, Calogero Volpe, reassuring him that the interests of the syndicate would be protected. (Volpe was a friend of the late Mafia Head, Don Calò Vizzini.)

All that Dolci knew, from his technicians, was that ERAS had offered $630 an acre for first-class vineyards and then more than trebled the offer; that the syndicate had demanded eight times the original figure, without consulting the majority of farmers involved, who were ignorant of the latest ERAS offer and many of whom were prepared to sell at $630.

Centineo arrived late, from the country, and was shortly joined by another man. "There's a lot of confusion," Dolci said. "We'd like to get the facts straight." Centineo replied heartily that to be against the dam would be "uncivilized"; their technician had made a report, consulted with ERAS—"We don't know any more," he said. Dolci probed patiently. "Could we see this report?"

"No, it isn't here. We haven't got the keys."

"Could we meet your technician? Where does he live?"

"I don't know. At Palermo."

"It could be important, this meeting," Dolci said. "Are you sure? You don't know where your own technician lives?" He appeared to smile.

"Look, Signor Dolci, it's useless to smile. I've told you to be against the dam is uncivilized. But I tell you something else—this land of ours is priceless. You say we don't want to reach an agreement——"

"No, I don't say that exactly. I say that from what you've just said, or haven't said, I'm not convinced you do want the dam built." There is something deadly about Dolci's quiet insistence. "I'm quite sure you want to reach an agreement, Signor Centineo. But it won't come if your prices are unreasonable."

"You've no right to come here and insult us. Who sent you?"

"Look, let's be frank. At the *Cassa* I've been told that bombs might be thrown. At Palermo the police persuaded ERAS to call off valuation surveys because of the threat to public order."

"We haven't said we'll throw bombs. We've said they'll have to walk over our bodies first to get on to the land." A moment later Centineo added, "We're organized."

"Well then," Dolci concluded, taking out a small ball-point and writing: "You say—one, "We are not against the dam"; two, "We want just prices for our land"; three, "At present we don't know how much we want for our land.' "

The man alongside Centineo sat silent and glaring throughout.

Reading a report of the meeting in Franco's typewriter next morning, I saw that Franco had added a postscript: "This sort of person is capable of anything."

A few days later Dolci received through a third person a warning from the syndicate. "Stop meddling," it said.

The Center was sharply divided. The critics counselled less haste and a less overtly dramatic form of protest than fasting. Old friends like Senator Parri were also sceptical. "This dam business is a typical tilt, Italian-style," Parri wrote. "Be consoled it isn't the only one. Bureaucracy and *camorra* run the whole of Italy today. Sadly, the most glaring examples seem to come your way. I don't agree with the fast. Not even the atom

bomb impresses people these days unless its bursts in their own
backyard. I would advise mass meetings. . . ."

"Dearest Danilo," a letter said, ". . . I can't imagine why you
stubbornly go on using a method which might have been effective thirty or forty years ago but not today when, so it seems, life
is no longer considered a precious gift from God, to be preserved
with the greatest care, but is thrown away with the greatest ease.
Frankly, I consider your gesture an attempt at suicide. How
easy it is to fall into heresy, even though one wants to do good,
when one loses sight of Christ. . . . With tender affection, Aunt
Agnes."

Eduard, away lecturing and raising funds in Germany,
wrote to say the fast was "ill timed," and told Dolci he feared it
would only antagonize the Government planners. Most of us
feared for Dolci's health. Franco feared for his life. Franco, his
warmhearted primitive shadow, became nervous and intense.
Only Dolci seemed cheerful, at times to the point of intoxica-
tion. He went about with his sleeves rolled up, and one day came
along in white ducks.

"If the dam fails our work in the area becomes useless,"
he told me during a long conversation. It was early morning,
barely six o'clock and already hot. We were sitting on the concrete steps outside his office. A few feet away eight big Red Bur-
gundy rabbits—the nucleus of Frank's breeding experiment—
crinkled fretfully against the netting of their cages, waiting for
Angelo, a Sicilian poet who came twice daily on a bicycle to
feed them. The bump of mule carts and the shouts of the cowherds, milking their animals from door to door, rang clearly in
the white morning.

"The greatest lack here," Dolci was saying, "is a lack of
faith in progress. Each man is alone. This is the cause of the
greatest depression. The Sicilian is a man like any other who
generalizes from his own experience. A man whose experience
has always been of a static society makes the generalization that
progress never occurs; he remains immersed in an ancient cul-

ture in which the distinction between power and truth is not yet made. But it's enough to show this man that progress is possible. . . .

"Our aim—we're not creating a pastoral idyll—our aim is to be a complex of pilot services of quality, to encourage the greatest possible development, and to be assimilated by local initiative."

"You may be overtaken by industry first," I suggested.

"It's possible. But there's a problem of quality and a problem of acceleration, and they have to be seen together. A new economy would naturally favor the development of a new (non-Mafia) culture. But this *isn't enough*. It's necessary to live and work in a direction that opens the way for new moral standards. You see, this is why a dam is so important. These people who are used to looking on the summer as an enemy that burns the earth, will find that the summer, with water, brings new life; what was dry, yellow, will become green. The water is important for their *hope*. If the dam doesn't come it means for these people groping in the dark for years, for decades of years to come, and this would be senseless."

"You're *convinced* about fasting again?"

"You tell me a better way to act so that everyone shoulders his responsibilities. Words, speeches, don't convince. But people who've known hunger, they understand—they feel compelled to take up a stand, as men, a position 'of courage.' And then the thing deepens and spreads——"

He gave me the best part of two hours. He spoke without rhetoric, and chuckled once when he said: "I'm not looking forward to fasting again, I can tell you." It was impossible to tell then that he was really frightened, but later it showed: he began to drop things, started when the telephone rang, and moved everywhere quickly.

I mentioned the fast to a mechanic I knew. He was underneath a truck at the time. He stuck an oily head out and said, "How long for?" "Ten days," I said. "Ten days?" he reflected.

"Ten days—without *living?*" His eyes radiated an expression of intense pity.

At that moment I understood. Others became convinced in much the same way. As the humanizing effect of Dolci's conviction spread through the Center, all scepticism vanished.

It was then 2 August. Dolci would stop eating on 7 September. He had barely five weeks.

Five weeks is not a lot of time to organize a campaign; not if you have to recharge from a cold start all the static particles of Partinico and district, then Palermo and then Rome, and at the end have only ten days flat on your back in which to alienate a vicious pressure group unconcerned with rules, so that all the various other bits fuse and create action. Simply, on 2 August the beacon of hope was thoroughly doused; there were five weeks in which to gather kindling and fire it; and ten days to fan it into a roaring blaze. This was Dolci's task.

He had a team of ten. Altogether he had 54 workers. But 44 of these were engaged on other essential tasks. He made do with Franco, three social workers, two technicians, two part-time office girls, a mailboy, and a liaison officer. Only Franco could type faster than 25 words a minute. He had one weapon: publicity. He used it.

Correspondence on the dam, covering nine years, now weighed some sixty pounds. In four weeks this doubled.

Thousands of letters, telegrams, phone calls, declarations went out to committees, newspapers, politicians, university and cultural bodies all over Europe. The declarations were duplicated. The letters Dolci wrote by hand early in the morning, while the others slept. As the incoming mail bulged, stray visitors to the Center, those with a gift for languages, were pressed into temporary service. "Would you mind translating this?" Dolci would say, piloting them to the nearest table. "I'll be back in a minute." He would reappear half an hour later, having attended a meeting, made several phone calls, seen the mayor, and trotted down to a bar in the Corso for a glass of milk. In this way he gained an extra liaison officer, a New Zealand school-teacher on holiday, Diana Fussell, who came for the afternoon and stayed three months. He sent out four workers on foot and by car. They were told to sound Mafia intimidation, clarify the compensation muddle, and marshal support. There were about seventy organizations to canvass.

Most of the landowners were scared. It was thought that only a few hundred were involved. It turned out that there were more than a thousand, many of whom, owners and part-owners of three- and four-acre strips, were illiterate and could not prove their land titles. And as Pippo, the Sicilian technician, discovered, how can you be sure you have won over a peasant anyway when, in one breath, he says enthusiastically: "Of course we want the dam—water's so short we dole it out to the kids like medicine, a spoonful at a time—and, in the next: "We say round here that those countries which have water all the year round have a different God"? Encounters had a tantalizing poetic flavor. At one gathering of peasants the following exchange took place:

"The dam will never be made, never, never. If all the Mafia at Partinico die, then perhaps it will be made."
"Water in Sicily controls man most, not Christ."
"What's the use of one man fasting?"
"Look—if there are a hundred sheep and there's no shepherd, what d'you do?"
"What a lot of rot. What d'you mean?"
"He's talking in riddles."
"No, he's not, he's talking about the sheep and no shepherd."
"But there *is* a shepherd."
"Who?"
"Yes, who?"
"Ah-h-hhh—you mean Danilo?"

Sometimes there were as many as seven meetings in a day. They began any time from six A.M. on, and involved every political, municipal, and student body within a radius of thirty miles. Dolci went to every one.

Encounters, however slight, were summarized, typed in triplicate, and discussed. These impromptu digestions took place with Dolci wherever he happened to be—in the corridor, at home, on the beach, in cars, cafés, newsstands, and barbers' shops.

He relaxed sometimes, driving to the meetings, and did not seem worried by the fact that the country roads over which he drove almost daily were visited by masked holdups which occurred regularly throughout the summer. He drove slowly, for an Italian, expressed a morbid fascination for prisons in passing villages, ate vast quantities of fruit which he bought from roadside vendors, and discussed tonal gradations in the landscape at every opportunity. Everything was scheduled to the minute. He allowed himself one luxury outing. This was an early morning drive to Scopello, a secluded tuna-fishing inlet beyond Castellammare Bay, a mile-long swim, a hill climb to admire the view, followed by breakfast at seven-thirty—fresh bread, soaked in oil, salami, figs, and lemonade. Dolci managed a loaf by himself. He led his companions on an architectural tour of a Saracen tower and ended up with his back against a boathouse, a beaming human ladder, while the others clambered one by one onto his shoulders, so they might peer down at the ark-like craft within. He changed on the roadside and drove thirty miles to Alcamo, arriving at nine-twenty-nine, a minute before the meeting was due to start. When it was over he drove straight to another meeting at Partinico.

Frequently he arrived back at the Center to find a busload of visitors waiting. Once there were forty German boy scouts sitting patiently in the courtyard. He would give more time to youth groups than to important visitors. If the VIPs were also pressed, he would take them along to the next meeting and chat en route.

Almost every meeting began late, at least three mayors

failed to show up to appointments. Lack of punctuality was the only thing that riled him. "And yet," he would say, more in sadness than in anger, bustling along the street, "how can you expect these people to conceive of the value of time when they don't yet know the value of human life?"

A meeting at Montelepre was arranged with the town councilors and unionists. He arrived punctually and was told: "It's the *festa*. They've gone to the races." Sighing, he walked up to the square and spoke to some men outside the café. A crowd gathered. He held his meeting impromptu. After a little he said: "What would you think of a demonstration to urge that the problem of water be resolved in the whole area?"

"If there were plenty of people the Monteleprans might join in," a peasant said. "If they could split up, lose themselves."

"*Lose* themselves?"

"Yes. The syndicate's got 'friends' here too—in the council, everywhere."

"But aren't the people concerned about water?"

"Yes, they're concerned," a student said. "When there's no water the women stand outside their doors and start praying, saying the rosary. But then, we know our people here. They wouldn't join a demonstration."

"What about students?"

"There are only three of us. I'm one. There's—but he's no good, his father's *in* the syndicate. I'll see if I can talk to the other one. . . ."

I saw Dolci give way to frustration only once. He became withdrawn, hunched into himself, almost tearful. He was trying at the time to get in touch with Bertrand Russell in Wales. He had booked a call via the fish shop, which was also Partinico's telephone exchange. The operators were two matronly fish vendors whose talents lay in that direction. It was difficult for either of them to believe that anyone in Partinico really wanted to converse with a philosopher named Russell, telephone number unknown, at a place called Plas Penrhyn Penrhyndeudraeth.

The call was kept in for three nights and cancelled in despair.

Cables and letters of support were pouring in daily.

The temperature rose steadily. For three days it hovered round 137 degrees in the street. Villagers walked the squares at night, unable to sleep. Hillsides of vineyards ignited spontaneously. The earth turned a sickly brown. Twenty of the rabbits died one noon, cooked alive in their cages.

There was no respite. While Italy went on holiday, discussions continued at the Center behind closed windows. To open them let in the *sirocco* which fanned the air like a furnace blast and made you want to faint. A vinegary smell, from a waterless lavatory and too much disinfectant, pervaded every room.

Dolci's occasional habit was to bound into the passage, seize you by the arm, and whisk you into his room, where you would be handed a summary of the latest meeting and asked for an immediate comment. For this reason it became rash to visit the toilet—it faced his office which lay three steps beyond. He worked facing the open door, his white shirtfront filling the frame, his head bowed over mounds of paper, and a spray of small blue-black ballpoints which he steadily wore out, one by one.

Eduard wrote from Switzerland, advising closer contact with Rome. Eyvind replied: ". . . a hundred different things are happening at one time. . . . Danilo doesn't do anything else but keep in touch with such people, La Malfa, Pastore, and so on. Yesterday he saw Gatto in the morning, Dragone was here in the evening, Gassman wrote a long letter, and I don't know how many phone calls went through. Now we go to the meeting in the town hall. In the afternoon a meeting to inform all the collaborators of the situation; tomorrow morning the monthly general meeting as usual. . . ."

Dolci was on a heart diet, but this—heavy on greens, light on sugar and salt—was about the opposite of a recommended pre-fast diet. He would disappear for sudden bursts of physical exercise and on Sundays appear briefly at the beach and plunge into the buoyant Tyrrhenian Sea, his tremendous flailing stroke outdistancing the other swimmers until he was almost out of sight. He would hurl quoits around violently and then lift one of the children on to his neck and meander away to the end of the bedraggled foreshore.

Gradually the whole Center was drawn in, subservient to his will. If the atmosphere at a meeting was cold he broke it down by getting the peasants to sing. Vincenzina seemed pensive. "Do you have any say in all this?" I asked one night over supper. She smiled good-naturedly. "Beh-h. . ." she said. "If I did it wouldn't change him, would it?"

Dolci informed Pastore of his plans, step by step. "If it is now understood in Rome that this work is in the public interest let construction start without delay," he wrote early in August. ". . . If the *Cassa's* authority be insufficient to deal with a small but powerful pressure group, let the Home Secretary intervene. As everybody knows the police force is the only thing in the area which is not underdeveloped. . . ." He added that popular pressure would be brought to bear, coincidentally with the hunger strike.

On 11 August Pastore sent six lines in reply. He asked Dolci to be "reasonable." Apparently it was hot in Rome too.

Dolci invited Pastore to the demonstrations.

September began with no further word from Pastore. *L'Ora* remarked: "The *Cassa* hesitates. While the Regional Government has, for some time past, been sleeping profoundly."

About half the provincial organizations canvassed pledged support. From the promises everything, or nothing, was predictable. Dolci had two elements in his favor. One was the recent rise of a center-left Government in Rome, tentatively pledged to social reform and representing the best change in Italian politics since Mussolini was shot. Diehard Christian Democrat Ministers were still in office, but the coalition contained two influential allies in Ugo La Malfa (Republican), the passionate Minister of Finance and Planning, and, ex-officio, a dynamic architect, Bruno Zevi, a member of the new commission for national economic planning. The other factor was the continuing heat. Water was short from the Po Valley to Puglia, and what had become the most punishing summer in twenty years promised to heighten Partinico's thirsty appeal.

On 4 September Dolci went home early and rested. Next day he had a light fever. On 6 September, the eve of the fast, he had a light supper of minestrone, salami, cheese, and olives. He ate fruit, drank water, and retired at ten-thirty. He slept well.

FAST
FOR A DAM

VIA IANNELLO is a crabbed and broken street 50 yards long and about 9 feet wide in the heart of Spine Sante. Number Six is a one-roomed hovel streaked with blue paint, a reminder of the Moors, like all the rest. When Dolci left Spine Sante in 1960 he installed a television set here for the quarter and kept the room for meetings and conversations with the peasants. It is here that he fasted. In the evenings the street is so cluttered with the poor and the contagion of the poor that a stranger might be forgiven for thinking he had stumbled on a desiccated reincarnation of a scene by Brueghel the Elder dating from the sixteenth century. Figures sit out amid hencoops and mule carts, eating, shouting, gesticulating, dozing, and every so often one will dart forward and scoop a yowling child out of the mud and, until the light reflecting off the blue-wash walls turns indigo and it is too dark to see, pick the day's lice from its hair. It is a street of inertia. Occasionally a resident is removed to or discharged from prison; this causes no surprise. On the corner of the next street, Via Giannola, is a fountain which serves 150 families. At night the families bolt themselves in behind enormous wooden doors. But for the light burning over the Madonna and the leaden gleam of pasta pots impaled on the stone walls these rooms might be dungeons.

Dolci came down to begin fasting at six A.M. on 7 September with Cielo, his eight-year-old son, and lay on a crumpled bed facing the door. The neighbors cried out that only the dead lay with their feet pointing that way, but Dolci said he wasn't superstitious and asked Franco to bring some DDT. Cielo fetched a bottle of water from the fountain and shortly Osvaldo, the mailboy, brought along a pile of telegrams which he put on the table by the bed and some of which Donna Filippa later mopped up when she cleaned out the room. There was a table, a partitioned hole-in-the-ground, a couple of posters (including Einstein's declaration), a pocket mirror by the door where Dolci shaved at five-thirty every morning, and another bed where Franco slept; this bed was always covered with press clippings and bodies, so that until ten o'clock when the door was shut (the only way to get the visitors out) Franco became a sort of homeless lamppost, ministering dazedly to the wants of all, but especially to Dolci whom he cared for as a mother. Their mutual understanding, joyous and intimate, evoked memories of older days when there were just the two of them, no Center, riding out together on a painted motor scooter, sharing the bloom of discovered stories in the wild virgin places. Vincenzina came every day with the children, but usually stayed in the background, shyly, as if not wishing to intrude. The room normally held ten, in comfort. When I arrived that first evening the only uninhabited part was the hayloft above Dolci's bed where in 1955 he had hidden the unionist, Salvatore Comparetto. After that there were never less than seventy people in the room, ten and twelve hours a day. The stifling heat continued. There were always flies and television cameras with flood lamps full on the bed, and it seemed rather pointless when on the third day Franco entered triumphantly with a fan, five inches across, to blow the air round. "*Macchè!*" an Italian journalist gasped, after two minutes in the room—"*What* air?" I saw Dolci grow impatient once, when a photographer's lamp blinded him, and he cried out sharply.

My view is necessarily one-eyed, because I saw events almost entirely from within, living between the fasting-room, the post office, and an improvised base at Number Ten, Dolci's old house. What follows is the result of daily conversations with Dolci, in diary form, because it happened that way:

FIRST DAY Dolci is violently attacked by Government Party organ, *Il Popolo*, in Rome. ("This Danilo Dolci who fasts —or pretends to; who in fact checks on him night and day? —is flanked by national and international communism. . . . The dam will be delayed just the same. . . .") This angers some of the mayor's local Christian Democrats, but Palermo CD headquarters dissuade them from retaliating. Hereafter no official or Right-wing paper mentions the fast.

I suppose about two hundred came today. One was a Communist regional deputy. Most of the seventy deputies in Palermo know our work, but —even on the Left—there's still diffidence. The mayor came. He heard on the radio that the Regional President and ERAS were behind the dam—not the fast, of course. I'd like a Government representative here for the demonstrations on Sunday: at Rome they say it's the Region's responsibility, and the Region says Rome is responsible. I'd just like them all to get together and say things very clearly.

I'm more relaxed. It's Franco and the others who do the work now. I'm curious to know what people think about the fast. Vincenzina is—she's resigned to these things. She didn't eat all day. I saw she was pale and then I asked one of the children and she didn't want him to answer me. There used to be a picture here, a Chinese picture. Ask Franco to look for it, would you? There's a vine with a leaf, and on the leaf are eight characters. I'm told they mean: "If you look ahead ten years you plant trees; if you look ahead a hundred years you plant men." It's very dear to me . . .

I wrote to my father three weeks ago, just saying things were going badly and that "a rather strong intervention" would probably be necessary. (*Smiles.*) He'll have already understood what's happening . . .

SECOND DAY Dolci discusses the demonstrations for tomorrow. Saragat and Russell send messages. Sicilian news bulletin announces the fast, the first authorized mention by state radio of Dolci's activities in ten years. He drinks two litres of water daily and is rigorously controlled by a Sicilian doctor.

There's something hard, something angular about Russell, but he's a man without vanity, with tremendous capacity for looking ahead, almost prophetic. This is what persuades you. Abbé Pierre is another who has this limpid vision.

A few key farmers came—none of the big landowners. (*Chuckles.*) I don't think they've any intention of showing the slightest solidarity.

This isn't like the other fasts. I feel a transition—from private to public action. Let me explain better. *If* we'd managed to work more profoundly there would have been no need for this fast because the political forces would have carried the work forward by normal means. But we haven't been able to make this happen. And so now it's become necessary to do violence—nonviolent violence.

My head's spinning a bit. It makes you ill when there are a lot of people. Evenings are worst. Franco's a rock. I found him in a night school—I told you. He was like a younger brother then; now, we're just brothers.

Some say this is theatrical—photographers, journalists, publicity for my books, so on. Often it's not the moments of publicity that are the best. Often there are those moments, dark, dark, when you work—as the mystics say—alone with God; those moments when everybody betrays. Those are the dark painful times. Those are the times when life is carried forward. Once I believed in "silence"—I didn't give enough importance to publicity. I'd taken up an attitude of direct contact with God, that is, with Truth, if you like. But then I came to understand that it wasn't authentic if it didn't come through men ... The important things for humanity are two or three. Once you've understood these, it would be stupid to go on thinking about them; you have to *do* them. And there's no need to say what they are.

We know them ourselves. Why is it necessary to do these things? Because the moment they start to preen themselves they become almost sacrilegious ...

About publicity: if more people read my books because of the fast I'm pleased. We don't write a book to amuse ourselves —we write it because it becomes an instrument for action. For me it's always an instrument. There's a need to clarify a situation, an argument, and a book is born. When a book comes out I keep it on my desk, it pleases me, but after a month I put it behind me. Personal attacks don't matter. They can spit in my face or say bravo. The important thing is that they should get together and get the dam built. Things like that article in *Popolo*, they make me sort of smile. And then I think that things which are *so* mistaken can provoke a reaction, and from this reaction other things take fire.

It's when there are friends who don't understand—then it's really painful. Yes, this time it's happening too. I don't know why it should be like that. Perhaps it's a form of conflict between a part of us—I don't know. I must think about it ... No, publicity doesn't give me that inner joy. The deep joy comes when I see things being transformed.

A late wire: "Tomorrow is the vigil of the nativity of Mary. May this anniversary bring concrete and visible hope to the people of Partinico and of all Sicily—Giorgio La Pira, Mayor of Florence."

THIRD DAY—SUNDAY Bruno Zevi chairs press conference attended by all political parties and national correspondents. Mafia plants claque and shouts down mayor who is also disowned by his own party for visiting the fasting room. Eduard, back from Switzerland, brings the news:

Marvellous! Now I really am *for* the fast, Danilo. It was very funny. They all began by attacking you and then got annoyed with each other. When they isolated the mayor all the journalists, even those of the Right, got so angry they issued a statement in your defense. Then the whole atmosphere changed

1962 FAST, THIRD DAY: *Dolci marches grim-faced in a 2,000-strong procession, is on his feet four and a half hours.*

—they forgot the fast and began crusading for the dam, which is exactly what we wanted. When I left they were all fighting to climb on the bandwagon ...

Afternoon: meetings, marches, speeches in Piazza Garibaldi from neoclassic marble dais, symbol of waste in Umbertine Italy. Regional Secretary for Agriculture speaks, politely ignoring the fast. Anti-Mafia posters displayed. Dolci marches grim-faced in 2,000-strong procession; is on his feet four and one-half hours. Mafia and Catholic organizations distribute pamphlets denouncing Dolci. No incidents. At night Vincenzina brings his slippers. He says his trousers are too loose and asks for a smaller pair.

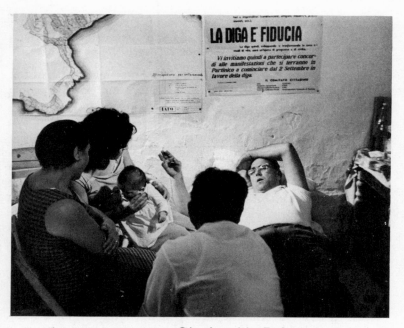

1962 FAST, FOURTH DAY: *Giustina visits Dolci in fasting room. The poster reads, "The dam is faith in the future."*

I'm not exactly content. Today was a confirmation. You see, in Italy all the political parties are eaten away by rhetoric. I think at the conference they were moved by a desire not to remain alone.

There's one thing: they say I'm out to line my own pockets, that we stand to gain eight per cent of the value of the dam—that's about $1,344,000. It's absurd. Some people think the money for the dam is coming from the President of Switzerland. They haven't even all got the same *mistaken* idea. But the whole town is talking; that's good. I don't think the Mafia will risk anything now. The Mafia strikes in darkness, but if you throw a sheaf of light on it there are always reflections.

I feel fine, still fine. Something's moving ...

FOURTH DAY Mafia whispering campaign, joined by Arch-priest, gathers force: "Dolci's getting a million .. 5 million dollars." Messages from Moravia, Levi.

A pity hatred's being worked up ... Last night my eyes felt dry inside—better now. Several things moved me. At first people just came, like that. Now they're hugging, kissing me—strangers. A man came, factory worker, from Palermo. I'd never seen him before. He brought a melon, for my children.

You saw Giustina. The woman from Trappeto whose baby died. She wants help for the passport, to join her husband in Germany. She's terribly sad—leaving four children, farming them out to sisters. Doesn't want her husband to be alone. When husbands leave their wives behind they forget them. This large-scale emigration, it can be harmful in the long run. Did you know the resources of this area are sufficient to provide an extra one and a half million working days a year?

The doctor is giving me antitoxin injections—lack of sugar. But look, I can still hoist Cielo up with one arm.

FIFTH DAY Government intervention assured within a week. Dolci still able to sit up at a table writing for two hours in the early morning. Acidosis worsens, but he refuses sugar solution. Mail includes letters from strangers in America and a London postman.

You have to get up, staying in bed makes you weak. Last night I went to sleep with a sort of tension. So much activity. This place is practically a public office. This arm's all numb. The injections help. The only thing I don't like, I know I've got bad breath—it worries me a bit when I talk to people.

My father wrote. He hasn't understood. He talks of "irre-sponsibility," and ... why am I telling you this? It caused me great pain. His generation—it didn't hesitate to leave wives, children, to go to war. They felt *this* to be right. And now my father says to me, "This is tragic irresponsibility—you're not thinking of your wife and children." But *how* I think of them! And we—I— others— do this, which isn't going off to kill anybody ... because we, even the children, are living in a new world with a new morality. In a short while it won't be possible to live if people haven't acquired this new morality ...

SIXTH DAY In the night Mafia destroys all crops on property of a dam supporter. Injections no longer control toxic condition; doctor orders five per cent sugar solution, otherwise coma within one day and death within three.

The rumor that we're speculating is growing yet. Now I understand that people can feel wounded, thinking we're getting thousands ... And when you think of the conditioning of Sicily it's quite legitimate they should think a person acts only for self-interest.

You asked about Don Zeno. He used to read—for example, the Bible. Had a fantastic ability to suck the essence out ... Used to read three lines, then close it and put it away, and I used to say to myself: "Why doesn't he go on?" Then I realized. When he found something important he'd make it a part of his life before he went on—the highest tribute to truth. He couldn't admit the possibility of knowing a thing without acting on it. That was the most powerful lesson I learned at Nomadelphia.

Franco's gone to investigate this new crop outrage.

Franco returns and types his report: "The man is a smallholder, open and courteous. He said: '... why did they cut down those vines? Couldn't they cut down the ones I've got at Giancaldara, where it would have been easier to cut them? We've got a saying—it's the gentle ox that pulls the heaviest load. They say that Danilo's getting eighteen per cent on the dam. Is that right?' ... 580 vines and five peach trees destroyed. The property borders on Centineo's ...'"

My thoughts are of work. Above all, work. And decisions. Nothing from Rome. I'm content, not happy. Content.

It would have been better to do without sweetened water. But if I got a cold I'd take aspirin. Still feel strong ... You know that when you "die of hunger" you don't die of hunger at all? It's a kind of poisoning you get. In itself a fast doesn't prove a

cause just—no. At the bottom is a desire for purification, im-
plicit; and it's true, that a man is purified by fasting. (*Chuckles.*)
It's enough to try it. But really it's a comradeship, an act of faith
—that others won't let you die without listening to you.

> The following letter comes from a woman in Tyddyn-
> Angharad, Merionydd, North Wales: "I wonder if it has
> occurred to you to get Danilo Dolci to take some of the
> Exultation of Flowers which I sent for the agricultural ex-
> periments ... You can spray the face, eyes, anywhere you
> fancy, but particularly the solar plexus ... Take the drops
> from the pipette frequently—if he will not drink that then
> spray very often ... When seriously ill give the drops every
> few minutes; if unconscious moisten the lips with it ..."*
> SEVENTH DAY Questions in the House. Pastore, asked the
> reason for the "frightful state of affairs" in Partinico, re-
> plies: "There is a halo of mystery." However, he says he
> will do something.
> The heat and glare of lamps is affecting everyone. Fran-
> co, a scarecrow, is almost a hospital case. Dolci's voice is a
> croak; his sentence structure periodically collapses. Peas-
> ants seem despondent and, out of respect, do not smoke.
> Dolci calls in children and has them sing.

> Strange, this business ... The atmosphere changes. Even
> the people change, physically—every day they seem more beau-
> tiful, especially the women with babies. There's a new light in
> their eyes, a special tension. They understand. There's a pro-
> found humanity in them.

> News comes that the Sicilian President, the Regional au-
> thorities, the prefects, the mayor, have left suddenly for
> Rome.

* Later Eyvind replied: "Our agricultural worker in Menfi reports that
... no result at all can be noted. He has therefore decided to discontinue the
experiment; also because he fears that the local farmers, whose confidence is
of prime importance to us, may fail to grasp the distinction between this
product and H_2O, and so believe that we are losing our sense of proportion.
The bad need for water in this zone, they rightly think, must be met on a
somewhat larger scale."

1962 FAST, SEVENTH DAY: *"Even the people change, physically —every day they seem more beautiful, especially the women with babies."*—DANILO DOLCI

This was one reason for the fast, that all the responsible people should get together. I've still got a doubt inside me. Someone asked if this will be the last fast. I think there will always be difficulties in the world and for the rest of my life I'll go on trying to solve them in the most perfect, most nonviolent way possible. A fast is part of a way of living. I always come back to thinking this, even if nobody knows about it.

Every so often I happen to take hold of one hand with the other, against the light, and it's thinner. One hand doesn't seem to know the other any more.

EIGHTH DAY In Rome the *Cassa* confers with all interested parties. Dolci keeps children out of the room.

1962 FAST, NINTH DAY: *Rome capitulates. Dolci, meeting with colleagues, agrees to start eating. On right, Eduard.*

Last night I calculated everything again. I thought, "Shall I stop fasting?" And then, "But they mightn't decide anything." Words aren't stones. We don't want promises, we want precise guarantees.

This morning I could only sit up writing for ten, fifteen minutes. Still think though, make notes ... Generally I write three or four pages a day. It's easy to express yourself, difficult to make yourself clear. But I've an advantage over most people —my colleagues. They reread, look over things, and then the small miracle of men thinking together happens again.

Evening: Unofficial word comes that an agreement is reached in Rome. Dolci is sitting up, working on draft statement to Pastore, when I arrive at 10 P.M. to bunk down alongside, and insists on getting up, shifting beds, table, to make room. Continues writing, discussing thoughts aloud until 11:30. He dreams; at 2 A.M. sends Franco scuttling outside at sound of police car, calling to make an arrest a few doors away. Dozes fitfully.

NINTH DAY Wakes at 5:30 as usual, rouses Franco; shaves. Polishes draft. Awaits morning papers anxiously; when they come reads Pastore's published statement: *Cassa* guarantees fresh valuation surveys, immediate compensation, and start of dam construction within five months.
After six minutes his voice goes altogether. He lies back.

I've called a meeting. Whatever happens we can't let up now. The Mafia will try and get in on subcontracting, try and wriggle in everywhere. The thing's not finished yet.
I think I've got a cold ...

10 A.M., all workers gather in fasting-room. Doctor orders Dolci to lie down. Dolci refuses and sits at meeting table, wearing a tartan choker. Meeting approves Dolci's statement and urges him to start eating again immediately as an "act of responsibility" towards the Government. At noon he breaks the fast with milky coffee, biscuits, and fruit juice, and goes home with Vincenzina "to sleep and think." Vincenzina is smiling.

Dolci had won, with a day in hand. In nine days he had forced decisions and actions from above which in the normal course of events would have taken years.
Bruno Zevi, one of the planners "from above," said: "Things are changing. Once I couldn't get the meaning of this 'fast' Danilo talked about, the mysticism and so on. Now he is deeply changed. He is grown-up. This fast was planned. It was the perfect mediator between the faith and belief of the population below and the apathy of the politicians above."
Eduard said: "Danilo transforms others. It's a kind of moral strength which can transform even politics."

The campaign drained the Center in the traditional way. In a letter to the Dolci Trust in London, requesting a loan, Eyvind described "our people here who are now making an involuntary fast because the voluntary one cost us half a month's budget. ..."
Dolci did not appear to notice the discrepancy.

1962 FAST, TENTH DAY: *Victory celebration in fasting room. Dolci borrows an accordion.*

On 16 September, the day after the fast ended, the people of Spine Sante threw a *festa* in his honor. Dolci came, wearing a blazer, played the accordion, and went home with flu. Vincenzina said he was "so weak he nearly fell on the floor." The following day, Monday, he rang the Center several times and worked by telephone. That evening he was seen driving, and on Tuesday was all day in Palermo. At five o'clock on Wednesday morning he was back at his desk. About noon he walked off in the direction of the sea, reappearing at two-thirty, having swum at a rock inlet halfway round the coast to Palermo airport, walked twelve miles and back, uphill, as far as the Trappeto turnoff, where he had felt a bit tired and hailed a lift the rest of the way from a motorist. He worked all that afternoon. The next day he went to Rome ...

The *Cassa* had pledged that work on the dam would begin by the end of February 1963. Dolci, in his statement of 15 September, warned Pastore that he would fast again if there were further delays.

On 27 February 1963 the contractors moved on to the dam site and work began. One of the first unemployed to be taken on was Sariddu, Dolci's former neighbor, who had been waiting sixteen years for a regular job. When I was last in Partinico scores of men were working in shifts round the clock. Soon the face of the dam would start to rise.

ON BEING ANTI

THE fast had a curious effect on Dolci's father. His is still an average Italian reaction, and it underlines the thorny—many would say the impossible—nature of the task Dolci has set himself as a political and moral educator.

During the fast Signor Dolci wrote to his son: "Millions have gone to fight wars, ethics don't come into it . . . the idea of destroying yourself in order to create is absurd." Waiting on a railway platform, between trains, Dolci wrote a long reply (later published in Clara Urquhart's anthology, *A Matter of Life*) in which he said, ". . . it is through ethics alone that humanitarian standards will finally be achieved, by feeding on the consciousness of each one of us." He added that public fasting was an ultimate weapon, to be used when all else failed.

Their friendly battle had been going on ever since Dolci left home.

Four months later, in February 1963, Signor Dolci came to Partinico, as he put it, "to scold my son." Franco drove him from the Center to Trappeto, to see Borgo di Dio, which Eyvind and his wife Kerstin, have converted into their home and one of Sicily's more relaxed villas. Kerstin describes a smallish, restrained man "with a certain nobility and a beautiful soft-keyed voice; a little white hair, and no impression of violence. You liked him immediately." Signor Dolci wore a suit, silk tie, salt-and-pepper overcoat, and remained standing. He stayed ten minutes. He told Kerstin and Franco:

Eyvind Hytten

"Everyone congratulates me for my son. But I'd be happy if he weren't my son, if he were somebody else's. I always come here to scold him.

"It's fantastic how the eucalyptus trees have grown. And how beautiful the iris blossom is! The almonds are finished, I see. It's ten, eleven years now since he came here to live among the poor. I thought he'd get over the idea. He had a blanket. He slept on it—there, in that corner. The blanket was too short, his head stuck out one side, his legs on the other.

"He's never had any money. He never learned to stick to

it when he got it. When he had the Lenin Prize I told him to make sure and keep half for his own children. Of course he gave it away, all of it. 'The money belongs to everyone's children and the children of everyone,' he answered.

"You can't imagine how my wife and I have suffered—him living in all this dirt, the poverty, the disease. The danger. Yes, yes—he's survived. We used to sit up there in the north reading about it, and . . . Why did it have to be *him*?

"It's true they're building the dam now. But, bah! Look at the sacrifice it's cost, the troubles; all this anguish. Of course, the work's organized now, there must be forty or fifty of you in your 'Study Center for——' whatever it is. We're thinking of his children. At least they're now living in a comparatively modern apartment, even if it is spartan. But children of eccentric parents will always have difficulties. How will it be for them later on with a father who has offered his life to helping others?

"The work *is* important for Sicilians. I understand that. Only I wanted someone else to do it. Now if it had been you, Franco—or you [Kerstin]—I would have encouraged and admired you. As it is now, I can only scold.

"I tell you one thing: when I read in a Christian Democrat paper that Danilo was fasting to earn thousands of dollars out of the dam, then I thought, 'Ah, at last! Finally a *sensible* reason for starving himself.' But, of course, it wasn't true, it was only newspaper bluff. I might have known. He's hopeless."

On this evidence alone it is not difficult to imagine why Dolci will remain an enigma to the Italians.

The fast did not confound the critics. But it won new friends—an exhibition in Milan to which leading national artists contributed raised $15,120 for the work—and blew away a little scepticism among still doubtful allies. Earlier Nino Sorgi, the lawyer, had remarked: "I respect Danilo very much. But have you ever seen any change brought about by one of Danilo's fasts? Never. He abandons struggles." This misunderstanding reflects merely on Dolci's bad public relations. Sorgi added: "The trouble is, he mistrusts political power." I doubt if Sorgi would say this now.

Dolci had now fasted seven times. His grass roots approach, "begin at the bottom" (pure Gandhi), had broadened; he was swaying the politicians as well as the people. He was protesting effectively for the first time. He was doing what his more conservative advisers, Eyvind and Eduard, had long wanted him to do—using the fast as political mediation while remaining uncommitted himself. Their only previous doubts had overlooked his instinctive genius for action. Now they were won.

Outside Sicily experts began to talk about "the Dolci Group."

Inside Sicily the unexpected happened. The Mafia made a mistake. On 30 June 1963 the Mafia booby-trapped an abandoned white Giulietta limousine in a Palermo suburb and blew up seven policemen and soldiers by accident. Even Sicily was shocked. At last the Parliamentary Anti-Mafia Commission woke up: it formed emergency police squadrons and began a purification offensive which continues today. Its latest victims include Gaspare Centineo who attempted to gate-crash a subcontract for the Iato Dam construction, was arrested, tried, and is now on parole under strict police surveillance; and Luciano Liggio, of Corleone, the youngest and most vicious *capo-mafia* in history. Officially credited with ten murders, Liggio had been at large for sixteen years. When arrested in May 1964 he was bearing false identity papers in the name of Gaspare Centineo. At his trial he said he had been using this name for sixteen years. Liggio is now in prison.

After eleven years Dolci's lonely battle had been joined by a nation.

Returning from a trip to Norway in July 1963 Dolci found that in his absence the Center had been raided. But nothing was taken. His Mafia dossier was safely hidden, elsewhere. The Commission prepared to call him as a star witness. When it did so he set off an impressive chain reaction by presenting, as a test case, sworn evidence of electoral complicity between the former gangster, Coppola, and the Partinico senator, Girolamo Messeri. There are some thirty affiavits, testifying to the help given Messeri by Coppola during the 1958 and 1963 national elections. The Commission thanked Dolci and invited him to testify again. Messeri called Dolci "a cad" and placarded the island with thousands of posters to emphasize the point. Shortly after this he was made Undersecretary for Foreign Commerce in the Moro Government. Coppola maintained silence. Dolci has not met Coppola, "though I dreamed about him once. I don't remember just what happened, but I know we didn't hug each other."

The Messeri–Coppola case made a furor in the press, and then apparently died. But it had created a new climate. It brought out, in a way that the Commission and therefore the Government no longer dared disregard, that the Mafia continued to survive because of a sophisticated political client system. In effect it publicly challenged the Commission to take its task seriously. The Commission has yet to make a full report to Parliament.

Dolci went on writing, lecturing, purifying. In the winter of 1963 he was in Britain, in the summer in Norway, in the autumn in Yugoslavia. His technicians watched the dam, giving the peasants free advice, doing the Government's work. *Waste* appeared in English. *The Times Literary Supplement* gave it half a page. Gavin Maxwell, writing in *The Observer*, said: ". . . to encounter anyone who found *Waste* boring would be to meet a moron." Norman Lewis in *The Sunday Times* wrote: "Dolci's resistance movement to the terrific story of exploitation told in this book is the one bright chapter in Sicilian postwar history."

Dolci turned more and more to his pacifist writings, clarifying his theory about group protests. "What's the use of working towards nonviolent education when a war will probably break out long before?" an Israeli economist said to him. Dolci replied: "The greater the popular voice, the greater the chance that those at the top will think twice. And even if there is no hope, *we* must act as sane people."

"For better or worse all my problems are problems of quality," he told me. "I'm all right in the big things; it's the little things that worry me." Little things irked him. Conferences at which delegates "smelled of onions and old underwear and talked of 'purity' "; fanatics who abused language and said things like "We must *work the masses up* into nonviolence." He sat at meetings in unflinching concentration, making marginal notes, despairing of small talk, smiling wanly at jokes, never getting ill. Once he had flu for half a day. "Not longer?" a friend said. "No," he replied, "I don't let it last longer."

Some people thought his task as a writer, as a poet of denunciation, was over. Basically it was. But he could not afford to relax. The social stagnation of Sicily had its counterparts all over the globe, in central and southern Spain, in Greece, the Middle East, in Latin America, and many parts of Africa. The idea of codifying a nonviolent technique with far-reaching influence preoccupied him. It was important, while maintaining an education framework, to knit his organization into a tight yet flexible pacifist propulsion-center.

"Dolci is no longer a Gandhi, he is more a Nehru," observers began to say. It was a fallacy. He did not have Gandhi's mistrust of technology nor was he the complete ascetic; but in all other respects he was more Gandhian than ever. He admired Nehru—"He is a man, a block," but Gandhi was greater—"Gandhi had no need of guns."

Christopher Driver has written that the reason the British anti-Bomb movement failed to develop organically is that the movement "never found a Gandhi." After many years the Dolci movement was evolving creatively precisely because it had one. But it was evolving in a way few realized.

There is a dogma that development agencies can work effectively hand-in-glove with established authority and with

the people, without ever touching politics. When an issue becomes political they tend to retire. This is the conventional
approach.

The dogma, Dolci's colleagues say, is "bunk." Dolci is more
polite. "Deep change is not possible this way," he says. He believes it possible for a technological agency to work in a political mold, towards a series of democratic explosions, without
ever aligning itself. Put another way, it is quite possible, even
desirable, to obtain democratic results by entirely undemocratic
means. This was the lesson of the Iato fast.

Having drawn the lesson, Dolci now proceeded to drive
it home.

In September 1963 he ticked off the irrigation map. There
were three dams—Carboi, Bruca, Iato. One was there, one was
coming, and one was wanting. The missing link was Bruca, on
the River Belice behind Roccamena, the dam in the geographic
middle.

Dolci fasted again. This time action did not come quite as
quickly as it had for the Iato. It took a day longer.

The bald facts are as follows:

Bruca, one and a half times bigger than Iato, had been
projected since 1930. Promises and plans all the way, but no
hint of action. Money had been set aside, only to vanish—diverted, during the 1963 election campaign. Dolci discovered
this in August. In September Roccamena peasants said they
would fast for one day. Dolci said he would join them and fast
for ten. He then went to Yugoslavia. When he returned he had
less than three weeks to plan the campaign. Roccamena was a
ghost town. Three-quarters of the able-bodied population had
emigrated. The administration had been in crisis since 1959.
Ignorance was such that peasants did not even have a word in
their vocabulary for "dam"—they called it "the big lake."

Dolci stopped eating on 26 October. Peter Moule, secretary
of the British Committee of 100, fasted with him. Small groups

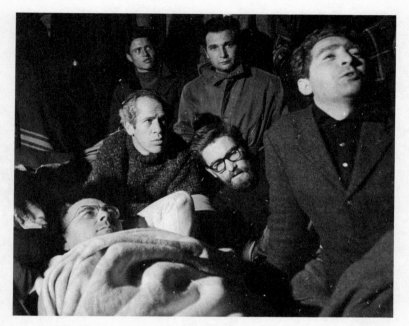

1963 fast for Bruca Dam: After starving for nine days, Dolci and Peter Moule joined a mass fast of friends and two hundred peasants, sleeping out in a village square. Dolci and Moule (bearded) shown here with author (in tweed sweater).

fasted in sympathy all over Europe. Dolci called for "precise guarantees" from Rome by the tenth day, 4 November.

The intellectual world backed him as usual, but for nine days the authorities kept their distance. Pastore was noticeably cool. On the eighth day one hundred fifty peasants began a 24-hour fast; at night half the square was filled with starving people. Dolci and Moule slept with them, lying out on a bed of hay. On the ninth day the whole village walked in symbolic procession four miles to the dam site. Women carried babies in their arms. Dolci and Moule went with them, still fasting and mounted. "Like Roland on horseback," an old peasant

*1963 fast for Bruca Dam: The following morning Dolci and
Moule rode four miles to the dam site. The whole village
walked behind.*

said. He was thinking perhaps of the folk hero Miraglia who
led a mounted cavalcade of peasants to occupy the Sciacca fiefs
in 1947 and was shortly afterwards machine-gunned to death
by the Mafia. This time the Mafia did not interfere. That ninth
evening the Regional authorities appeared in Roccamena and
guaranteed support. Rome came to life the following morning.
At five minutes to ten an official car drew up in the square and
two Government representatives alighted and walked into the
fasting-room with the pledge the villagers had requested. Dolci
had called for action "by ten-thirty A.M."

The jigsaw was complete.

Had I not seen it myself, day by day, I would have thought, as many must think after reading this, that it was all "arranged." But a moment's thought will show that no Government in the world *wants* to appear foolish.

I have no doubt that Bruca will be built, as Iato is now speedily being built. In a few years' time the Italian Government will boast an enlightened fifty-six-million dollar irrigation network from the steppes of Partinico to the Mediterranean coast which will be the envy of bigger states. And "how" it all came about will doubtless be forgotten, which in the long run is as it should be. For the moment, however, it should be remembered.

There is probably no man living who can galvanize deadened or recalcitrant human material as creatively as does Dolci. It is not so much that he makes the Government look sheepish. Rather, that he has perfected a technique of civil resistance which enables the people consistently to shame the Government into action.

It is a gentle way, the way of the peacebuilder.

It enables poor folk to become men first and subjects afterwards; and it allows foolish politicians to act at last and retain their dignity—and also the credit for the operation.

It shows that Gandhi is still the strongest part of him and that the French journalist's phrase, "*le Gandhi de la Sicile,*" is not a bloated fantasy. Gandhi pioneered passive resistance to external authority. Dolci has successfully extended it to internal authority.

He has repolarized the Gandhi system and given it a potential universal meaning.

One asks, how?

Dolci's policy is active nonviolence. This means positive development work, the work of the centers. But when sane development is blocked this also means positive action. Dolci's role changes to political catalyst. He calls up a kind of emergency pincer group. It compresses dormant or corrupt forces

towards an inevitable clash so that sparks fly out and a democratic transformation takes place.

It is a risky method, open to fire on all sides. In a way it is
absurd. But it works. One suspects that it needs supermen, but
Dolci and his colleagues claim that, as a method, it can be passed on. The Service Civil International, one of the biggest development networks in the world, agrees: it has begun to use
the method in Africa, working closely with Dolci's advisers.

The next step is the founding near Partinico of an international teaching institute for development workers. The
institute will be an ideological extension of the Center, but
a separate unit in which—desirably, I think—Dolci would not
have singular control. It would draw practical sustenance from,
for example, some of the very real community development
begun in Partinico in the last three years (four cooperatives
working) as a direct result of the presence of Dolci social and
agrarian teams.

At present his Center is the only place where any reliable
information on the sociological anatomy of the south and on
Mafia as a social phenomenon are available. But this primitive
archive is neither designed nor tempered to teach.

The Center is now a magnet for social scientists the world
over. They have long argued the need for a pilot institute. It
makes sense. One has only to glance at Southern Europe, and
the depressed emergent nations in and below the Mediterranean Basin. Sicily, in fact, is already a focal study point for the
Basin where, excluding Africa, twelve millions still live in conditions of total or semidestitution. Sicily itself is changing faster
than at any time before. But there are yet no deep changes. The
malaise of "outlawry" remains. The last of the big estates, Bronte, has only just been handed over to the people. The Church
sleeps on. The *per capita* income is still only half that of North
Italy. Half a million Sicilians, ten per cent of the population,
have emigrated in the last ten years; the emigrant trains to
Switzerland, Germany, France, Belgium, are still full. And,
while Mafia as a business racket may crumble, Mafia as a cult

—as an ideology of silent respect for "keeping oneself to one-self"—will persist: the cult of the lonely and the backward and the proud. Because of this the island will continue to provide the most disturbing, as well as the most fascinating sociological pattern of the age. Other countries contain one or two of the major ills of backwardness. Sicily, awaking fitfully from the wreckage of sixteen past civilizations, contains elements of them all.

"We even venture to suggest," Dolci says, "that some of the basic social problems of our more evolved societies could be resolved more easily through a clear analysis of the tasks we have set ourselves in this developing region."

A teaching institute, divorced from the Center but based on its methods, has long been Dolci's dream.

"We like to throw a lasso to the stars," Eduard says. But Dolci, unlike some reformers, does not seek refuge in dreams. He has always been a builder of dreams; but he has always been also an extremely practical visionary. He is one of the few pacifists who realize that to achieve a moral revolution you need organization and precise aims.

He is not ambitious in the normal way, neither for money nor social prestige nor political power. He *would* like to construct a worldwide pacific revolution in the hearts of men. It is consistent with everything he has ever said or done.

Paradoxically, Dolci's very consistency makes the future uncertain.

The illusion is that his Center will become respectable. The fabric of Italy's twenty-one development organizations has officially acknowledged its role. Angela Zucconi, the mastermind of CEPAS, the prestige Italian social welfare school, visited the Center in 1958 and was appalled; but recently she came again and revised her opinion. She is now an enthusiastic supporter. Vice-Presidents of the Common Market and Italian Ministers occasionally drop in.

However, the visitors seldom come officially, and when they do there is usually a row. La Malfa's 1963 visit, for example,

earned him a rebuff from Rome, presumably because in an impromptu speech he praised the Center and said he would like
to join its heroic band. (The speech reached Stockholm where
Ingrid, secretary of the Swedish Dolci Committee, distributed
hundreds of copies to friends, including the Italian ambassador
there. Next day the ambassador rang her, furious. "It's a mistake!" he said. "No Minister of the Republic would *ever* say a
thing like that." He told her to get a denial from La Malfa. Ingrid passed the message to Partinico. The Center cabled back:
"La Malfa speech tape-recorded.") Nor is Rome ever likely to
admit that its sudden dam-building activity south of Partinico,
for instance, has anything to do with a man who fasted. And
even if the Government does offer some official funds, Dolci is
unlikely to accept. He will take nothing "with strings."

It is safe to assume that in twenty years he will still be
leading a rebel outpost, aloof, independent, beggarly, and—when
necessary—against the Government.

Dolci's dogged antiauthoritarianism, the key to his character, puzzles almost everyone. One result is that, given his reformer's autocratic temperament, it makes for obedience, not inno-
vation: a surround of disciples rather than a welcome inclusion
of scientists with ideas as original and as valuable as his own.
In practice, however, this is not a grave disadvantage. Dolci
no longer attracts the ubiquitous Pasqualinos, the anarchical
Doglios, the unorthodox Gerrits, but instead less brilliant, quietly qualified people who are more constantly in tune with his
working methods. They are courageous, talented, hardworking,
sometimes enterprising—they are not yes-men. But they are
mostly Italian or Sicilian, and they are disciples. They understand Dolci as no northerner (without chagrin) readily can;
and he, them; and they are not tempestuously upset by his
foibles. Significantly, where once there were two foreigners in
the group to one Italian, now the ratio is reversed.

Dolci's preferred outlaw status is really a good thing. The
arguments in its favor, in favor of nonrespectability, far out-
weigh any disadvantages.

One is the pincer method. In the final analysis only a closely knit rebel group can exploit it.

Another is that there is strength in being uncommitted to either Church or political party. To keep his revolution open and flexible Dolci has never, amid the hothouse of Sicilian temptation, succumbed and crossed into any political camp. This is one of his more remarkable achievements, though it puts him on an uncomfortable tightrope. He knows that if he aligns himself, he stands to lose useful contact with at least half the population and runs the risk of being smothered by political embraces. Nonaligned, he thus remains open to varied commitment. His enemies call it "duality." But Dolci is in a rare position. He cannot remain strictly neutral either. If he sits on the rope, on the Sicilian political fence, he becomes by the very act of nondoing, committed. He plays directly into conservative (i.e., Mafia) hands. Fence-sitting of itself becomes a political attitude. Neutrality is impossible.

It is this openness of revolution, the continual experimenting, which has led to the pincer method. One really has, I suppose to thank the Mafia. It would be welcome irony if it turns out that a criminal body with a vested interest in social stagnation should have fostered a major advance in global humanitarianism.

There is a final argument for rebel status. Official chaperons require hard results in a given time. Development work is a more primitive field than sociology; it is excruciatingly slow; results cannot be measured in the normal way.

Five years ago, in 1961, there were three big development projects in southern Italy. One for the Abruzzi, one for Sardinia, and one for Sicily. The first was state-subsidized. It collapsed. The second was sponsored by the state and the OECD (Organization for Economic Cooperation and Development). It was flourishing, but it was on a time-expiry basis. When the time expired, it collapsed. The third was Dolci's private development project for thirty-five rural communes in West Sicily. This is the socioeconomic excursus (the *pianificazione*) elaborated by Faber, Doglio, and Co. in 1961–2; among other things it has helped shame the national Government into admitting the need for starting its own regional planning. Meantime it remains as a testimonial, the only one of the three which survives.

ψ

ψ XXVIII ψ

ψ

DOLCI'S TRAVELS

DOLCI is an incurable traveller. On tour he sows the whirlwind.

He takes no luggage, save a satchel, no entourage, no secretary—the interpreter does the lot—and if there is no committee to stand the expense he pays his way by writing a series of newspaper articles, usually at white heat, on his return to Sicily. If there is no interpreter available, he goes anyway.

One is reminded of Churchill's penetrating judgment of T. E. Lawrence: "A rare beast; will not breed in captivity."

Travel is necessary to Dolci. It is his safety valve, the only time he can let off steam (he nearly stopped the Carlisle express in 1963, trying to pull the emergency cord with his head), have fun, be a boy again.

Apart from the fund-raising aspect which is necessary to keep his organization afloat, he is driven chiefly by a restless empiricism. Part of him believes, with the folk hero Miraglia, that "a man should understand everything, know everything, comprehend everything"; and Dolci is an activist as well as an experimenter. He will not take "Yes," or books, or "Well, they do it this way there" for an answer, but must go and see for himself. So he goes to England to peruse the miracle of adult education, to Sweden to study the neuroses of overcivilization, to Israel to extract the benefits of communal farming, and so on. He meets community leaders, thinkers, planners, asks endless questions, allows the results to flow and fuse in post-tour discussions with his colleagues, and finally distills the essential experience into his life's pattern. The rest he forgets. If he sometimes carries this questing to the wildest extremes of time and space it is nonetheless Dolci at his most honest, most down-to-earth, and, his interpreters remark, his most human. A post-card from one of them is likely to read: "Danilo bright as a but-ton—very huggy—singing in the street."

This chapter is mainly about that *other* Dolci, the side seldom revealed, even to friends. He keeps his friends blocked off, compartmented with the facets of his personality. There are scores of Dolcis. It is one reason why he is so elusive, why one can never presume to know him.

Since he got the passport back in September 1959 Dolci has been to Britain (twice), India (twice), Israel, the United States, Russia (twice), Scandinavia, and the West European countries (frequently), Yugoslavia, Africa—every continent, in fact, except Australia and South America. He is sometimes away two months.

In 1960 and 1961 he took Vincenzina with him to Britain and Russia. She was not very happy with English food—some-one took them to a Chinese restaurant for a "traditional English meal"—so at Manchester Professor Waller gave her the run of his kitchen. She had "a whale of a time." In Moscow they went to the Bolshoi every night, and also to Lenin's cottage in the Kremlin, where Vincenzina broke down because "none of the crockery matched." She was surprised to discover how big Rus-sia was. "I thought it would be like Palermo," she said.

In Russia Dolci had trouble with his trousers again. He lost them in a hotel. Now when he is away Vincenzina writes regu-larly, begging him not to lose any more things.

British reporters liken him to a tweed teddy bear, a jumbo-sized Pickwick, a giant film star. In 1963 he arrived at London Airport wearing dark suit, habitual white shirt buttoned to the neck, no tie, beret, tweed overcoat, and thick woollen scarf. "Oh, isn't he *sweet!*" the *Daily Mail* woman said, jumping up and down. "How much do you weigh?" the men asked. "I don't know," Dolci said (he doesn't). His benign crispness and occasional patting gestures—he may clutch his listener just above the elbow and shake him, gently, to get the point home—endears him to the flintiest pressmen. Reporters are told his eldest child is nine and are perplexed when he says, seriously, that he is a grandfather (Vincenzina's eldest boy, Turi, has a child).

He is unfailingly courteous. Once in Sweden, arriving to address a meeting of Quakers, he found his audience sitting in silence, apparently praying. He tiptoed in at the back and sat down. After about half an hour somebody gave a violent snore, and the rest of the hall woke up.

He travels as he works, breakneck all the way, leaving a trail of shredded warm impressions which have magnified the myth. The saint legend is necessary, he realizes, but it embarrasses him. He studies his news clippings assiduously, but the question he always asks the interpreter is not "What do they say?" but "Have they understood?" His authentic *mana* is difficult to capture. But in Russia, eastern and other delegates to the 1962 World Peace Congress knelt down when he arrived; in London taxi drivers send crumpled pound-notes to the Dolci Trust in Gt. James Street and refuse to take any fare; in Switzerland railway porters do the same and slip money into his pockets; elsewhere exiled Sicilian barons turn up to his meetings and collect money at the door ... One is likely to be buttonholed in the most unlikely corners of Europe and offered hospitality merely because one happens to know him. People who meet him socially for five minutes become lifelong supporters, and BBC actresses donate their fee on the strength of slighter connection. Sometimes he has merely said "*ciao.*" Dolci has a way of saying hullo which makes it seem he is inviting you to a party. It is partly his books, translated into ten languages, but largely the alchemy of his epic personality. Even in a motor car he has stage presence. He holds audiences by a simple presentation of the realities. His voice is effortless. He stands stock-still on the platform, gazing benignly about and nods imperceptibly while the interpreting is going on. He has the knack of projecting his personality through an interpreter to the back of the draughtiest hall. Women tend to go ga-ga. Lionizing only troubles him. He withdraws from what he calls "the facile laugh" and "the nonviolence of the limp handshake" and says such things as: "You'd think it wouldn't matter, this saint business, but everything produces a reaction, and it's impossible to tell what the result of these inexactitudes may be."

It is normal for him to travel, second-class, three thousand train miles in a fortnight, with appointments timed to the minute every day and lectures on twelve nights out of fourteen. He burns up interpreters regularly. They adore him for it. Diana Fussell, his last interpreter, writes: "The best part was just talking in the train for hours and hours. I learned things about him I'd never even suspected—his sharpness, charity, humor, and especially a kind of wholeness that he has. ... I started the trip observing him, but finished up loving him."

Occasionally, at exhaustion or crisis point, when the interpreter breaks down and weeps, Dolci seems bewildered and offers a large white handkerchief.

He will shop, but only for music. He never buys gifts or indulges a weakness for good food, though he enjoys it when offered; in the provinces he eats in modest back-street Chinese restaurants.

A tour may bring a committee fourteen hundred dollars. The 1960 British tour brought about eight thousand dollars, enough to staff the center at Menfi for one year.

England seems to be his favorite country; he has been there five times. He hates English beer and fashions and claims—this in the West End—that the most beautiful head covering for a woman is a scarf. He loves the churches, suspension bridges, and especially the system of local government. The last he discovered under the aegis of the Mayor of Carlisle. Dolci thought the mayor had invented the system and asked for "a blueprint." The architect in him despises provincial red brick, and he finds it difficult to believe that new housing communities, like the Sheffield Park Hill project, have actually been designed. "Draughtsman's architecture," he mutters, stamping his feet.

He is never afraid to ask a silly question. "And what do you do?" he said to his host at a dinner in London given by the Marquess of Anglesey, who is treasurer of the Dolci Trust. Lord Anglesey replied: "When I fill in a form I put Peer of the Realm." Dolci read him peasant conversations from his latest book with the coffee. And for one who is the archenemy of ignorance, he is remarkably patient with mayors who introduce him as "Do Dolly" and "Danillow Dolcillae." In Glasgow a university professor presented him with the words: ". . . this country, Italy, which, as you all know, has given us those two great men, Machiavelli and Dolci."

In Glasgow he saw the Gorbals, one of the worst slums in Britain, and wept.

In Carlisle some Partinico emigré tailors came to the meeting. One had decorated the hall with an Italian flag five yards long, instead of five feet, because he didn't understand his instructions very well.

After meetings he likes to stroll up hills, to see the view. "Which hill?" his hosts inquire. "The biggest hill." His hosts usually drive up and wait for him on top.

Like the film director Fellini he has a passion for water. A Bristol hostess said: "What would you like to do?" "See the sea," he said. "Would the river do?" she asked anxiously. At Stavanger in 1963, between sessions of the War Resisters' International Conference, he was usually to be found by the beach. He went deep-sea fishing and late one night was approached on the wharf by a strange Norwegian fisherman. They stared at each other. "Do you believe in Jesus Christ?" the fisherman boomed. "I hold him in great esteem," Dolci replied pleasantly.

Before meetings there is a ritual "quiet time." He wanders off, immersed. In Belgrave Square, before addressing the Italian Institute, he paused in the middle of the road to consider a plane tree outlined against the night sky. A taxi missed him by inches. His attitude to British motorists may be inferred, perhaps, from a remark made to the assistant secretary of the Dante Alighieri Society in Glasgow. She was driving him to a meeting in Down-

hill Street at the time. "Madam," he said, leaning across, "you
drive just like Carlo Levi." She flushed with pleasure. (Dolci did
not explain that, until someone corrected him, Levi used to
start in third and drive everywhere round Rome in that gear—
"I thought all these modern cars went that way," Levi said.)

Trains soothe him. He writes on them about nonviolence
with the same ease that a well-known English writer compiles
thrillers commuting on the southern line. He gives his notes—
an upright scrawl on scraps of paper—to the interpreter to
work up, and sighs for a good Italian newspaper. "When I can't
get the papers it's worse for me than it is for you when you can't
get a cigarette." He travels in reverie and bursts of boyish curiosity.
For example: Crewe junction, the train spotters' mecca—his companions (Trust secretary, Robin Dixon, and Diana) ill with fatigue
—10:30 on a desperate Sunday morning:

"Where's everybody?" (*brightly*)

"In bed," Robin says.

"They can't be. They must have gone away for the weekend—they've left the milk bottles out."

"They're in bed." (*firmly*)

"Well, what are *they* doing?"

"Taking down the numbers of trains."

"Don't be silly—of course they're not!"

"They're called train spotters. I used to be one."

"Oh, yes, but you've stopped."

At breakfast next morning he was shown a small boy at
the table. "Danilo, there *is* a train spotter." The boy nodded.
Dolci looked at the boy for a very long time, amazed.

Expressionistic attitudes and faces, like facts, revive and
stimulate him. On the 1963 British tour, numbed by a succession
of eighty lectures and appointments between the West Country
and Dundee in eleven days, he brightened immediately when
taken, secretly, to a late afternoon game of bingo in the North.
He stared at the head-up-head-down tension of hundreds of
pasty-faced women, many in overcoats and curlers, playing furiously. "Look at that, look at that!" he exclaimed. "*Mamma mia*

— it's pure film material!" He asked for a bingo card as a memento and became engrossed. Some time later a policeman tapped him on the shoulder. "Are you Dannylow Dolchee?" the policeman said. Dolci nodded. "Come along, you're wanted urgently at the meeting." Dolci put the bingo card in his pocket and went.

Exhaustion does not affect the steamrolling rhythm of his program. He forbids interpreters to tell organizers when he is upset, angry, or tearful with tiredness, and at worst forgoes his late-night stroll, gets a taxi to his lodgings, and climbs the stairs for bed, very slowly, leaning heavily on the interpreter and murmuring: "If this keeps up I'll get to the stage where my mind wanders while I talk, and that's horrible, horrible. You become a machine, not a man." In 1963 friends smuggled coramine drops, for the heart, into the various liquids he drank round England—until, forgetting Vincenzina's advice, he left the drops in a kitchen in Carlisle. He would retire about eleven-thirty and be alert at four. In London he woke at three-thirty and sat up until breakfast time reading music scores. He had bought these the day before at Peters in Oxford Street. He called for the complete stock of Bach organ music and then turned to Diana and asked her to inquire how much discount there would be. "Danilo, you can't ask for a discount *here*," she reminded him. (In Sicily it is standard practice.) "Never mind," he said. "Go on— ask them." She did. Peters gave him a discount of twenty-five per cent.

He nearly bought an organ as well, but modified his enthusiasm and left word for a bowler hat to be sent to Partinico instead—"for the children, so they can play at Charlie Chaplin." Dolci took the organ music, his biggest item of luggage, round Britain and on return to Partinico scoured the town to find an organ; he was offered the use of an instrument in a neutral church.

Meeting him, days after a tour has ended, is still to experience something of the whirlwind. About the time the bowler hat came, I drove into Partinico from Cammarata and passed him driving the other way, by the music podium. He swerved to a stop, narrowly missing a baker's boy, jumped out, straightened his beret, hugged me, and gave a crisp shorthand version of the trip in the middle of the Corso—"Tremendous, tremendous," he said. "And you," I chafed, "were worn out when you got back." I think he beamed. "Not worn out. I didn't exist. For three days I didn't exist."

Interpreters *say* that travel is his way of relaxing.

✴

✴ XXIX ✴

✴

CONVERSATION
IN ROCCAMENA

MANY people would like to see a *rapprochement* between Dolci
and the Catholic Church in Italy. This would appear to be
about as likely as the idea that he may one day be canonized.
The gulf is not merely wide; the two sides are light years apart.

Cardinal Ruffini's Easter message for 1964 is a pastoral
letter which opens with a warning to his flock to beware of the
three deadly sins which plague Sicily: the Mafia, *The Leopard*,
and Danilo Dolci. This is His Eminence's first public statement that organized Mafia is in any way to be deplored—or indeed even exists. So it appears at first glance. In fact, the letter
smears Dolci, and comes close to whitewashing the Mafia.

Dolci's last public remark about the Church, deemed provocative, was at Lugano in March 1960; nowadays he does not
bother to mention its opposition to him, unless pressed, and then
is at pains to say nothing which might create further enmity—
indeed, he recently defended the Vatican so hotly to Lord Russell that the old man, who is truculently anti-Catholic, rattled
his teacups in surprise. Yet Dolci is still regularly accused of
attacking the Church. On balance it seems to be the Church
which does most of the attacking.

A head-on collision is almost inevitable, considering the
man who has been in the Palermo See for the last two decades
and the general backwardness of the Sicilian clergy. Men like
the ardent young Jesuit, Father Noto, who denounces Mafia
connection with the Church party and wants to enlighten the

fixed old-world attitude which blights Sicilian seminaries, are
unhappily still rare. Most Sicilian clergy are from laboring or
artisan stock. The spirit of St. Francis or the parable of the Good
Samaritan have no part in their preaching. Backwardness is
such that in rural areas priests have yet to learn the news of
Pope John's encyclical, *Pacem in Terris*. Not long ago one told
me that Dolci lived in Russia. It made no difference when I
corrected him, saying I had just come from Dolci's house a few
miles away. The priest interrupted: "No, no, he's an out-and-
out Communist; he lives in Russia." These men *preserve*. Their
opposition to Dolci is human. In their eyes he wants to destroy
most things they hold dear. Thus, they call him a "swindler,"
and refer to that grand old preserver, the late Mafia Head, Don
Carlò Vizzini, who was a murderer, as a *"galantuomo"*—a man
of respect, and *"la buonanima"*—the good soul. (Don Calò had
the right connections. One of his uncles was a bishop; a cousin
was titular Bishop of Noto and founder of the monastic order of
Maria Santissima de Carmelo; two brothers were priests, one a
monsignore. Among the many mourners at Don Carlò's funeral
in 1954 were priests from far and near, in lines, chanting
and swinging bowls of incense.) It is not only Dolci. Pastor
Tullio Vinay is having a worse time in Riesi; he cannot buy
another acre of land to expand his Christian Service there. Father Duynstee was forced out of Palma di Montechiaro by the
Church, and he is a Catholic. But he is also a sociologist.
And it is not so long since a young poet-priest, Alfonso di Gio-
vanna, was quietly extracted from his country parish and muz-
zled in Agrigento because he dared champion a politician who
broke away from the CD party.

    Cardinal Ruffini's reference to *The Leopard* leads one to
suppose that Lampedusa's prelate is not a wholly fictitious character: "He was not a Sicilian. . .and many years before he had
tried to leaven with Nordic activity the inert and heavy dough of
the island's spiritual life in general and the clergy in particular . . .
But soon he had to realize that he was, as it were, firing into cotton
wool; the little hole made at the moment was covered after a few

seconds by thousands of tiny fibres and all remained as before, the only additions being cost of powder, ridicule at useless effort, and deterioration of material."

Cardinal Ruffini is not Sicilian. He is from the Po Valley in the northwest alps, the son of a haberdasher. He was a brilliant scholar and came to Palermo as archbishop in 1945. Pius XII made him a Cardinal the following year. He is handsome, with a fine patrician face and roving beady eyes, and still looks a young man, though he is seventy-six. At the height of his powers he bestowed largesse, opened churches, oratory schools, and old folks' homes with a panache reminiscent of Mussolini dedicating one of his monolithic post offices. In 1959 Ruffini returned from a trip to Spain a Franco enthusiast, rejoicing in the union of Church and State there as a model for the Catholic world. Statements to this effect earned him a snub from the Vatican. (Ruffini later denied he made them.) In 1960 after a series of harrowing Mafia murders involving some of Sicily's proudest families he is reported as saying: "We may be a little backward as regards hygiene, but statistics show that crime and moral dissolution are far worse in the north." (In 1959 there were 254 murders in Palermo, eight times as many as in any city in the north. Not very long ago I picked up a Sicilian newspaper and saw, on one page, the following headlines: "Palma di Montechiaro, mother and son killed by neighbor after quarrel; Agrigento, 21-year-old carpenter stabs young wife eight times; Messina, aged peasant hangs himself; Altofonte, corpse of forty-year-old found in wood; Enna, vandals destroy six hundred vine plants and two hundred almond trees; Partinico, masked youngsters rob six cars and seventeen passengers; Germany, Sicilian emigrant stabs brother to death.")

"Prisons should be penal settlements," Ruffini told an Italian editor named Osmani. "But visiting prisoners is one of the seven corporal works of Catholic mercy," Osmani observed timidly. "Visit them, yes; but allow them enjoyment, no," the Cardinal replied.

Between the prelate and the apostate it would appear that

antipathy is mutual. "Don't talk to me about Danilo Dolci!"
Ruffini interrupted when Osmani introduced the name in conversation. At a fairly recent concert in Monreale Cathedral,
when a friend remarked to Dolci that Ruffini, who was present,
had an intelligent face, Dolci's features darkened. Dolci's last
mention of Ruffini, in 1960, was that the Cardinal would like a
form of Government along the lines of that in Franco's Spain.
This was reported accurately in a Lugano newspaper. Ruffini
sent the paper the following cable: "I deny the affirmation at-
tributed to me and I pray you not to heed pseudobenefactors
who bring nothing to Sicily but dishonor. I bless you." One suspects nowadays that the Cardinal is a disappointed man who
rather enjoys basking in his self-cast role as one of Italy's more
aggressive reactionaries.

In Rome there is "no such thing," I was told, as an official
Church opinion about Danilo Dolci. But the present Pope,
Paul, has sent his gratitude and blessing to Ruffini for the sen-
timents expressed in his latest pastoral letter.

However, it is not Dolci's actual split with the Church, I
think, which is so interesting. He is anticlerical rather than anti-
Catholic. As humanist spokesman for an entire cultural bloc
in Latin Europe, he seems to me to symbolize a widespread discontent with what is most decadent in modern Catholicism.

In the beginning it was the lay culturalists of the north
who criticized Dolci, when he signed himself "Yours in God."
Nowadays, a statement like "All his principles derive from the
Gospels" is enough to make reasonable Jesuits bang tables and
to blight friendly conversation with intelligent Latin Catholics.
(*Waste*, which has a deep Christian message, was banned in Ire-
land.) A BBC program "Danilo Dolci and his Critics," in which
I leaned so far to the Catholic view that the Dolci Trust itself
was annoyed, brought a flood of complaints from Catholics in
England. Only one of the many Italian priests I interviewed
for this program had read any of Dolci's books (though Cardinal
Ruffini's secretary thought His Eminence had once heard a

poem recited); a Jesuit editor in Rome whose journal had published two bitter attacks observed that the Vatican was "indifferent" to Dolci, but agreed to be interviewed only if his identity were concealed. The commonest remark was "What a *shame* Dolci isn't a good Catholic."

A glance at the surroundings in which he lives does not readily yield an insight into his beliefs. At home one is likely to surprise him in shorts at the piano, playing a Bach prelude and singing lustily in a mellow bass accompaniment. The house is roomy and underfurnished. Cielo's bike sometimes strays into the kitchen. If a common burglar broke in he would be disappointed; the place is devoid of material possessions. Dolci's office is equally utilitarian. The floor is stoneflagged, and the feel is of space and hard brown furniture. The rafters are pitted by dry rot and a frayed light cord dangles from a beam. The cold wall face is broken by posters, peasant pottery, a hand-woven mat from Erice, and some potted plants. Everything is well dusted. There is a plain wooden table, seating ten, for minor meetings. His desk reveals a pile of papers, a few architectural doodles, a telephone, a lamp, and little else. Alongside it, glassed in, is a small select library—Gandhi, Tolstoy, Jungk, Capitini are there; no fiction. In a flyleaf of Gandhi's *Autobiography* is written: "Please! This is the only copy! Return it to Danilo's bookcase after you have read it. Thank you!" Pride of place is taken by three images: faded photographs of Gandhi and Epstein, and a tapestry sketch of Lenin sent to Dolci by Russian workmen. It is very much a man's room. The impression emerges of one of life's uncontaminated travellers, whose sustenance comes from somewhere beyond the rotting rafters.

He is called Christian, heretic, mystic, atheist, pantheist, evangelist, theist, and various other "ists." His religious belief, like his method, is expanding all the time. Dolci is profoundly religious, but more now in the honest-to-God than in the mystical way. Perhaps Father Bruno Scott James, who is a Catholic convert, is nearest the mark when he says, "I think he is a humanitarian—a humanitarian who puts us Christians to shame."

Dolci finally defined his own attitude during the Bruca
fast in October 1963. Various circumstances had interrupted
earlier attempts. We had begun to talk about religion in September, but first Yugoslavia, then the Bruca campaign intervened. On 16 October his father died of heart failure. On 25
October we were continuing the conversation in his office when
he complained of a heart pain. He stood up, breathing in gasps
and leaning heavily on the desk. He took a couple of steps and
fell forward on top of me. I took him home, and later, when I
called to see how he was, he launched back into the theme
without preamble. But he tired quickly, and it was only after
three days of fasting at Roccamena, when he was more relaxed
and cheerful than he had been in weeks that the conversation
was completed. What follows is an amalgam of these talks. He
said:

"People get the wrong idea about fasting. These aren't
medieval fasts any more."

"There's no death wish now, you mean?"

"If you like, yes. There's no masochism. What would it
serve by dying?"

"You wrote to Eduard last year about taking fruit juices."

"That's right. Gandhi took citrus juices. This confirmed to
me that he didn't have the 'taste of dying' either. I took juice
in 1957, towards the end, when the poisoning got serious. Last
year a five per cent sugar solution. This year, too, if the doctor
orders. In 1956 nothing; I came through well that time. I'd
never take sweetened water on the first few days—what a charlatan I'd be! That would be reinforcing myself, it wouldn't be a
fast at all. A fast is a sacrifice, but a joyful one."

"You've said that Sicily isn't Christian. At your trial Vittorini spoke a lot about castes."

"I think he's wrong. We're not saints and Sicilians are not
Indians. This is not India. There are no castes here. It's a blend
of paganism, magic, superstition. These cults are still strong."

"Why did you leave the Church? There were many factors,
but what was the real reason?"

"I'll tell you. We of the north always thought that the priests here at least gave alms to the people, but at Trappeto I discovered there wasn't a tradition of charity *even on the alms-giving level.* It's the same today, ask anyone who lives there. Then, I remember two sermons. In one the priest got furious because the people hadn't brought anything for the collection; he called them 'a lot of Jews.' You remember, the people were starving then. And the other—he said, 'Just as you shouldn't approach a leper for fear of getting leprosy, so you shouldn't approach sinners' ... You understand? Not only that. I didn't leave the Church only because it was uncharitable. But because it was actually a *subversive* element, not only in Trappeto but in the whole zone. What was it that upset me most? After the war throughout that whole rising of the poor, when the people turned 'outlaws' in order to live— I realized that the priests could have stopped this, they could have *tried* to stop it. But not one priest stepped in to help the people, to stop the police, to stop the firing, to stop the tortures. Not one."

"You don't use the word God any more."

"When I understood that the word 'God' was likely to bring more confusion than clarity—we talk to be clear, don't we?—then I stopped using it. I don't believe in a personal God, not in the old traditional sense, any more. For me the key is *creativity.* 'To create'—how do we create? It can be 'by the will of God,' and if there's no fatalism involved then this is also creative in an educational sense. But for me this isn't enough. Man must also intervene to try to change things, to modify and perfect, and this is outside the traditional religious concept. St. Paul says man must be a *co-creator* with God—which is the same idea, though Paul doesn't expand it. Jesus was ambiguous, or rather you find both viewpoints in him. In the parables there is the thought of the condemning God. This is the old world. But he also says, 'my God is the God of life'–and, you remember, he talks about the seed having to die before it can bring forth fresh fruit. What matters is that man should be creative. There's nothing higher in man. But is this religious? Some say it is. Here we're trying to graft this possibility of autocreation onto a fixed old-word *attitude*. Western Sicily is our experimental field—to try something which may become valid for the rest of the world."

"You've *almost* answered my question."

"Look: and in this sense it seems I am religious—for me the *Why?* of everything remains the *Why? Why* are we here? This is something that modern culture largely ignores or eliminates. And I think it's wrong."

❦ XXX ❦

ENIGMA

IT is one of the eternal riddles of the human condition that the more a man does for it the more he attracts the calumnies of others. Dolci has been called a "liar" and a "criminal" by members of the Italian Government, a "buffoon" and a "drum-stealing seahorse" by the Church, and, at various times by embittered colleagues, almost everything under the sun. Most of these former judgments, together with the people who made them, can safely be jettisoned; few withstand close analysis, and in the long run they merely testify to the largeness of mind of a man who, at bottom, remains an enigma.

One wonders though about the colleague-critics; one wonders, too, about the human wastage, why so many people leave Dolci—why, though he changes them and gives them a stabler purpose, some do not remain so grateful to him. Inevitably their opinions are extremist and highly personal, though this does not invalidate them: Gerrit, who calls Dolci a "mixed-up social engineer" and "very Machiavellian," also adds—"This is just my view, influenced, of course, by the fact that he ruined my program." The wastage of men (a sad irony, remembering that Dolci is the author of *Waste*) is more serious.

The answer I think, is a very old one—there is an abnormal gap in the spectrum, between the private and the public image; and it has always been apparent throughout Italian history wherever great men, good and bad, from Cola di Rienzo down to Benito Mussolini, have exerted their genius and then been subjected to the detached scrutiny of Anglo-Saxon or Nordic eyes. Dolci's dissatisfied colleagues expected or hoped that his diplomacy *in camera* would match his genius at interpreting the hopes of an underprivileged people. They were disillusioned. Dolci was not an administrator—nor will be; he was irrational, contrary, sensitive to criticism, and (like Nehru) a strange failure in management; and perhaps for this reason alone he will always lose good men. It was always possible to work for him, under him, alongside him, or even without him, but never actually *with* him.

In other words, he does not delegate. Many leave out of sheer frustration.

This happened in the most recent crisis (1964). A group of social workers, including two Americans, submitted for publication a paper on the Center—without his knowledge. The paper, though well meant and informative, criticized Dolci's approach, especially his autocracy and interference with work programs. The criticism—as was Dolci's anger when he made the discovery—was justified. But instead of calling a general meeting and discussing the fundamental complaint, Dolci saw the whole thing as a personal insult and would discuss it with the rebels only individually. Tension reigned. The atmosphere was boiling for weeks. In the end, he lost eight valued colleagues, including Eyvind.

Dolci's crises, like his books, seem to come at regular two-year intervals—this was the third schism since 1958—and, just as regularly, he manages to mismanage them until the morale at the Center is so pinched that a general pique sets in and a whole group walks out. Dolci appears to watch with a sad, slightly sweating, almost bemused detachment. Or, as now, he will become theatrically dictatorial, imposing his veto on a majority ruling and inflating ·to breaking point an issue which, handled more rationally, would have fizzled and died. Sometimes he is *schlau* and evasive—as when, faced with an uncomfortable administrative decision, he will ponder, begin doodling, then shrink away, escaping into a sort of sardonic featurelessness—

until he shuts off his personality altogether and mumbles "Thank you" when he really means "Goodbye."

He is a man who does not appear to learn from experience. Yet sometimes the "closing down" is necessary, for him to keep going.

The recent leave-takers have given allegiance to the new teaching institute, now in embryo stage. Eyvind, at their head, plans to establish it near Palermo. The idea of a university-type structure, sprung from Dolci, based on Dolci, and in Dolci territory, but in which he is not significantly involved, may prove salutary. Some of his more astute admirers in the European universities are almost relieved that, like Garibaldi a century before him, Dolci may not in the end be the man to carry out the moral revolution he has so nobly inspired.

Dolci has emerged from the latest crisis quite unruffled. Before it was over he had completed revisions to a new book about his travels, *A New World in the Making*, which has just appeared in English, both in Great Britain and the United States. His band is reduced; it is nearly all of Italian stock, but it is probably better this way. In the final analysis, only Italians or Sicilians can work deep changes. His social team is more manageable, and, with less administration about his shoulders, he is free to watch over the coming chain of irrigation dams. In itself this is a herculean task. Already in 1965, in Partinico and Roccamena, he has had to lead protests to insure that construction proceeds without Mafia or other interference. "We have to watch this work," he told me, "not month by month, not week by week, *but day by day*."

More than any other, the latest crisis has thrown into relief a big segment of Dolci's character: namely, the dichotomy in the man himself of which he is only partly, or subjectively, conscious. He feels this cleavage—the frequent meaninglessness of his theories on nonviolence in the face of his authoritarianism within his own Center—subjectively; objectively he is totally unaware. This is the personal tragedy of Dolci. There is a conflict,

at times a raging conflict, within him; and he is to this extent
his own worst enemy. The danger is, as in the current upheaval,
that hidden defects—personal vanities, pride—may emerge, as
when a productive machine, uncoupled from its work load, will
reveal sinister whining notes, before racking itself to pieces.
Sensitive ears have many times detected warning notes of ca-
tastrophe in Dolci's makeup, and every time he has halted the
work output and instinctively adjusted the defective parts before surging on again at full bore. The danger of personal ca-
tastrophe, however, always remains; and it may well be that one
day he will end by crucifying himself on the cross of his own
best intentions. But I do not think so. There has always been a
conflict; and Dolci does not give up struggles easily. He goes on
fighting himself all the time.

His blunders *in camera* are not excusable. They are limitations and a pity. But they do not mean he is a charlatan. They
mean he is ineluctably an Italian. And that much less of a saint.
Either that, or a very human kind of saint. Dolci has influenced
European thought on the whole question of southern poverty; he
has drawn the eyes of the civilized world to a forgotten corner
of Europe. This much is fairly clear. The most and the least that
can be said of Danilo Dolci is that he is a man of his time who
sincerely wants to do good. Any wider definitive judgment is for
posterity. He himself makes no extravagant claims to achievement,
just as he claims no consistency of method or originality of action.

And while it may be true that his admirers tend to over-
look the changes that are taking place in the south quite apart
from his reform ideas, it would appear nonetheless that a good
deal of the current official activity is a direct result of his stubborn needling over the years. Offhand one thinks of massive rehousing and slum-clearance plans for Palermo, for Palma di
Montechiaro, for Licata; of moves to woo northern industry, to
snap the gutstring of Mafia monopolies, to overcome illiteracy;
of starter measures towards organic regional planning—towards
the sort of awareness, for instance, that if you build housing
settlements on remote hillsides you must connect water and

light *before* you can expect peasants with large families to live in them. One cannot say that Dolci is responsible for all or any of these changes. He appears merely to have hastened them by a generation or two.

He is now a powerful figure, with considerable pull in Rome, especially at the Left and Center. Power has not corrupted him. He stands alone, head and shoulders above parties and creeds. As Professor Waller has written, he stands amid the denied and the destitute for what a hundred years of adult education have stood in the more fortunate democracies—"the extension of knowledge so that men and women everywhere may have more abundant life."

President Kennedy read *Report from Palermo*, which became a direct source of inspiration for his founding of the Peace Corps.

Bertrand Russell has written: "He carries the burden of conscience for us all."

He is a master publicist, a master showman ("masterful" is one of the adjectives his friends use most). His is usually an honest performance, without cant. I think Dolci does like acclaim, more than is apparent. He is quite open about some vanities. He once told me: "When I see myself listed alongside men like Russell and Schweitzer, this pleases me. I know I'm forty years younger than they are."

Withal, he remains basically a modest person. A remarkable thing about him is his encyclopedic knowledge, embracing the entire Italian cultural—and much of the European sociological—world. He is on Christian-name terms with almost all the leading figures, and will pepper a conversation with astute shorthand judgments on each in two crisp sentences. There is never a whiff of name-dropping. If there is an element of megalomania in his character, it is largely unconscious and hardly surprising. He has already done more for Sicily than any man in the island's twenty-six centuries of recorded history.

Dolci is above all a writer and an *educational* reformer. He seems, for many Italians, the quintessence of the moral and spiritual drive which came out of the Resistance Movement. Equally, for many more people, as the enemy of slum-thinking and the chaos born of nepotism and bureaucratic apathy, he is a kind of universal moral detergent—like that bottle of liver pills we can none of us do without: we keep it on the shelf, slightly to one side, and do not boast of it to guests; but from time to time we are forced to take one and are profoundly grateful for the good it does us.

He is also many other things, and it is part of the riddle, as it is part of his greatness, that there is a paradox behind his almost every quality. He reminds me often of Orwell. He exhibits the same anger at injustice, in all its forms; he has the same obsession with poverty which stops just short of fanaticism; and he brings the same fearless approach to his writing and yet remains an artist, never a mere pamphleteer. In some ways he is a frustrated artist. His accounts have a searing muddled beauty, and at best, for economy of language and naked power of description, no Italian writer can touch him. Parts of *Outlaws* and of the dialogues on the meaning of living and dying in *Conversations* read like an Introduction to the Gospels. He is deeply Italian in temperament and, within the iron mold of his moral consistency, utterly unpredictable. He makes a mockery of the thesis that only the bad are interesting. Nothing about him is small, especially the failings, but in the end the limitations shrink and it does not seem to matter that he burns up colleagues or meddles or is a bad administrator—one is dealing with a typhoon, not a tally clerk; in the end it is the saga of goodness that takes over, with all the infinite variations he is able to ring on the theme. After a time, watching him biting on the kernel of living, getting rid of obstacles like spitting out the shell, one ceases to be amazed and accepts the fact that time and circumstance have created someone quite heroic. What matters, it seems to me, is the original total sacrifice—this and the courage and the awesome tenacity of purpose. In the end it is not the personality—which can be almost too impressive—nor the achievement, nor even the work which really matter. What carries you along, what convinces, is the living example.

At Trappeto today a cow and a calf live in Giustina's basement where her first baby died, but it has been done up and is
in rather better condition than when Dolci fasted there in 1952.
"That's where he did penance for the Lord," the neighbors still
say. People who visit the Center in Partinico will see the sign
Center for Studies and Action towards Full Employment on the
outer wall, and if they spend any time at all on the island will
discover that it is far from an anachronism. The great barn of a
building preserves a farmyard approach; grimy children play in
the rucks of mud and beg ten lire from visitors; on a concrete
pad by the meeting room an alien Evangelist group continues
to burst into revivalist song at no set hour; upstairs, where the
social section is harbored, children throng the *doposcuola* and
their wild industry echoes through the spartan corridors; downstairs, Senator Messeri's poster, calling Dolci "a cad," dominates
the stone vestibule and the towel in the toilet still smells of vine-
gar; peasants clump in, cap in hand and exceeding polite, and
workers in austerity clothing greet visitors with handshakes of
iron and move quickly about the rooms; at the farthest recesses
Dolci's voice may be heard booming softly for Franco.

There are some twenty-five workers, half of them Sicilians,
living on about eighteen dollars a week. Some earn less than
nine dollars a week. Salaries take nearly two-thirds of the annual
budget ($70,000) which comes more or less equally from volun-
tary committees in seven countries, from private businessmen
(mostly northern Italians), and from Protestant and student
bodies in Europe and the United States.

Americans see him in comic-strip terms—as the goodly white
saint *versus* the evil black hand (of the Mafia), or as the pawn
of Communists. Either this, or they do not see him at all. They
have yet to grasp the spirit of his work, his fundamental platform of moral reform. He, himself, by his bad system of public
relations, has unwittingly contributed to the misunderstanding.
Yet despite the tag of Communist, with which Catholic propaganda has smeared his name, he is supported in America by
such Establishment figures as Auden, Fromm, Mumford, de

Santillana, in fact almost the Parnassus of American culture, as well as by people like Norman Thomas, leader of the Socialist party.

The biggest committee is in Britain (3,500 subscribers, growing all the time) which reflects Dolci's impact on audiences there. "When I talk to an English audience," he told Richard West, "it is like playing on a violin. They seem to understand what I want to say. The English have a love of culture . . . they understand about underdeveloped countries, and they are excellent organizers." The British Dolci Trust sends some seven thousand pounds a year to Menfi. Its sponsors include such non- or anti-Communists as the Bishop of Manchester, Sir Laurence Olivier, Count Michael de la Bedoyère, the Liberal leader Jo Grimond, Lord Sainsbury, Professor Sir Denis Brogan, and a Jesuit priest, Father Thomas Corbishley. Dolci's British press is generally jubilant, irrespective of political affiliation. In Italy, while he has no blanket support from either Socialists or Communists, the picture is just the reverse. Three of the five newspapers which regularly champion his cause—*L'Ora, Paese Sera,* and *Unità*—are Communist or fellow-travelling; the others are the Socialist paper *Avanti!* and *L'Espresso,* the tabloid *New Statesman* of Italy. His most ardent supporters are among the Communist intelligentsia. "Why are so many of your cultural friends Communists?" a Sicilian engineer asked him. "You show me a Christian Democrat who is cultured," Dolci replied. Naturally enough some Sicilian Communists work in his centers. The emphasis is spread between peace and development work, and politics: in Sicily they cannot be divorced from each other. Outside his centers, many Sicilian people themselves —those who have heard of him—dislike and mistrust him, as they would mistrust any humanitarian who worked in a glow of publicity. "Once he was humble, walked everywhere, and was one of us. Now he lives in an apartment, drives a car, and travels the world. Here is another foreigner who has risen on our backs." This is the line of their reasoning. Ther is no Dolci committee in Sicily.

Most days Libera, his eldest child, comes along and dusts

the office. There are five Dolci children, Maria-Libera (or Libera-Maria: Vincenzina isn't sure) who is eleven, Cielo (ten), Amico (eight), Chiara (six), and Daniela (four). It is said that Dolci decided against increasing the population further after his last horrified inspection of the birthrate in India. Vincenzina wanted to call all the children after him, but succeeded only with Daniela. The other names, chosen by Dolci, are symbolic, especially Amico's. Amico (Friend) has five names— Amico Aldo Norberto Lucio Enrico—commemorating Dolci's 1957 success in obtaining a *rapprochement* among Italian cultural leaders who normally couldn't stand the sight of one another.

Vincenzina remains a stoical, contented, if shadowy figure, nostalgic only for the crusading days of Borgo and the People's University. At home she is often dynamic, shouting at her children as vehemently as the neighbors shout at theirs—but not usually when Dolci or visitors are present. She is probably relieved that her five children by her first husband—all sons and all working in the north—lead normal lives and have shown no wish to become involved in the Dolci movement. She reflects his aura with a quiet dignity, and is naturally humble. It is always from some other person that one learns about her—about how, for example, when she was married to the peasant Luciano and living with his people in Trappeto, she was once beaten so hard for a peccadillo that two ribs were broken and she had to continue making the beds for the entire household on her knees; or of how in 1961 she was expected to prepare supper for thirty people, with the usual alacrity, despite the fact that she had given birth to Daniela only a week before. Vincenzina is a remarkable woman, a blend of uncompromising Sicilian fibre rooted in Greek tragedy and of the slow dawn of the modern Sicilian woman. She remains utterly devoted to Dolci and says, simply: "I understand I have changed because our life is different." Once, asked why it was that Sicilians sang so much, she explained in these words: "When I lost my husband and I'd given all the bread to the children I always used to sing, and the hungrier I was the more I sang, just to have it *here* in my head,

*Dolci with Vincenzina and three of their five children on the
roof of their Partinico home.*

not in my stomach. But my sister-in-law knew. When she heard
me singing at the top of my voice she would say, 'Listen to the
wretch, her stomach's full of nothing again.' "

Not long ago Tullio Vinay came to see me in Cammarata,
on his way from Riesi to Palermo. He is one of the famous pas-
tors of Europe and came to live, and work in Riesi—a despairing
town in Caltanissetta province—in 1961. It was early morning
when he called. The peasants had long begun their two-hour
trek to the fields; Peppino the goatswain was finishing his round,
milking from the teat straight into the housewives' bottles; and
the narrow inclines rang with the thud of hawkers' mules sliding down, and the pestering cries of women and families thread-
ing their way up, towards the hills, for the end of the olive har-

vest. We stood on the little wrought-iron balcony looking across the village to the Tumarrano Valley and the eight or nine villages, their populations cut in half by emigration, which smudged its broken featureless gullies. The valley rolled in a gray cataract to the far horizon, a ridge of blue-black mountains which marks a confine of three provinces. It was on these feudal estates that Mafia began.

Vinay was not surprised to learn that I had to work in Cammarata anonymously, chiefly because the priests—and therefore the ruling clique—considered Dolci a militant Communist. "It is the same in Riesi," he said. "It is easier for the clergy to condemn Communism than to incarnate the faith they profess."

After a while he said, in English: "You know Dr. Müller-Ganghoff wrote an idea about the Third People of God. The First People of God was Israel, and they betray the Lord. And in His Freedom the Lord chose another people, the Church. But the Church is now betraying the Lord. And the Lord is free to choose other men, *sine nomine*, as His people. And Danilo is surely one of the Third People."

There is something prophetic, almost preordained about these words. It is linked in my mind with Dolci's principle of self-immolation in order to create ("to know how to die is to know how to live ... all things can be changed"); and with the uncanny nature of his survival. His life is a modern fable.

Vinay's visit at the end of 1963 coincided with Dolci's historic denunciation of Messeri and the ex-gangster Coppola before the Parliamentary Anti-Mafia Commission. Dolci's watchdog activities, as a sort of private detective (uncommissioned, unpaid) to the Commission have continued unabated; and it seems fairly clear, as a result of his and other testimonies coming forward, that the Mafia's role as a vote-getting machine for the Christian Democrats will never be the same again. In 1964 Messeri resigned his Ministry post. In the same year, where previously Government action had managed to detain only rank-and-file members of the secret society, there were waves of arrests of major *mafiosi*. In 1965 Coppola and other leaders of the drug traffic underworld

linking Sicily and the United States were arrested, on both sides
of the Atlantic. Meanwhile, the feudal king and the acknowledged
Head of the Sicilian Mafia, Giuseppe Genco Russo, had been
jailed. Russo, whose twisted moral code provides a revealing
chapter of *Waste*, inherited Don Calò's mantle, was an intimate
of priest and politician, and had been regarded as "untouchable." At his trial he was convicted for being "a danger to society" and sentenced to exile in the northern Alps. He is contained there now, without a telephone, an arthritic self-pitying
hulk of seventy-two, in a remote lakeside district northeast of
Milan where as a boy Dolci once walked with his father and
dreamed his first dreams about the gift of goodness. The wheel
of destiny has completed a revolution.

Dolci is in the prime of life.

Assuredly he will not be canonized. He may continue to
try the patience of his sponsors, but I doubt that he will exhaust
it. He will probably not—like Bellini (who died in Paris), like
Pirandello (who died in Rome), or like Verga (who lived mostly in Milan), all three of whom have monuments in their native Sicily—be honored in concrete or marble. But his spirit will
carry on.

He told a conference in Norway recently: "With diligence
I am continuing."

BIBLIOGRAPHY

EXCEPT where specially significant, the newspaper and magazine commentaries I have consulted are not included, chiefly for reasons of space. Many specialized articles and monographs by Dolci and his colleagues are available in Italian and English from Centro Studi, Partinico, on request.

Abba, Cesare, *Da Quarto al Volturno*. Bologna, Zanichelli, 1912.

Alongi, G., *La Mafia*. Turin, Bocca, 1877.

Barbera, Lorenzo, *La Coscienza di Roccamena*. Bari, Laterza, 1964.

Barzini, Luigi, *The Italians*. New York, Atheneum, 1964.

Capitini, Aldo, *Rivoluzione Aperta*. Milan, Parenti, 1956.

——, *Danilo Dolci*. Florence, Lacaita, 1958.

Carli-Ballola and Narzisi, "*Il Grano Rosso*: vita e morte di Salvatore Carnevale." Milan, *Avanti!*, 1956.

Carlyle, Margaret, *The Awakening of Southern Italy*. London, New York, Oxford University Press, 1962.

Centro Studi, *Notes for friends*. Partinico, 1958-64.

——, *Convegno sulle condizioni di vita e di salute in zone arretrate della Sicilia Occidentale*. Palma di Montechiaro, 1960.

Dolci, Danilo, *Voci nella Città di Dio* (poems). Mazara, Società Editrice Siciliana, 1951.

——, *Da Borgo di Dio* (pamphlet). Trappeto, 1953.

——, *Fare presto (e bene) perchè si muore*. Turin, De Silva, 1954.

———*, *Banditi a Partinico*. Bari, Laterza, 1955.

———, "Volevo scoprire l'anima della vita" (autobiographical soliolquy). Milan, *Tempo*, 1956.

———, *Poesie*. Milan, Canevini, 1956.

———, *Processo all' articolo 4* (with others). Turin, Einaudi, 1956.

———*, *Inchiesta a Palermo*. Turin, Einaudi, 1956.

———, Series of travel articles in *L'Ora*. Palermo, 1958.

———, *Una politica per la piena occupazione* (with others). Turin, Einaudi, 1958.

———*, *Spreco*. Turin, Einaudi, 1960.

———, *Conversazioni*. Turin, Einaudi, 1962.

———*, *Verso un mondo nuovo*. Turin, Einaudi, 1964.

Fisher, Louis, *The Life of Mahatma Gandhi*. New York, Harper, 1960.

Franchetti and Sonnino, *La Sicilia*. Florence, Vallecchi, 1876.

Galtung, Johan, "Gandhi, Dolci e noi" (article). Florence, *Il Ponte*, 1957.

Ganachaud, Guy, *Les Bandits de Dieu*. Paris, Seuil, 1957.

Gandhi, Mohandas K., *An Autobiography*. Boston, Beacon Press, 1957.

Gentile, Nicola, *Vita di Capomafia*. Rome, Riuniti, 1963.

Gliozzo, Calogero, "Danilo Dolci e gli intelletuali francesi" (article). Rome, *Civiltà Cattolica*, 1958.

Grasso, Franco, "A Montelepre hanno piantato una croce." Milan, *Avanti!*, 1956.

Hobsbawm, Eric J., *Primitive Rebels*. New York, Praeger, 1963.

Kefauver, Estes, *Crime in America*. Garden City, Doubleday, 1951.

Lampedusa, Giuseppe Tomasi di, *The Leopard*. New York, Pantheon, 1960.

* Published in New York by Orion as *Outlaws* (1961) and *Report from Palermo* (1959) and by Monthly Review Press as *Waste* (1963) and *A New World in the Making* (1965); and in London by MacGibbon & Kee as *The Outlaws of Partinico* (1960), *To Feed the Hungry* (1959), *Waste* (1963), and *A New World in the Making* (1965). *Outlaws* includes extracts from *Fare presto (e bene)*, *Articolo 4*, and *Una politica*; *Waste* includes a portion of *Conversazioni*.

Levi, Carlo, *Words Are Stones*. New York, Farrar, Straus & Cudahy, 1958.

Lewis, Norman, *The Honored Society*. New York, Putnam, 1964.

Mack Smith, Denis, *Cavour and Garibaldi, 1860*. Cambridge University Press, 1954.

———, *Italy*. Ann Arbor, University of Michigan Press, 1959.

Maxwell, Gavin, *God Protect Me from My Friends*. London, Longmans Green, 1957.

———, *The Ten Pains of Death*. New York, Dutton, 1960 (c. 1959).

Mazzetti, Roberto, *Memorie di Don Zeno e di Nomedelfia*. Parma, Guanda, 1956.

Noto, Giuseppe, "Danilo Dolci e lo 'spreco' in Sicilia" (article). Rome, *Civiltà Cattolica*, 1960.

Nott, Kathleen, "Danilo Dolci: Non-violence in Italy" (article). New York, *Commentary*, Vol. 31, Feb., 1961, pp. 119-26.

Pantaleone, Michele, *The Mafia and Politics*. London, Chatto & Windus, 1964.

Pitré, Giuseppe, *Usi e costumi del popolo siciliano*. Milan, Cappelli, 1961 (first published 1848).

Runciman, Steven, *The Sicilian Vespers*. Cambridge University Press, 1958.

Russo, Paolino, and Alia, Toni, *Due pescatori siciliani raccontano la storia del Borgo di Dio*. Milan, Il Gallo, 1954.

Sciascia, Leonardo, *Il Giorno della Civetta*. Turin, Einaudi, 1961.

Sibley, Mulford Q., *The Quiet Battle*. New York, Anchor, 1963.

Steinmann, Jean, *Pour ou Contre Danilo Dolci*. Paris, Cerf, 1959.

Thoreau, Henry, *On the Duty of Civil Disobedience*. London, Peace News, 1963 (first published 1849).

Urquhart, Clara, *A Matter of Life*. London, Cape, 1963.

Verga, Giovanni, *Little Novels of Sicily*. New York, Grove, 1953.

Vittorini, Elio, *Conversation in Sicily*. London, Penguin, 1961.

Waller, Ross, *Danilo Dolci* (monograph). Manchester, 1960.

Wätjen, Eduard, *Danilo Dolci—his life and work* (monograph). Partinico, Centro Studi, 1963.

West, Morris, *Children of the Shadows*. New York, Doubleday,
    1957 (published in London by Heinemann as *Children of
    the Sun*).

INDEX

DATE DUE

DEMCO 38-297